Interactive

Language Development Teaching

INTERACTIVE LANGUAGE DEVELOPMENT TEACHING

The Clinical Presentation of Grammatical Structure

BY

Laura L. Lee, Roy A. Koenigsknecht, and
Susan Mulhern

NORTHWESTERN UNIVERSITY PRESS
Evanston, Ill., 1975

Library of Congress Catalog Card Number: 74–82560
ISBN 0–8101–0451–2
Printed in the United States of America

Portions of this research were supported by the United States Office of Education grant OEG–0–71–0949 (607).

The project presented or reported herein was performed pursuant to a Grant from the United States Office of Education, Department of Health, Education, and Welfare. However, the opinions expressed herein do not necessarily reflect the position or policy of the United States Office of Education, and no official endorsement by the United States Office of Education should be inferred.

Laura L. Lee is Professor of Speech and Language Pathology at Northwestern University.

Roy A. Koenigsknecht is Associate Professor of Speech and Language Pathology at Northwestern University.

Susan Mulhern is Associate in Speech and Language Pathology at Northwestern University.

Contents

List of Charts

List of Tables

Acknowledgments

THE AUTHORS WISH TO ACKNOWLEDGE the support for this project by the United States Office of Education Grant OEG–0–71–0949 (607). They wish further to acknowledge the valuable support of the parents of the clinical children who were included in the project and the tremendous contribution of the children themselves. Appreciation is extended to the graduate student clinicians at the Northwestern University Speech and Language Clinics, whose questions and discussions often led to new insights and revised approaches to clinical language training. Finally, credit should be given to Philip Friedman, Diane Hill, and Sharon Conger, all of whom participated at various times and in various capacities in the development of these teaching materials.

INTRODUCTION

INTERACTIVE LANGUAGE DEVELOPMENT TEACHING is a clinical procedure for presenting grammatical structure to children with language-learning problems. It was developed at the Northwestern University Speech and Language Clinics and has been used extensively with groups of children for whom the learning of grammatical structure was the primary goal. These were usually children who already had an expressive vocabulary of thirty to forty words and were beginning to use word combinations occasionally but whose sentence structure and use of syntactic forms were considerably below expectations for their chronological and mental ages. These language groups have usually consisted of four to six children in the preschool age range of three to six years. With one-hour clinical sessions four times a week over a one-year period, and sometimes a two-year period, it was imperative to find a procedure that would maintain interest and enjoyment for such young children and would, at the same time, be an effective language-teaching device. Unstructured methods of simple "language stimulation" have not always produced the desired results in clinical teaching, while highly structured, imitative drill sessions sometimes diminish the interest of both clinicians and children over extended periods of treatment. Interactive Language Development Teaching attempts to avoid these two extremes by presenting language in a controlled developmental sequence while preserving, at the same time, the natural child-adult interaction of normal language learning.

The developmental aspects of language learning are set forth in great detail in another book, *Developmental Sentence Analysis* (Lee, 1974),[1] which is a kind of companion piece to this present volume. In *Developmental Sentence Analysis*, two procedures are presented, one for the evaluation of children's utterances which are in pre-sentence form, and the other for the assessment of grammatical growth found within complete

1. Full publication data for this and other works cited will be found in the References section at the end of this book.

sentences in children's spontaneous speech. These studies provide the clinician with a guide for presenting syntactic and morphological forms in carefully graded developmental steps. Clinical language lessons should be planned to follow the normal progression of language learning whenever possible, and Interactive Language Development Teaching makes maximum use of this information.

The verbal interaction between parent and child, which is the natural setting for language learning, can be simulated in the clinic. Children can be engaged in conversation around a subject or story, where the semantic content of language is clear and apparent. If the verbal interaction of clinician and child is related to ongoing events, then purely imitative speech will be avoided or will be reduced to a minimum. Children will be led to formulate language, not merely to imitate it. Furthermore, the constant shift between listener and speaker roles allows a child the opportunity for both receptive and expressive language learning. The clinician's careful control of the language spoken to the child allows for the introduction of new grammatical forms as comprehension tasks before the child is asked to produce them himself. Structures can be presented in meaningful semantic contexts many times to insure the child's comprehension.

In a clinical setting, where a lesson must occur at a designated time, it is difficult to produce an interesting and profitable conversation "on call." However, the preparation of a simple story which relates familiar events is a good substitute for the content of parent-child conversations. A language story can discuss common home and community activities, it can introduce the kinds of people whom the child already knows, and it can contain the level of thinking, problem-solving, and anticipation of future events that are within his cognitive capacities. Furthermore, the story can be written with more control of grammatical structure than spontaneous conversation usually allows. The language of such a lesson can contain both aspects of natural language acquisition that the clinician needs to incorporate into clinical teaching: the developmental and the interactive.

Interactive Language Development Teaching has gone through many stages of modification and refinement at the Northwestern University Speech and Language Clinics over the past ten years, and it has been used with a great number of children in clinical language training. Up to the present time this procedure has been used primarily with children who are within the normal range of intelligence and who show normal hearing sensitivity, as described in detail in Section III. It is possible that this procedure could be adapted for language training with mentally retarded and hearing-impaired children, but this has not yet been demonstrated.

More than a hundred student clinicians have been trained in this procedure, and many of them are continuing to adapt it to their own clinical needs in a variety of professional settings. This text has been written with both the student and the practicing clinician in mind. It is designed to be both an instructional approach for the training of student clinicians and a practical tool for speech and language clinicians in handling children with language problems. It is not intended to be a rigidly administered procedure, nor should the sample language stories contained in this book be considered as a series of workbook lessons to be presented, one by one, to any clinical group. Instead, it is hoped that students and clinicians will find ways of incorporating the interactive and the developmental aspects of language teaching into whatever methods and techniques they already use. The sample stories should provide creative clinicians with guidelines for composing their own stories built around the particular interests, cultural patterns, and common experiences of the children they serve, as well as their individual language needs.

This book is divided into three general sections. Section I discusses the Interactive Language Development Teaching procedure, giving background information and rationale for its use, information on writing effective stories, suggestions for the story presentation, ways of evaluating the teaching effectiveness of this method, and a transcribed language lesson to illustrate the procedure. Section II presents thirty stories written for children at a beginning level of syntactic development and thirty-two stories for children at a more advanced stage. The language goals for each lesson are listed, and the weighted DSS scores for all the elicited sentences are included, following the procedure of Lee's *Developmental Sentence Analysis*. Thus, the sequential order of language development is evident in this progression of language lessons. Section III discusses the results of a three-year continuing study of Interactive Language Development Teaching at the Northwestern University Speech and Language Clinics and evaluates the effectiveness of this method with a population of clinical children. It is hoped that this information will be of interest and value to speech and language clinicians who provide extended ongoing treatment for children with problems in learning language.

Interactive

Language Development Teaching

Section I

Interactive Language Development Teaching

INTERACTIVE LANGUAGE DEVELOPMENT TEACHING is based on the developmental model of grammar that is described in *Developmental Sentence Analysis* (Lee, 1974). One part of the DSA procedure is the Developmental Sentence Scoring (DSS) technique, which establishes a developmental order in eight grammatical categories: indefinite pronouns, personal pronouns, primary verbs, secondary verbs, negatives, conjunctions, interrogative reversals, and wh-questions. By assigning weighted scores to items in these eight categories on the basis of their early or late acquisition, an over-all assessment of language level can be determined from a child's spontaneous language sample.

Chart I shows the DSS chart of developing grammatical forms and the weighted scores assigned to each item. The classification and nomenclature of traditional grammar have been modified in the DSS procedure since it is the developmental grammar of children, not adults, which is being evaluated. Words with similar semantic content or syntactic function have been grouped together, giving rise to such classifications as quantity words, indefinite pronouns and noun modifiers, personal pronouns, secondary verbs, wh-pronouns, wh-conjunctions, etc. These groupings frequently borrow from both traditional and more recent psycholinguistic terminology, but they adhere strictly to neither one. For example, the classification called ''indefinite pronoun and noun modifier'' includes demonstratives, cardinal numbers, and even such quantifying adjectives as

Chart 1. The Developmental Sentence Scoring (DSS) Chart

SCORE	INDEFINITE PRONOUNS OR NOUN MODIFIERS	PERSONAL PRONOUNS	MAIN VERBS	SECONDARY VERBS
1	it, this, that	1st and 2nd person: I, me, my, mine, you, your(s)	A. Uninflected verb: I *see* you. B. copula, is or 's: *It's* red. C. is + verb + ing: He *is coming.*	
2		3rd person: he, him, his, she, her, hers	A. -s and -ed: *plays, played* B. irregular past: *ate, saw* C. Copula: *am, are, was, were* D. Auxiliary *am, are, was, were*	Five early-developing infinitives: I wan*na see* (want *to see)* I'm gon*na see* (going *to see)* I got*ta see* (got *to see)* Lemme [to] see (let me [*to*] *see)* Let's [to] play (let [us *to*] *play)*
3	A. no, some, more, all, lot(s), one(s), two (etc.), other(s), another B. something, somebody, someone	A. Plurals: we, us, our(s), they, them, their B. these, those		Non-complementing infinitives: I stopped *to play.* I'm afraid *to look.* It's hard *to do* that.
4	nothing, nobody, none, no one		A. can, will, may + verb: *may go* B. Obligatory do + verb: *don't go* C. Emphatic do + verb: I *do see.*	Participle, present or past: I see a boy *running.* I found the toy *broken.*
5		Reflexives: myself, yourself, himself, herself, itself, themselves		A. Early infinitival complements with differing subjects in kernels: I want you *to come.* Let him [*to*] *see.* B. Later infinitival complements: I had *to go.* I told him *to go.* I tried *to go.* He ought *to go.* C. Obligatory deletions: Make it [*to*] *go.* I'd better [*to*] *go.* D. Infinitive with wh-word: I know what *to get.* I know how *to do* it.
6		A. Wh-pronouns: who, which, whose, whom, what, that, how many, how much I know *who* came. That's *what* I said. B. Wh-word + infinitive: I know *what* to do. I know *who(m)* to take.	A. could, would, should, might + verb: *might come, could be* B. Obligatory does, did + verb C. Emphatic does, did + verb	
7	A. any, anything, anybody, anyone B. every, everything, everybody, everyone C. both, few, many, each, several, most, least, much, next, first, last, second (etc.)	(his) own, one, oneself, whichever, whoever, whatever Take *whatever* you like.	A. Passive with *get,* any tense Passive with *be,* any tense B. must, shall + verb: *must come* C. have + verb + en: *I've eaten* D. have got: I*'ve got* it.	Passive infinitival complement: With *get:* I have *to get dressed.* I don't want *to get hurt.* With *be:* I want *to be pulled.* It's going *to be locked.*
8			A. have been + verb + ing had been + verb + ing B. modal + have + verb + en: *may have eaten* C. modal + be + verb + ing: *could be playing* D. Other auxiliary combinations: *should have been sleeping*	Gerund: *Swinging* is fun. I like *fishing.* He started *laughing.*

NEGATIVES	CONJUNCTIONS	INTERROGATIVE REVERSALS	WH-QUESTIONS
it, this, that + copula or auxiliary is, 's, + not: It's *not* mine. This is *not* a dog. That is *not* moving.		Reversal of copula: *Is*n't *it* red? *Were they* there?	
			A. who, what, what + noun: *Who* am I? *What* is he eating? *What book* are you reading? B. where, how many, how much, what . . . do, what . . . for *Where* did it go? *How much* do you want? *What* is he *doing?* *What* is a hammer *for?*
	and		
can't, don't		Reversal of auxiliary be: *Is he* coming? *Isn't he* coming? *Was he* going? *Was*n't *he* going?	
isn't, won't	A. but B. so, and so, so that C. or, if		when, how, how + adjective *When* shall I come? *How* do you do it? *How big* is it?
	because	A. Obligatory do, does, did: *Do they* run? *Does it* bite? *Did*n't *it* hurt? B. Reversal of modal: *Can you* play? *Won't it* hurt? *Shall I* sit down? C. Tag question: It's fun, *isn't it?* It isn't fun, *is it?*	
other negatives: Uncontracted negatives: I can *not* go. He has *not* gone. Pronoun-auxiliary or pronoun-copula contraction: I'm *not* coming. He's *not* here. Auxiliary-negative or copula-negative contraction: He was*n't* going. He has*n't* been seen. It could*n't* be mine. They are*n't* big.			why, what if, how come how about + gerund *Why* are you crying? *What if* I won't do it? *How come* he is crying? *How about* coming with me?
	A. where, when, how, while, whether (or not), till, until, unless, since, before, after, for, as, as + adjective + as, as if, like, that, than I know *where* you are. Don't come *till* I call. B. Obligatory deletions: I run faster *than* you [run]. I'm *as big as* a man [is big]. It looks *like* a dog [looks] C. Elliptical deletions (score 0): That's *why* [I took it]. I know *how* [I can do it]. D. Wh-words + infinitive: I know *how* to do it. I know *where* to go.	A. Reversal of auxiliary have: *Has he* seen you? B. Reversal with two or three auxiliaries: *Has he been* eating? *Could*n't *he have* waited? *Could he have been* crying? *Would*n't *he have been* going?	whose, which, which + noun *Whose* car is that? *Which book* do you want?

every, *any*, *some*, and *more*; they are classified together whether they modify nouns or stand alone as shortened noun phrases. The possessive adjectives *my*, *your*, *his*, *her*, and *their* are classified as personal pronouns because children learn them as members of a pronoun group. *Who* and *what* have been assigned to the personal-pronoun classification; by recording them under the same heading, the clinician can more readily ascertain whether the child has made the human-nonhuman distinction that they require. These modifications of conventional grammatical description have been made in order to reflect the child's developing grammatical and semantic word classes and to provide clinicians with a developmental guide for the analysis of children's language.

Other departures from traditional standards of grammatical usage result from the fact that we are analyzing conversational rather than written language. Even adults use contractions such as *gonna*, *wanna*, *gotta*, and *lemme* in their casual speech to children; and when the children begin to produce these structures, they articulate them in the same manner. Therefore, the DSS chart lists these words as legitimate verb forms of children's spoken language. In the beginning stages of grammatical training with clinical children, certain "substandard" forms are allowed and accepted because the grammatical distinctions required by the standard forms are too fine for a child at a low developmental level: *who* for *whom*, *in* for *into*, *can* for *may*, *like* for *as*, etc. Even the clinician's speech to clinical children should ignore these very precise grammatical distinctions and should concentrate on those forms that are within the children's semantic and syntactic capabilities. The conversational quality of spoken English and the developmental nature of children's grammar are both reflected in the DSS classification system.

Koenigsknecht (1974) has discussed the norms that were developed when the language samples of two hundred carefully selected, normally developing children were analyzed by the DSS procedure. These norms can be used for comparison with the language samples of clinical children to determine their levels of language development. Koenigsknecht's (1974) statistical findings indicated that the DSS was a valid and reliable assessor of grammatical usage and that it could be repeated at four-month intervals to determine a child's rate of progress during the period of remedial teaching. While the DSS was originally designed as an evaluation instrument, it can also be used as a guide to language teaching. The sequence of grammatical learning that is shown by normally developing children provides the clinician with a progression of lesson goals for children with language-learning problems.

RATIONALE FOR INTERACTIVE LANGUAGE DEVELOPMENT TEACHING

The information gained from the analysis of a child's spontaneous speech allows a prescriptive remedial approach based on the comparison of his grammatical usage with the normal acquisitional order. Not only can immediate teaching goals be determined from a child's DSS, but, from periodic language samples, progress can be accurately measured and long-range program planning can be projected.

Language growth develops in two ways: (1) more mature grammatical forms appear in the child's language and (2) he is able to combine more types of grammatical structures into a single sentence. Thus, both the maturity and the frequency of grammatical forms contribute to the increasing grammatical load which a child shows in his spontaneous speech. Even at the earliest stages of expressive-language usage, syntactic structures and morphological forms do not occur in isolation. Children who have impaired language skills can often use a particular structure accurately in a short phrase or in isolation but cannot utilize that same structure in combination with others. The grammatical load of the sentence appears to be a critical variable. One important aspect of treatment is expanding the child's ability to handle an increasing grammatical load and to maintain appropriate use of newly learned language structures in combination with other structures. Interactive Language Development Teaching seems particularly well suited for this goal since, in the conversational interchange between clinician and child, language structures are presented in combination, not one by one.

Interactive Language Development Teaching approximates as closely as possible the conversational setting of normal language development. Parents do not ask children to imitate their speech but instead talk to them in simplified language concerning environmental events. The semantic content of language is emphasized more than grammatical precision; and if new words or grammatical constructions are needed, the social context always provides immediate meanings for them. Parent-child conversations also require a child to shift speaker and listener roles constantly. Either person can initiate topics or ideas, and either one can ask or answer questions. Thus, if clinical teaching is to capitalize on these features of normal language acquisition, it must create a setting where language can be spontaneous, nonimitative, and meaningful and where both receptive and expressive skills can be practiced. Since such conversations cannot be left to chance in a clinical setting, storytelling provides an effective substitute. A child-clinician interaction can be centered around a simple story presentation which duplicates the common, everyday experiences that parents and children talk about.

Normally developing children are capable of generalizing grammatical rules from the conversational speech of parents, but clinical children have shown reduced ability for the self-discovery of grammatical rules. A structured interchange between clinician and child helps to highlight the grammatical problems the child is encountering. The clinician needs to reformulate, remodel, correct, or expand a child's utterances in an effort to elicit more mature language from him. While parents may produce these corrections or expansions only occasionally, clinicians need to do it constantly. This interchange encourages a child to pay closer attention to grammatical forms, to listen more carefully, and to find the meaning of what is being said in the social context.

In Interactive Language Development Teaching, the child responds to questions or prompts which develop out of the plot line of the narrative. He is not asked merely to repeat preselected lists of sentences. At times he will even be led to ask questions. It is natural for a child to answer a question and for someone to comment on his response. In turn, it is natural for the child to feel free to elaborate upon or respond to a prompt or question within the exchange. This process develops a tolerance for the demand of spontaneous language formulation. Drills based entirely on rote repetition of phrases and sentences do not provide this experience.

Interactive Language Development Teaching incorporates many aspects of normal language acquisition into a clinical procedure. The lessons are developmentally organized and presented in storytelling form. The clinician reads a few lines of the story, then asks the child a question to elicit a target response which contains one or more of the grammatical goals of the lesson. The clinician then uses a variety of techniques for helping the child to produce a more mature response than he originally gave. In this way grammatical structure is presented to children in verbal interaction with an adult through discussion of subjects that are familiar and meaningful to them.

THE STRUCTURE OF THE LESSON

The lessons in Section II were designed for small groups of three to six children in a fifty-minute clinical session, but Interactive Language Development Teaching can be modified to meet other time requirements and other clinical settings. It is recommended that the session begin with a three-to-five-minute period of routine activity to get children settled and ready to listen. A calendar activity, in which children place their printed name cards under the appropriate day of the week, has been found most satisfactory for this purpose. Children learn to recognize their names, learn the names of the other children and the clinician, and are exposed to the names of the days of the week. Children are not expected to learn the serial order of day names but are expected to become familiar with this vocabulary and with the linguistic patterns of referring to time. Stereotyped phrases such as "I am here on Tuesday" serve to establish listening and responding behavior, to emphasize taking turns, and to provide a classroom atmosphere.

The story presentation takes thirty to thirty-five minutes of a fifty-minute session. A different story theme is used for each lesson as the vehicle for presenting and teaching language structures. Although all the children in a group hear the same story, the clinician treats each child individually when he responds to questions. Some children may progress at a faster rate than others, and more can be expected of them in terms of the target sentences. By carefully selecting and modifying the questions she asks of each child and by using the appropriate level of prompts for expanding each response, the clinician adapts the general procedure to individual needs. The children are called upon in random order, but an attempt is made to provide each child with an equal number of opportunities for response.

It is advisable to have a short break after thirty minutes of concentrated listening and responding to the story. Children may help rearrange the room, put away story materials, or get a drink, so that they have a moment of relaxation. The final ten to fifteen minutes of each lesson is devoted to a group activity in which material related to the story is presented in a new form. Pencil and paper activities may include drawing, tracing, coloring, cutting, and pasting; real-life activities, such as washing windows and dishes, decorating cupcakes, and hiding and finding objects, may be appropriate; imaginative activities, such as dressing up, playing store, and role-playing could be used. In all cases, the activities should relate to the theme, concepts, vocabulary, and grammatical structures presented during the story period, and the children should be encouraged to use in a spontaneous way the language that was presented to them first in a structured story form. Transcripts of the children's utterances during this section of the lesson are useful for judging their progress and for modifying the treatment goals in subsequent lessons. Thus, there is continuity in the sequence of lessons based on the prescriptive needs of the individual children in the group.

WRITING THE STORY

Lesson goals are derived from the Developmental Sentence Analysis of a child's spontaneous language sample. Long-range goals include a variety of pronouns, verb forms, negatives, conjunctions, and questions which he may be using inconsistently or which are one step above his demonstrated expressive-language level. Any one lesson selects four or five items from the many possible structures that would be developmentally appropriate and places them as target structures to be elicited from the child as responses to questions. Thus, the format of the story provides one column for the clinician's narrative, interspersed with questions, and another column for the anticipated target responses of the child. By reading the list of sentences in the target-response column, one can easily ascertain the language goals for any particular lesson and can judge the level of the language the child is being asked to produce. Section II contains one set of stories with beginning language goals and another set with more mature language structures, where this progression of language development is evident.

The lessons contained in Section II are not intended to be a workbook for a clinician to follow in rigid sequential order with any one child or group of children. They are intended to illustrate the type of language presentations which clinicians themselves can create. The following guidelines should help clinicians write effective language-development stories that highlight the grammatical structures of the lesson, clarify their meanings, and increase the probability that the child's response will come as close to the target as his capabilities allow.

Guidelines

1. *Select a story topic that is within the child's experience.* The theme of a story must reflect the experience and background of the children for whom it is written. New information and unfamiliar ideas should be avoided when the goal of a story presentation is language development. Children should not have to struggle with both content and grammatical structure at the same time, and closer attention can be given to structure if the content is familiar. Therefore, such subjects as Eskimos and igloos, butterflies and cocoons, are inappropriate for this purpose. Also, the story themes should be realistic rather than fanciful; witches and elves are not suitable characters. Animals that talk to one another are common enough in television cartoons to be acceptable to clinical children, but stories in which humans and animals talk together should be avoided as too unrealistic. Stories which anticipate Christmas have been found distracting to the

goals of a language lesson, and sad or tragic stories, involving injury, accident, and death, are apt to be upsetting or even confusing.

Suitable themes for language-development stories are the common, everyday experiences involving family members and their activities: going to the store, planning a birthday party, playing in the snow, caring for pets, or making visits to the park, the beach, or the airport. Such topics are within the experience of middle-class suburban children but would have to be modified for urban or rural groups or for institutionalized children. Story themes should provide action, dialogue between characters, and some degree of suspense, which makes it possible for the children to guess, infer, and anticipate events. Stories about putting out a fire or going to Kiddyland will hold interest better than writing a letter to Grandma. Three or four characters are sufficient; more than that may be confusing. All characters should be named by proper names. Attempts to utilize a continuing plot through several stories have not proved successful, since children with language problems may have difficulty in maintaining the continuity of a plot from one day to the next. Each story should be independent and should come to a logical conclusion. The stories in Section II illustrate the types of subjects which have been found most satisfactory for interactive language teaching. By glancing through their titles, the clinician will gain ideas for further story presentations suitable to her own group of clinic children.

2. *Provide sufficient narrative to keep the children's attention.* The number of sentences in the narrative prior to the elicitation of a target response can vary. Children in beginning language-development groups may have such limited attention spans and such poor receptive skills that three or four sentences of narrative are all they can handle at one time. The clinician will need to intersperse questions and elicit responses frequently in order to make sure that the story is clear and understandable to them. This example from Level I, Lesson 6, illustrates a fairly short narrative presentation with little content to remember:

NARRATIVE	TARGET RESPONSE
This is the fire station. The fire truck stays there. Here is a man. See him. He's by the fire truck . . . right here. He is the fireman. Who is he?	He is the fireman.
And look what else is here. It's a dog. This is the fireman's dog. This is Spot. Who is this?	This is Spot.

More advanced children can be expected to follow the story line through seven or eight sentences of narrative. The clinician must constantly evaluate a child's receptive capacities and provide adequate opportunity for him to follow the unfolding of an idea through longer and longer stretches of narrative. However, since language production by the child is the ultimate goal, the clinician should not become so carried away with her own storytelling that she neglects to provide adequate opportunity for verbal interaction with the children. The following example from Level II, Lesson 32, illustrates a longer narrative presentation:

NARRATIVE	TARGET RESPONSE
Bobby gets on the back of Timmy's new bike.	
They ride to the corner.	
They turn the corner.	
Timmy sees his house.	
He sees his mommy.	
His mommy is sweeping the sidewalk.	
She is sweeping the sidewalk.	
What is she doing?	She is sweeping the sidewalk.

3. *Provide adequate build-up of semantic content for the target structures.* Since one of the chief goals of interactive language teaching is to present language in a meaningful context rather than as an imitative drill, careful attention must be given to the informational content of the narrative which precedes a question. Sometimes the three to eight lines of narrative present the same information in a variety of ways, so that the semantic content is repeated while the grammatical structure is changed. The following example from Level I, Lesson 1, is illustrative:

NARRATIVE	TARGET RESPONSE
This is Bobby's school.	
But who is this lady?	
It's his teacher.	
This is Bobby's teacher.	
She is the teacher.	
Who is the lady?	She is the teacher.

Sometimes the narrative can provide simplification of a difficult grammatical structure through a series of built-up sentences, as in this example from Level II, Lesson 12:

NARRATIVE	TARGET RESPONSE
The horse has no place to live.	
He has nobody to live with.	
The horse is sad because he has nobody to live with.	

He is sad because he has nobody to live with. Why is the horse sad?	He is sad because he has nobody to live with.

Sometimes a sentence with a conjunction is more easily comprehended if its component sentences are presented separately, as in this example from Level II, Lesson 16:

NARRATIVE	TARGET RESPONSE
Timmy says: The sun is shining. It is warm today. It is warm today because the sun is shining. What does Timmy say?	It is warm today because the sun is shining.

Sometimes a new or difficult target structure can be included in the narrative twice before a child is asked to produce it, as in this example from Level II, Lesson 30:

NARRATIVE	TARGET RESPONSE
Bobby says: Which sidewalk goes to our house? Which one? Which sidewalk goes to our house? What does Bobby say?	Which sidewalk goes to our house?

Sometimes the narrative stresses related vocabulary, so that the meaning of a target response is clarified by the association of lexical items. In the following example from Level II, Lesson 16, the words *cut paper*, *need help*, and *can't do* emphasize the meaning of the reflexive pronoun *myself:*

NARRATIVE	TARGET RESPONSE
Timmy says: I will cut the paper. I will cut the paper, but I need help. I can't do it myself. Susan, will you help me? Will you help me because I can't do it myself? What does Timmy say?	Will you help me because I can't do it myself?

As the clinician writes the story, she should try to anticipate what difficulties the children may have with the semantic content of the target responses. The narrative can then be written to increase the probability of grammatical comprehension.

4. *Introduce new structures as receptive tasks before eliciting them as targets.* The narrative need not be confined to those grammatical items which are to be elicited from the children. Indeed, it would be difficult to write an interesting story using only the earliest grammatical forms. There is great value in having children hear plural pronouns, modal verbs, infinitives, and tag questions within the meaningful story context before they are asked to produce them. As one reads the stories in Section II, one can see that the narratives often contain items that become target structures in later lessons, as in this example from Level II, Lesson 4:

NARRATIVE

Mommy says:
I need some carrots,
Timmy.
Look in the refrigerator.
See if we have *any* carrots.
Timmy looks in the refrigerator.

The word *any* is not introduced as a target structure until Lesson 17, but it has been presented as a receptive task long before that time. The clinician must use good judgment in choosing the structures to be included in the narrative, avoiding grammatical items that are too far beyond the children's expressive level. In general, the narrative can contain structures one or two DSS levels above those expected as target responses.

5. *Provide frequent review to stabilize structures previously introduced as target responses.* Once a structure has been presented, it is important to continue to use it in succeeding sessions. Lesson planning should be cumulative, and structures that have received primary emphasis as target responses should continue to receive occasional secondary emphasis in later lessons. As a general rule, primary emphasis means at least five presentations in a single lesson, while secondary emphasis is considered to be three or four presentations. The secondary emphasis is used sometimes to introduce new grammatical forms and at other times to review or stabilize them; the primary emphasis is reserved for intensive work on the lesson goals. Each of the two levels of lessons presented in Section II is preceded by an index that indicates which stories give primary and secondary emphasis to the structures that are lesson goals. The structures that will receive primary and secondary emphasis are also listed at the beginning of each lesson. The continuity of grammatical presentation is thus readily observable.

6. *Clarify the concepts underlying the contentive vocabulary.* While Interactive Language Development Teaching is designed primarily for the

presentation of grammatical structure, attention should be given to the vocabulary of lexical nouns, verbs, and adjectives included in the stories. Vocabulary and grammatical structure reinforce and clarify each other in a conversational context, and there are many opportunities to explain vocabulary by way of grammar and often to explain grammatical structure by way of vocabulary. For example, word opposites and negative forms often occur together, as in this example from Level I, Lesson 7:

NARRATIVE	TARGET RESPONSE
The pony is standing over here. It's a little one. It is not big. See. It is a little pony. The pony is not big.	
Is the pony big?	No, it's not. The pony is not big.

Sometimes the superordinate structure of vocabulary can be introduced into a story, as in these examples from Level II, Lesson 15:

NARRATIVE	TARGET RESPONSE
Mommy says: Here is the fruit. What kind of fruit should we buy? What kind of fruit can they buy?	
Can you guess?	(Elicit responses from the children.)
Timmy says: Can we buy some apples? Can we? Can we buy some apples?	
What does Timmy say?	Can we buy some apples?
Mommy says: We need some dessert. Let's buy some dessert. What can they buy for dessert?	
Can you guess?	(Elicit responses from the children.)
Timmy says: I like ice cream. Can we buy ice cream? Can we? Can we buy ice cream?	
What does Timmy say?	Can we buy ice cream?

In almost all story presentations there is opportunity to include contentive vocabulary related to a general theme and thus to strengthen common word associations. The vocabulary stressed in each lesson in Section II is listed at the top of the story. For example, Level I, Lesson 14, associates *seed*, *flower*, *tomato*, *corn*, *hoe*, *digging*, *watering*, and *planting*; Level I, Lesson 15, associates *cookies*, *oven*, *stirring*, *baking*, *spoon*, *dough*, *soft*, *hard*, *round*, and *star*; and Level I, Lesson 21, associates *beach*, *towels*, *dry*, *wet*, *ball*, *swimming*, *wading*, and *watch*. Thus, the clinician can introduce various kinds of vocabulary-building opportunities involving opposites, superordinates, word associations, and word recall, all of which strengthen a child's ability to handle his lexicon of contentive words.

7. *Include questions which elicit creative thinking*. Not all questions in a narrative must necessarily elicit predetermined target responses. Sometimes children are asked to make spontaneous guesses from clues within the story. At other times they are asked to draw upon their own past experiences without such clues, as in this example from Level II, Lesson 3:

NARRATIVE	TARGET RESPONSE
Timmy says: This is the last car. It is on the end of the train. It is a funny car. Daddy says: That car has a funny name. It has a funny name. Timmy says: What is the name of the car? What is it? What is the name of the car?	
What does Timmy say?	What is the name of the car?
Do you know what the name is?	(Elicit answers from the children.)

Frequently the clinician can depart from the prepared story to ask questions which occur to her on the spur of the moment or in response to some spontaneous remark of a child. Interactive Language Teaching is particularly well suited to this type of conversational interchange which occurs fortuitously in a lesson. It provides an opportunity not only to observe the children's spontaneous language formulation but also to introduce creative and inferential thinking, logical problem-solving, and other abstract verbal tasks.

PRESENTING THE STORY

Interactive Language Development Teaching was designed primarily for use with a group of three to six children, but it can be used in individual lessons. While this technique was intended for preschool and primary-grade children, it has occasionally been modified for use with older children. A small room should be used, but one large enough to accommodate the group without crowding. Usually the children are seated at a table during the story presentation. It is most convenient to use a circular table or a V-shaped table arrangement. A flannel board on an adjustable easel is placed to the side of the clinician's hand of preference. The children's line of vision and height when seated should be considered in determining the height and angle of the flannel board. If possible, the clinician's chair should be on casters to facilitate ease of movement.

The clinician is allowed considerable flexibility in reading the prepared narrative. She may depart from the script whenever her own judgment dictates, she may repeat sections, she may elaborate spontaneously, and she may introduce new material as it occurs to her. A natural conversational pattern of emphasis should be used. Many beginning clinicians have a tendency to emphasize target structures unnaturally in language training, but children's interest is not enhanced by exaggerated prosodic emphasis. One can highlight structures in the story through repetition or use of exclamations but should not slow down or change the natural prosody of the utterances. Singsong or monotone presentation of the narrative and language models should also be avoided. However, presentation can be too rapid. Children with language problems often seem to require more time to process utterances than other children do. It is important not to rush through the narrative. Providing appropriate pacing and tempo in the story cues the children to be prepared to respond; too slow a presentation tends to result in lethargic participation by the children.

The verbal presentation should always be accompanied by visual materials, such as flannel-board cutouts, pictures, puppets, toys, and objects. The materials should be extremely simple, just enough to keep the subject of the story in visual attention, since auditory attention alone may be insufficient. Experience has shown that flannel-board materials are the easiest to make and to handle during the lesson presentation, and they are by far the least expensive. Moreover, since they can easily be placed out of the children's sight, they provide an element of surprise and novelty during the story. It has been found advisable to keep materials out of the children's reach as well, since manipulating toys, puppets, and even pictures during the story can be distracting to the lesson goals. Appropriate materials have been listed at the beginning of each lesson in Section II.

Eliciting the target response is the focal point of expressive-language teaching. Children are called upon individually, but several children may be asked the same stimulus question in turn. If the child's response is less than the target, the clinician engages in an interchange with him in an effort to elicit a longer or more accurate version of the target sentence. There are a number of techniques that the clinician has at her disposal for this purpose, and there is a general order in which they should be applied. Some interchange techniques offer a child more help than others, and a clinician should be aware of each child's abilities and the degree of help he needs in bringing his initial response closer to the target. The following interchange techniques are listed in the order of most to least help offered to the child.

Interchange Techniques

1. *Complete model.* A repetition of the desired target response, which the child then imitates, is typically used as a first step in establishing a response. This is an imitative task, in which the child is provided with the exact utterance expected. For example:

STIMULUS QUESTION	TARGET RESPONSE
Were they hot?	They were hot.

INTERCHANGE

Child: They hot.
Clinician: They were hot.
Child: They were hot.

2. *Reduced model.* A clinician may repeat a part of the desired target response, usually an element omitted in the child's original response. The child is expected to reformulate his response to include the elements presented in the reduced model. For example:

STIMULUS QUESTION	TARGET RESPONSE
Were they hot?	They were hot.

INTERCHANGE

Child: They hot.
Clinician: Were.
Child: They were hot.

This elicitation technique is typically used after a child can consistently imitate a complete model. The child's task is not imitation but rather reformulation of an utterance, with assistance, to include the critical elements. One exception to the use of the complete model as the first step in teaching is the introduction of interrogative reversals. The critical point in question formulation is the reversal of the subject of the sentence and the first auxiliary of the verb. A reduced model has proved to be the most efficient means of highlighting the critical elements of this structure. Thus, reduced models are the first prompts used to establish question responses. For example:

STIMULUS QUESTION	TARGET RESPONSE
What did Bobby say?	Can I go out?

INTERCHANGE

Child: I go out?
Clinician: Can I?
Child: I can go out?
Clinician: Can I?
Child: Can I go out?

3. *Expansion requests.* Next in the general hierarchy of these techniques is the request for a child to expand his incomplete response without a model from the clinician. No clue as to which element has been omitted or incorrectly attempted is given to the child. The child is merely told that his response is incomplete. Expansion requests can take various forms: "Tell me the whole thing"; "Tell me some more"; "Say all of it." In this task the child is encouraged to be less dependent on the clinician for modeling or monitoring his response. For example:

STIMULUS QUESTION	TARGET RESPONSE
What is Bobby doing?	Bobby is going to the park.

INTERCHANGE

Child: Bobby going park.
Clinician: Tell me the whole thing.
Child: Bobby is going.
Clinician: Tell me more.
Child: Bobby is going to the park.

4. *Repetition request.* The next in this series is a request for the child to repeat his response to the stimulus question. This, like the expansion request, can be used to indicate to the child that his response is incomplete or in error and that he should reformulate it. The repetition request is less specific than the expansion request because the child is not told that anything has been omitted from his utterance. This prompt can also be used as a means of stabilizing and reinforcing a correct response. The repetition request typically takes the form "Tell me that again" or "What did you say?" For example:

STIMULUS QUESTION	TARGET RESPONSE
What did he do?	He went to the store.

INTERCHANGE

Child: He goed to store.
Clinician: What did you say?

Child: He went to the store.
Clinician: Again.
Child: He went to the store.

5. *Repetition of error.* Sometimes it is useful to repeat the child's own error. In a sense, the clinician is thereby asking the child to pick out the error in the utterance and to reformulate it correctly. At times the clinician may aid the child in recognizing the error by repeating the child's responses with a questioning facial expression or intonation. For example:

STIMULUS QUESTION	TARGET RESPONSE
What did he do?	He went to the store.

INTERCHANGE

Child: He go to the store.
Clinician: He go to the store?
Child: He goed to the store.
Clinician: Goed?
Child: Went. He went to the store.

Although on the surface this appears to be more specific than the two prior techniques, our experience has shown that verbalizing the child's error before the child can respond consistently to expansion and/or repetition requests is confusing. At an early stage, children appear to use the repetition of their errors as models to be imitated rather than as clues for correction, and this should be avoided.

6. *Self-correction request.* The clinician asks the child whether his response was correct or incorrect. This is a less specific prompt than repeating the child's error, and, like the repetition request, it can be used in two ways. When a response is in error, a self-correction request can be used to stimulate reformulation and correction. This prompt can also be used to stabilize and reinforce correct responses. In the latter instance the child may merely affirm the correctness of his response. The self-correction request usually takes the form "Is that right?" or "Is your answer right?" For example:

STIMULUS QUESTION	TARGET RESPONSE
Is he going home?	He is not going home.

INTERCHANGE

Child: He not going home.
Clinician: Is that answer right?
Child: He is not going
home.
Clinician: Is it right now?
Child: Yes.

7. *Rephrased question.* When there have been several intervening interchanges between the stimulus question and the elicitation of the correct target response, it is effective to restate the original question or rephrase the question to re-elicit the target response. Often a question form simpler than the original is used. This new question may elicit an incomplete response, but generally the response moves in the direction of a closer approximation to the intended target. The rephrased question is also a means for stabilizing a correct response to the stimulus question. For example:

STIMULUS QUESTION	TARGET RESPONSE
What did Bobby do?	Bobby went to the circus.

INTERCHANGE

Child: Bobby go to the circus.
Clinician: Went.
Child: Bobby went to the circus.
Clinician: Did Bobby go to the circus?
Child: Yes, Bobby went to the circus.

For purposes of illustration in the above discussion, each elicitation technique has been used in isolation. In clinical application the clinician might use a combination of these techniques to elicit the desired response. Following are some examples of typical combinations and sequences of prompts.

INTERCHANGE A

Clinician: Karen says: I'm hot.
What can we do?
I want to cool off.
I don't want to be hot.
I don't like being hot.
What can we do to cool off?
What does she say, Anthony?
Anthony: What can we . . . . What Karen have for cool off?
Clinician: What can we do?
Anthony: What can we do for cool off?
Clinician: What can we do to cool off?
Anthony: What can we do to . . .
Clinician: You're right. What can we do to cool off?
Anthony: What can we do to cool off?
Clinician: Very nice. Tell me that one more time.
Anthony: What can we do . . .
Clinician: What can we do to . . .
Anthony: What can we do to . . .
Clinician: Tell me the whole thing.
Anthony: What can we do . . . to cool off?
Clinician: Good.

INTERCHANGE B

Clinician: Timmy and Karen ran into the house.
They ran into the house.
They found Mommy.
Timmy says: Mommy, we are hot.
It's very hot outside.
We want to cool off.
But we don't know what to do.
We don't know what we can do.
How should we cool off?
We don't know what to do.
What did he say, Wendy?
Wendy: We don't know what to do.
Clinician: Very good. Tell me again.
Wendy: We don't know what to do to cool off.
Clinician: Very nice.

INTERCHANGE C

Clinician: What did he say?
What did Timmy say, Mark?
Mark: What could we do cool off.
Clinician: Almost.
He said: We don't know what to do.
Mark: We don't know what to do.
Clinician: Tell me again.
Mark: We don't know what to do.
Clinician: Good.

INTERCHANGE D

Clinician: Mommy says: I know.
I know what you can do.
I'll help you cool off.
I know what you can do.
What does she say, Anthony?
Anthony: I know what can do.
Clinician: I know what can do?
Anthony: I know what *you* can do.
Clinician: Was that right?
Anthony: Yes.
Clinician: Good. Tell me again.
Anthony: I know what you can do.
Clinician: Very nice.

INTERCHANGE E

Clinician: Timmy and Karen and Bobby ran through the sprinklers.

They weren't hot any longer.
They were cooling off.
They were having lots of fun.
They weren't hot any longer.
Were they still hot, Wendy?
Wendy: They wasn't hot any longer.
Clinician: They wasn't?
Wendy: They were not hot any longer.
Clinician: Good. They weren't.
Wendy: They weren't hot any longer.
Clinician: Were they hot, Wendy?
Wendy: No, they weren't hot any longer.
Clinician: Good.

Interactive Language Development Teaching allows a clinician considerable flexibility in deciding how to handle any one interchange with a child. Individual children respond differently to the variety of interchange techniques, and the clinician must select appropriate procedures for each child. The clinician must also use her own judgment in deciding how long to persist with a single interchange and when to accept a less-than-accurate target response as a child's best performance. The attention of the group may be lost during an unduly long interchange with one child, and that must be avoided.

EVALUATING THE LESSONS

The refinement of any clinical technique is directly related to the adequacy of objective assessments of both the children's and the clinician's performances. The extent and rate of children's learning must constantly be reassessed so that future lesson-planning will be appropriate to their progress. Likewise, the clinician must submit her clinical performance to systematic analysis so that her effectiveness will be increased.

Evaluating Children's Progress

It is important to judge a child's progress not only by his performance during the lesson periods but in a setting quite apart from the clinical classroom. Progress should be assessed not only by his response to structured lessons but by the quality of his spontaneous speech in conversation with an adult, using novel stimulus materials. The Developmental Sentence Scoring procedure (see Chart I, pages 4–5), which evaluates a child's grammatical development from a tape-recorded language sample, affords this kind of objective assessment. Previous research on the temporal reliability of repeated application of the DSS procedure indicates that it can be used at intervals as brief as four months.

The over-all performance on the DSS language sample allows a clinician to quantify the general level of grammatical usage in spontaneous speech. The child's DSS score can be compared directly to the chart of norms (see Chart II) for children between 2–0 and 6–11 years of age. By plotting an individual child's successive DSS scores on the norm chart, his rate of language growth can be compared either with children of his chronological age or with children at his stage of language development. A set of cumulative DSS scores, thus displayed, gives a picture of a child's language growth during the remedial training period and provides strong evidence of the effectiveness of the clinical teaching.

The information which is most useful in planning a remedial program is derived not from the child's over-all DSS score on his language sample but from an analysis of the structures he produced within individual grammatical categories. The clinician should examine the entries in each DSS category and ascertain which items the child is correctly formulating. Once a child is spontaneously formulating a language structure correctly 50 per cent of the time, it is no longer necessary to give primary emphasis to this structure in the remedial program; it may continue to receive emphasis, however, at a secondary level or in combination with other structures.

The next step is to examine the attempt entries within each category of the DSS which were incorrect. These are strong indicators of the child's language needs. They indicate that the child has or is developing a concept for which he does not have an appropriate syntactic or morphological form. These attempts should guide the clinician in selecting future remedial goals. Another factor which should be examined is the DSS categories which the child does not use. Remedial work in these categories should begin at the receptive level, since the child has not indicated concepts underlying their usage.

Another way in which a child's progress can be evaluated is through the type of prompts that are required for eliciting the target structures during an interchange with the clinician. Children in beginning language training may need complete models frequently but later may show that they can approximate the target structure with only a repetition request or with the clinician's repetition of the error. Sometimes a child may correct himself spontaneously or may give even more information than the target response required. Over a series of lessons the clinician should look for movement away from the earliest types of prompts to more subtle prompting. A child's continued reliance on the most explicit types of prompts over a long period of time may indicate that the level of difficulty of the target utterance is inappropriate. If, on the other hand, a child is responding consistently to less explicit prompts, this indicates a need to increase either the

CHART II. NORMS FOR DEVELOPMENTAL SENTENCE SCORING (REWEIGHTED)

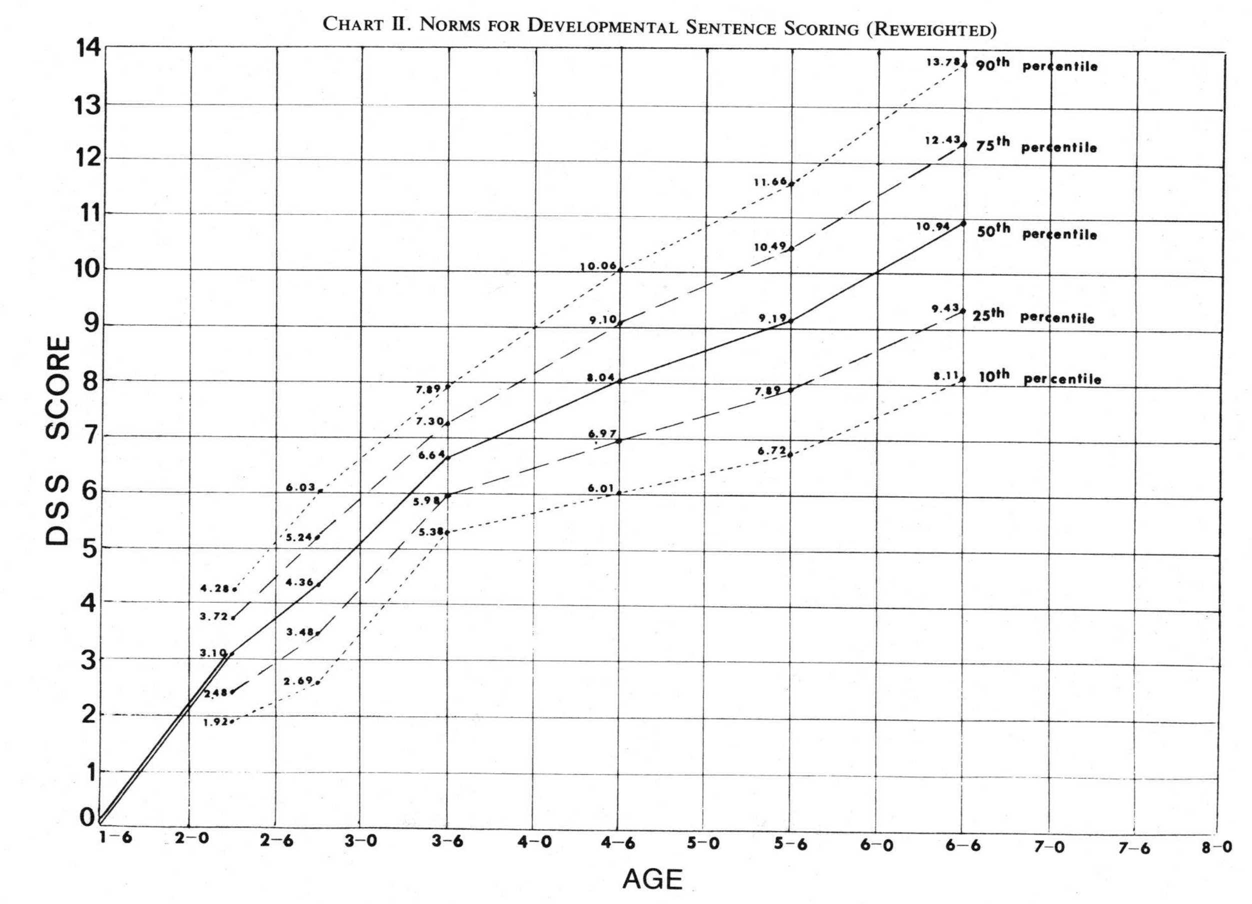

maturity of the syntax or the length of the target response. The clinician should consistently upgrade the child's formulation skills by moving through levels of difficulty in terms of both reliance on prompts and the demands of the response requirements.

Another gauge of progress in language learning is the child's ability to formulate novel, spontaneous sentences with the structures that are receiving emphasis in the lessons. Sometimes the child may expand the sentence that is a target response, as in the following examples:

NARRATIVE	TARGET RESPONSE
Bobby and Susie are going to the park. They are gonna go on the swings. They are gonna play on the swings. They are gonna play on the swings. What are they gonna do?	They are gonna play on the swings.

INTERCHANGE

Child: They are gonna play on the swings.
Clinician: Good.
Child: They are gonna go on the slide, too.

NARRATIVE	TARGET RESPONSE
Timmy says: Mommy, we are hot. It is very hot outside. We want to cool off. But we don't know what to do. How should we cool off? We don't know what to do. What did he say?	We don't know what to do.

INTERCHANGE

Child: We don't know what to do.
Clinician: Good.
Child: We don't know what to do to cool off.

Another indication of the child's facility with newly learned structures is his demonstration of self-monitoring through spontaneous self-correction. Some children appear to do more self-correction, while others evidence more expansion behavior. This is another example of the individuality children demonstrate in learning. The related creative activity and other nonstructured periods in the lesson provide an opportunity for informal assessment of a child's use of language structures. A child's appropriate usage of primary-emphasis structures in nonstructured activities should be a clear indication to the clinician to move forward in lesson-planning.

Group performance can be analyzed by combining and charting the performances of the individual children. In addition, the clinician should take note of the general pattern of group behavior. In order to judge whether the story plot is being understood and whether high interest levels are being maintained, a clinician should note whether the children are able to resolve logical questions from clues in the narrative and whether they develop hypotheses or speculate on what is going to happen next in the story. Another index of group performance is the degree of participation of all children in the lesson, as indicated by the tempo of response. It is immediately obvious to an observer, or to a reviewer of an audiotape of a lesson, when the lesson is dragging.

Evaluating Clinician Effectiveness

The obvious measure of a clinician's effectiveness lies in the progress of the children whom she is teaching, but there are also other ways in which her performance can be evaluated. It is possible to chart the order in which the clinician uses the types of elicitation techniques within each interchange with a child. This information identifies which prompts are most effective for each child and indicates when a clinician is not capitalizing on the basic treatment method of moving the child from reliance on explicit prompts to more subtle forms.

Chart III, the Interchange Chart, lists the various types of prompts a clinician can use as interchange techniques. These prompts are displayed in a left-to-right order of diminishing amount of help a child receives from the clinician. For example, the most helpful kind of prompt, after the Stimulus Question, is the Complete Model, which is the target sentence repeated by the clinician for the child to produce. The Reduced Model gives less help, and the Expansion Request and Repetition Request give no help at all in remodeling the target structure. The clinician's Repetition of Error requires the child to recognize his own mistake in her speech, while the Self-Correction Request gives no hint as to what the error was. The Rephrased Question is the least helpful of all, for it merely repeats the Stimulus Question, and that was the source of the initial failure. The interchanges between the child and the clinician are numbered and classified on the Interchange Chart according to the type of prompt which was given. The child's success or failure to produce the target structure is noted by a + or − after the number of the interchange. Through this charting one can identify clinicians who consistently use one or two

CHART III. The Interchange Chart

Interchange	Stimulus Question	Complete Model	Reduced Model	Expansion Request	Repetition Request	Repetition of Error	Self-Correction Request	Rephrased Question
A	1 –	3 – 4 +	2 – 6 –	7 +	5 –			
B	1 +				2 +			
C	1 –	2 +			3 +			
D	1 –				4 +	2 +	3 +	
E	1 –		3 +			2 +		4 +

The numbers on this chart indicate the order of usage of the elicitation techniques. The + and – notations indicate the correctness of the child's response.

methods of eliciting a response, regardless of their effectiveness. One can also identify clinicians who persist with the same prompt when it is not eliciting the desired behavior.

To illustrate the use of the Interchange Chart, the interchanges on pages 21 and 23 have been recorded on Chart III. For example, in Interchange A (Chart III) the child failed to respond accurately to the Stimulus Question (1 −) and also failed to respond accurately to the Reduced Model (2 −). The clinician then wisely went to the most helpful interchange technique, the Complete Model, and the child failed on its first presentation (3 −) but succeeded on the second attempt (4 +). The clinician did not stop there but proceeded to give the more difficult Repetition Request, which the child could not do (5 −), nor could he accurately produce the structure from the more helpful Reduced Model (6 −). He then performed accurately on an Expansion Request (7 +), after which the clinician returned to the story. This clinician correctly judged the child's inability to cope with more subtle interchange techniques and returned to more helpful types of prompts when necessary. She did not persist in prompting him at one level only but actively aided the child to produce the desired target structure by giving him many kinds of cues.

In Interchange D (Chart III) the child was capable of success with the subtler forms of prompts. Although he failed to produce the target structure accurately in response to the Stimulus Question (1 −), he was able to correct it when the clinician gave a Repetition of Error (2 +). In order to give him a little more practice, the clinician then went to more difficult prompts, the Self-Correction Request (3 +) and the Repetition Request (4 +), before returning to the story.

The child in Interchange E (Chart III) was also able to make use of the more subtle prompts. Although the Stimulus Question (1 −) was answered incorrectly, the clinician's Repetition of Error (2 +) elicited it. The clinician then gave the contracted form of the target structure in a Reduced Model (3 +), which was also successful. Before returning to the story, the clinician gave the most demanding prompt of all, the Rephrased Question (4 +), which was answered correctly. Thus the child had several opportunities to produce the target structure under a variety of elicitation conditions.

This kind of charting of a clinician's performance can best be done by the clinician herself from a videotape, where she can see and evaluate her own clinical style. It can also be done by observers who are familiar enough with the procedure to keep up with the tempo of the lesson. It can be done informally, from recall of the sequence of events within a lesson;

this method is less successful, but it can provide a clinician with some guidelines for the moment-to-moment interchange with children. In reviewing the lesson, the clinician's effectiveness should be judged on the following points:

1. Did the clinician always provide feedback to the children? An interchange should not end without some indication of the child's success or lack of success. This is particularly important at the end of a lengthy interchange.

2. Did the clinician reinforce only correct responses of the children? Clinicians can inadvertently reinforce an incorrect response with a stereotyped "OK" or through nonverbal cues, such as head-nodding and smiling. A particular danger lies in reinforcing unintelligible or ambiguous responses, in which the criteria of the target sentence were not clearly met.

3. Did the clinician pursue a target response by using appropriate prompting techniques in the interchange? The goal of each interchange is the accurate formulation by the child of the target response specified in the lesson. Sometimes a clinician may move on to another child too quickly if a target response is not immediately correct. A child should be given more than one opportunity to formulate the target sentence. Sometimes the clinician may use inappropriate prompting procedures, so that the child is not really aided in giving a correct response. The clinician may discover that she has been relying on only one or two prompting techniques, with the result that her lesson administration has become stereotyped and repetitious. She may discover that she is using such subtle or complex prompts that a child cannot be successful with them; she may also find that she is not increasing the level of difficulty for those children who are capable of responding to more subtle prompting techniques.

4. Did the clinician modify the demands of the target response for individual children? Rigid adherence to the specified response is not always desirable. When it becomes obvious that a child is unable to formulate the exact target, the clinician must determine what an acceptable response is for him. A child with a word-retrieval problem may not be able to call up the specific lexical items in the target, but he may give a response which contains the correct grammatical features being stressed. In a case like the following, the clinician could consider the child's response as acceptable:

TARGET RESPONSE	ACCEPTABLE RESPONSE
The salesman is measuring Bobby's foot.	The shoe man is measuring Bobby's foot.

A child with limited auditory-memory skills may shorten the target response but correctly demonstrate mastery of the critical grammatical features, as in the following example:

TARGET RESPONSE	ACCEPTABLE RESPONSE
Did Bobby's mommy find the blue sock?	Did Mommy find the sock?

5. Did the clinician repeat the target sentence when she called upon a second child? During an interchange with one child, the initial target sentence may fade from memory or go through so many variations that succeeding children will not have success in producing it. As the clinician proceeds from one child to another, it is often advisable to repeat the target before asking the question in order to refresh the children's memories and increase their chances of success.

6. Did the clinician provide adequate opportunities for response from each child in the group? Note should be made of the number of times each child responded per session and of the amount of the clinician's time devoted to each child. Slight discrepancies in this distribution in an individual story presentation are permissible, but the distribution should be equal over a series of three or four lessons.

7. Did the target responses planned in the story adequately challenge the children's formulation ability? When high percentages of correct responses to initial stimulus questions occur, it indicates that the structures selected for treatment are already in the children's usable grammar. This may be desirable occasionally as a review, but the purpose of Interactive Language Development Teaching is to induce new language usage.

TRANSCRIPT OF A LESSON

Two films are available from the Northwestern University Film Library for the purpose of illustrating the clinical procedures described here. *Developmental Sentence Scoring: A Demonstration Film* (Koenigsknecht, Mulhern, and Lee) shows the elicitation of a language sample from a clinical child and the technique of analysis which leads to prescriptive language training. *Developmental Language Teaching: A Demonstration Film* (Koenigsknecht, Mulhern, and Lee) shows the administration of language lessons to various clinical groups, using the interactive approach to language training. Here, however, a clear illustration of the teaching method can best be given by the transcript of an actual lesson. The reader can see how swiftly or slowly the story moves, how the clinician interacts with individual children in a group setting, how much time is taken in a single interchange, and what sequences of prompts can be used to elicit the desired responses. In the following transcript these points become clear. The children, aged four and five, are in a rather advanced group, where the language goals include possessive pronouns, wh-word with infinitive, the conjunction *because*, the infinitive of purpose, avoidance of the double negative, and considerable length of target responses.

CLINICIAN: This is Timmy.
Timmy is a boy.
Timmy is the boy in our story.
Who is this, Donald?

DONALD: This is Timmy.

CLINICIAN: Okay.
This is Karen.
Karen is Timmy's sister.
Karen is the girl in our story.
Who is this, Rachel?

RACHEL: Karen.

CLINICIAN: Tell me the whole thing.

RACHEL: This is Karen.

CLINICIAN: Good.
Who is this, Greg?

GREG: Karen.

CLINICIAN: Tell me the whole thing.

GREG: This is Karen.

CLINICIAN: Okay. Good.
Timmy and Karen are outside.
They are playing in the sandbox.
They are building sand castles.
They are playing in the sandbox.
What are they doing, Greg?

GREG: They are building a sand castle.

CLINICIAN: Sandbox.

GREG: They are playing in the sandbox.

CLINICIAN: Good, Greg.
They are playing in the sandbox.
What are they doing, Michael?

MICHAEL: They're playing in the sandbox.

CLINICIAN: They are . . .

MICHAEL: They are playing in the sandbox.

CLINICIAN: Very nice.
They are playing in the sandbox.
Timmy said: It's sure hot today.

I'm hot.
Are you hot, Karen?
Are you?
Are you hot, Karen?
What did Timmy say, Billy?

BILLY: Are you hot, Karen?

CLINICIAN: That's right.
Are you hot, Karen?
What did Timmy say, Donald?

DONALD: Are you hot, Karen?

CLINICIAN: Good, Donald.
Karen said: Yes, I'm hot.
What can we do?
I want to cool off.
I don't want to be hot.
What can we do to cool off?
What did Karen say, Rachel?

RACHEL: What we can do to cool off?

CLINICIAN: What can we . . .

RACHEL: What can we do to cool off?

CLINICIAN: Good, Rachel.
What did Karen say, Michael?

MICHAEL: What we can do to cool off?

CLINICIAN: Can we . . .
What can we . . .

MICHAEL: What can we do?

CLINICIAN: To cool off.
Okay.
What can we do to cool off?
What do you do to cool off, Greg?
When you're hot, what do you do to cool off?

GREG: I don't know . . .
Sometimes when there's heat . . . in the nighttime, we turn on the air conditioner.

CLINICIAN: You turn the air conditioner on.
That's one way to cool off.
What do you do to cool off, Billy?

BILLY: I turn my bedroom air conditioner on, too.

CLINICIAN: Okay.
But Timmy and Karen are outside.
They can't turn on an air conditioner.
What can they do to cool off, Donald?

DONALD: Turn on the air conditioner outside?

CLINICIAN: They don't have an air conditioner outside.
They have to find another way to cool off.

Timmy said: I don't know what to do.
Let's ask Mommy, because she will know what to do.
Let's ask Mommy, because she'll know what to do.
What did Timmy say, Greg?

GREG: Let's go ask Mommy, because she'll know what to do.

CLINICIAN: Right.
Timmy and Karen ran into the house.
They found Mommy.
Timmy said: Mommy, we are hot.
We want to cool off.
But we don't know what to do.
We don't know how to cool off.
We don't know what to do.
What did Timmy say, Billy?

BILLY: We don't know how . . .
We don't . . .
What can we do?

CLINICIAN: We don't know what . . .

BILLY: We don't know what.

CLINICIAN: To . . .

BILLY: To do.

CLINICIAN: Do it once more.

BILLY: We don't want to . . .

CLINICIAN: We don't know . . .

BILLY: We don't know.

CLINICIAN: What to do.

BILLY: What to do.

CLINICIAN: We don't know what to do.
What did Timmy say, Billy?

BILLY: We don't . . .
I said it already.

CLINICIAN: I want you to say the whole thing.
We don't know what to do.

BILLY: We don't know what we can do.

CLINICIAN: What to do.

BILLY: What to do.

CLINICIAN: Okay.
Say the whole thing.

BILLY: We can . . .

CLINICIAN: We don't . . .

BILLY: We don't know what to do.

CLINICIAN: Good, Billy.
We don't know what to do.
Mommy said: I know.
I know what you can do.
I'll help you cool off.
I know what to do.
What did Mommy say, Rachel?

RACHEL: I know what to do.

CLINICIAN: Good.
What did Mommy say, Greg?

GREG: I help you . . . I know what to do.

CLINICIAN: I know what to do.
Right.
What did Mommy say, Michael?

MICHAEL: I know what to do.

CLINICIAN: Very good.
Mommy said: First you must take off your playclothes.
Put on your swimming suits.
Take off your playclothes and put on your swimming suits.
What did Mommy say, Donald?

DONALD: Take off your playsuits and put on your swimsuits.

CLINICIAN: Okay.
Take off your playclothes and put on your swimsuits.
What did Mommy say, Billy?

BILLY: Take off your playclothes and put on your swimsuits.

CLINICIAN: Good. Very good.
They're going to put on their swimming suits.
What are they going to do, Rachel?

RACHEL: They are putting on they swimming suits.

CLINICIAN: Their swimming suits.
What are they going to do, Rachel?

RACHEL: They are putting on they swimming suits.

CLINICIAN: Their swimming suits.

RACHEL: They are putting on their swimming suits.

CLINICIAN: Okay.
Timmy ran to his bedroom.
He took off his playclothes.
He put on his swimming suit.
He ran to his bedroom and put on his swimming suit.
What did Timmy do, Greg?

GREG: He runned . . .
He ran to him room and put on him swimming suit.

CLINICIAN: He ran to *his* room.
Try it again.

GREG: He ran to he bedroom and put on he swimming suit.

CLINICIAN: His bedroom.

GREG: His bedroom.

CLINICIAN: Okay.
He ran . . .

GREG: He ran.

CLINICIAN: Go ahead.

GREG: He ran to he bedroom.

CLINICIAN: His.

GREG: His bedroom and put on him bathing suit.

CLINICIAN: His.

GREG: His bathing suit.

CLINICIAN: Okay, Greg.
Good try.
He ran to his bedroom and put on his bathing suit.
What did Timmy do, Rachel?

RACHEL: He ran to he bedroom and put on he bathing suit.

CLINICIAN: His.

RACHEL: His bathing suit.

CLINICIAN: His bedroom, his bathing suit.
Try it again.
He ran . . .

RACHEL: He ran to he bedroom.

CLINICIAN: His.

RACHEL: His bedroom and put on he bathing suit.

CLINICIAN: Good try, Rachel.
He ran to his room and put on his bathing suit.
Karen ran to her bedroom.
She took off her playclothes.
She put on her swimming suit.
She ran to her room and put on her bathing suit.
What did Karen do, Michael?

MICHAEL: He ran to his bathing suit, and he put on his bathing suit.
And he going swim?

CLINICIAN: I think *she's* going swimming. Listen.
She ran to her . . .

MICHAEL: She ran to her . . .

CLINICIAN: Room.

MICHAEL: To get her swimming suit on.

CLINICIAN: Okay.
She ran to her room and put on her swimming suit.
What did Karen do, Rachel?

RACHEL: She ran to her bedroom and put on he bathing suit.

CLINICIAN: Put on her bathing suit.

RACHEL: Put on her bathing suit.

CLINICIAN: Good try.
She ran to her room and put on her bathing suit.
Karen and Timmy ran to find Mommy.
Karen said: What are we going to do?
What are we going to do?
Are we going to go swimming?
What did Karen say, Donald?

DONALD: What are we going to do?

CLINICIAN: Good.
What did Karen say, Greg?

GREG: What are we gonna do?

CLINICIAN: Very nice.
Mommy said: Come with me.
Let's go into the garage.
I'll get out the sprinkler.
Then you can cool off.
I'll get out the sprinkler so you can cool off.
I'll get out the sprinkler so you can cool off.
What did Mommy say, Rachel?

RACHEL: I can't.

CLINICIAN: I'll get . . .

RACHEL: I get . . .

CLINICIAN: I'll get . . .

RACHEL: I'll get the sprinkler so you cool off.

CLINICIAN: So you can . . .

RACHEL: So you can cool off.

CLINICIAN: Okay. I'll get out the sprinkler so you can cool off.
What did Mommy say, Michael?

MICHAEL: I'll get out the sprinkler so you can cool off.

CLINICIAN: Good, Michael.
Timmy said: Good. We can cool off now.
We can cool off under the sprinkler.
What did Timmy say, Greg?

GREG: We can cool off now.

CLINICIAN: Good.
Under the sprinkler.
We can cool off under the sprinkler.
What did Timmy say, Billy?

BILLY: We can cool under the sprinkler now.

CLINICIAN: Cool off . . .

BILLY: Cool off under the sprinkler.

CLINICIAN: Okay. Tell me the whole thing.

BILLY: Last night my sprinkler was on.

CLINICIAN: Was it? Oh!
What did Timmy say?

BILLY: And I didn't run in it.

CLINICIAN: Okay. But what did Timmy say?

BILLY: We can cool off under the sprinkler.

CLINICIAN: Good, Billy.
Mommy got out the sprinkler.
There's the sprinkler.
She put it in the yard.
She got out the sprinkler and put it in the yard.
What did Mommy do, Rachel?

RACHEL: I don't know.

CLINICIAN: What did Mommy do, Donald?

DONALD: Mommy put out the sprinkler.

CLINICIAN: Got . . .

DONALD: Put out . . .

CLINICIAN: Got . . .

DONALD: Got.

CLINICIAN: Mommy got out . . .

DONALD: Mommy got out the sprinkler so we can cool off.

CLINICIAN: Good try.
She got out the sprinkler and put it in the yard.
What did Mommy do, Mike?

MIKE: She got out the sprinkler so they can cool off.

CLINICIAN: Okay. And put it in the yard.

MIKE: And put it in the yard.

CLINICIAN: Try it again, Mike.

MIKE: She put out the sprinkler in the yard so they go under the sprinkler.

CLINICIAN: Okay.
She got out the sprinkler and put it in the yard.
What did Mommy do, Rachel?

RACHEL: I don't know.

CLINICIAN: She got out the sprinkler and put it in the yard.

RACHEL: She got out sprinkler and put it in the yard.

CLINICIAN: Good.
She got out the sprinkler and put it in the yard.
Timmy got the hose.
He connected it to the faucet.
The faucet is where he'll get the water.
He connected the hose to the faucet.
He connected the hose to the faucet.
What did Timmy do?

DONALD: He connected the hose to the faucet.

CLINICIAN: Right. He connected the hose to the faucet.
What did Timmy do, Rachel?

RACHEL: Connected the hose to the faucet.

CLINICIAN: Tell me again.
He connected . . .

RACHEL: He connected to a hose . . .

CLINICIAN: He connected the hose.

RACHEL: Hose to a faucet.

CLINICIAN: He connected the hose to the faucet.
What did he do?

RACHEL: He connected a hose to a faucet.

CLINICIAN: Good, Rachel.
He connected the hose to the faucet.
Timmy said: When can I turn on the water?
Tell me when, Mommy.
Tell me when to turn on the water.
What did Timmy say, Greg?

GREG: Tell me when to turn on the water.

CLINICIAN: Good, Greg.
Tell me when to turn on the water.
What did Timmy say, Billy?

BILLY: Tell me when turn on the water.

CLINICIAN: When to turn.

BILLY: When on turn the water.

CLINICIAN: When to turn . . .

BILLY: When on turn the water on.

CLINICIAN: To turn.

BILLY: To turn on the water on.

CLINICIAN: When to turn on the water.

BILLY: When on.

CLINICIAN: When to turn.

BILLY: When turn.

CLINICIAN: When to turn.

BILLY: When to turn to . . .

CLINICIAN: On . . .

BILLY: On the water.

CLINICIAN: Tell me when to turn on the water.
What did Timmy say?

BILLY: Tell me when turn on the water.

CLINICIAN: When to turn.

BILLY: When on to the water.

CLINICIAN: When to turn.

BILLY: When on to . . .

CLINICIAN: When to . . .

BILLY: When to . . .

CLINICIAN: Turn on . . .

BILLY: Turn on the water.

CLINICIAN: Good try, Billy.
Tell me when to turn on the water.
What did Timmy say, Donald?

DONALD: Tell me when to turn on the water.

CLINICIAN: Good, Donald.
Mommy said: Wait.
I have to get out of the way.
I don't want to get wet.
I have to get out of the way
because I don't want to get wet.
What did Mommy say, Mike?

MIKE: I wanna get out of the way so I won't get wet.

CLINICIAN: Good.
I have to get out of the way.

MIKE: I have to get out of the way so I . . .

CLINICIAN: Because.

MIKE: Because I don't want to get wet.

CLINICIAN: Good, Mike.
I have to get out of the way because I don't want to get wet.
What did Mommy say, Greg?

GREG: I have to get out of the way because I can't get wet.

CLINICIAN: Because I don't want to get wet.
Greg, what did Mommy say?

GREG: I have to get out of the way so I don't get wet.

CLINICIAN: Because I don't want to get wet.

GREG: Because I don't want to get wet.

CLINICIAN: Okay, try the whole thing.

GREG: I have to get out the way so I don't get wet.

CLINICIAN: Because I don't want to get wet.

GREG: 'Cause I don't want to get wet.

CLINICIAN: Because . . .

GREG: I have to get out of the way because I don't want to get wet.

CLINICIAN: Good, Greg.
Mommy got out of the way.
Mommy said: I'm out of the way now.
You can turn the water on.
I'm out of the way, so you can turn the water on now.
I'm out of the way, so you can turn the water on now.
What did Mommy say, Rachel?

RACHEL: I'm out of the way, so you can turn on the water.

CLINICIAN: Good, Rachel.
I'm out of the way, so you can turn the water on now.
What did Mommy say, Donald?

DONALD: I'm out of the way, so you can turn the water on.

CLINICIAN: Right.
Timmy said: Okay.
He turned on the water.
He turned on the water.
The water went through the hose.

It went to the sprinkler.
The sprinkler started to go back and forth.
The water made the sprinkler go back and forth.
Back and forth.
The water made the sprinkler go back and forth.
What did the water do, Greg?

GREG: The sprinkler made the water go back and forth.

CLINICIAN: The water made the sprinkler . . .

GREG: The water made the sprinkler go back and forth.

CLINICIAN: Good, Greg.
The water made the sprinkler go back and forth.
What did the water do, Billy?

BILLY: The water made the sprinkler go back and forth.

CLINICIAN: Good, Billy.
Karen ran through the water.
She got wet.
She ran through the water and got wet.
What did she do, Mike?

MIKE: She ran through the water and got wet.

CLINICIAN: Good.
What did she do, Rachel?

RACHEL: She ran through the water, and she got wet.

CLINICIAN: Very nice.
Timmy ran through the water.
Timmy ran through the water.
He got his hands wet.
He got his feet wet.
He got his face wet.
He got his swimming suit wet.
What did he get wet, Billy?

BILLY: He got his foots . . .

CLINICIAN: His feet.

BILLY: His feet wet.

CLINICIAN: Tell me that again.

BILLY: He got his feet wet.

CLINICIAN: Greg, what else did he get wet?

GREG: He got his feet wet.

CLINICIAN: What else?

GREG: And he bathing suit wet.

CLINICIAN: His.

GREG: His bathing suit wet.

CLINICIAN: Okay, he got . . .

GREG: He got . . . I don't know.

CLINICIAN: He got his . . .

GREG: He got his bathing suit wet.

CLINICIAN: Good.
Rachel, what else did he get wet?

RACHEL: He got he face wet.

CLINICIAN: He got he face?

RACHEL: His face.

CLINICIAN: Good, say it again.

RACHEL: His face wet.

CLINICIAN: He got . . .

RACHEL: He got he face wet.

CLINICIAN: He got his . . .

RACHEL: He got his face wet.

CLINICIAN: Good. He got his face wet.
What else did he get wet? Michael?

MICHAEL: I think his head got wet.

CLINICIAN: You think his head got wet. I think so, too.
Here comes Bobby.
Here comes Bobby.
He's wearing his swimming suit.
He's wearing his swimming suit.
What is he wearing, Billy?

BILLY: He's wearing his swimming suit.

CLINICIAN: Right.
What is he wearing, Rachel?

RACHEL: He's wearing he swimming suit.

CLINICIAN: His.

RACHEL: He is wearing he swimming suit.

CLINICIAN: Good try.
Bobby said: Can I play with you?
Can I run through your sprinkler?
Can I play with you and run through your sprinkler?
What did Bobby say, Donald?

DONALD: Can I play with you and run through your sprinkler?

CLINICIAN: Good. Can I play with you and run through your sprinkler?
What did Bobby say, Billy?

BILLY: Bobby said: Can I play with you and run through your sprinkler?

CLINICIAN: Good answer.
Timmy said: I have to ask my Mommy.
Mommy, Bobby wants to run through our sprinkler.
Can he?
Can Bobby run through our sprinkler?
What did Timmy say, Michael?

MICHAEL: Can Bobby run through our sprinkler?

CLINICIAN: Can Bobby run through our sprinkler? Good, Michael.
What did Timmy say, Rachel?

RACHEL: Bobby run through our sprinkler?

CLINICIAN: Can Bobby . . .

RACHEL: Can Bobby run through our sprinkler?

CLINICIAN: Good. Can Bobby run through our sprinkler?
Mommy said: Of course he can.
He can cool off.
He can run through our sprinkler.
What did Mommy say, Greg?

GREG: He can run through our sprinkler to cool off.

CLINICIAN: Right. He can run through our sprinkler.
What did Mommy say, Mike?

MIKE: He run through our sprinkler.

CLINICIAN: He can . . .

MIKE: He can run through our sprinkler.

CLINICIAN: Very nice, Mike.
Timmy and Karen and Bobby ran through the sprinkler.
They weren't hot any longer.
They were cooling off.
They were having lots of fun.
They weren't hot any longer.
Were they still hot? Donald?

DONALD: They wasn't hot any longer.

CLINICIAN: They wasn't?

DONALD: They were not hot any longer.

CLINICIAN: Good. They weren't.

DONALD: They weren't hot any longer.

CLINICIAN: Very good.
Were they still hot? Michael?

MICHAEL: They wasn't hot any longer.

CLINICIAN: They weren't.

MICHAEL: They wasn't hot any longer.

CLINICIAN: Wasn't?

MICHAEL: Was any . . .

CLINICIAN: They were not. They weren't.

MICHAEL: They were not hot any . . . any more.

CLINICIAN: Good. Tell me once more.

MICHAEL: They were not any hotter.

CLINICIAN: They weren't any hotter? They were not hot any longer.

MICHAEL: They weren't any more hotter.

CLINICIAN: They weren't hot any longer. They were nice and cool.

Clinicians should be flexible and creative in their use of Interactive Language Development Teaching and should not feel constrained to follow the detailed description given here. Clinical settings vary in their ability to handle groups and in the types of language cases they include; children vary in their ability to attend to conversational speech; clinicians vary in their own predispositions toward certain clinical procedures. Interactive Language Development Teaching has been described here in great detail to provide as much information and as many suggestions as possible. Clinicians must select from this array of clinical techniques those aspects which are suitable, appropriate, and workable for the individual children they serve.

Section II

Language Development Lessons

INTRODUCTION

THIS SECTION CONTAINS sixty-two sample lessons which illustrate the story format of Interactive Language Development Teaching. These stories show the types of themes and language-structure combinations which have been found clinically useful. This particular set of lessons should not be considered as a workbook for a clinician to follow rigidly with any individual child or group of children. There is no assurance that any child will progress at the precise rate of grammatical development that these lessons exemplify. Some children will progress more slowly and will need many additional story presentations designed for the early-developing structures; other children will probably skip the early stories entirely and begin with the more advanced ones. The stories are presented as suggestions to clinicians for writing and presenting their own lessons and as models to follow in organizing grammatical structures into a systematic developmental order.

The lessons are divided into two levels. Level I lessons emphasize the acquisition of basic sentence structure and the earliest grammatical forms used by normally developing children. Level II lessons introduce grammatical forms that are developed somewhat later, and they also stress the combination of several grammatical structures within a single sentence. While the main purpose of these lessons is to teach grammatical structure, considerable thought has been given to the underlying concepts and vocabulary which they incorporate. These items are listed at the beginning of each story, along with the materials suggested as visual aids to the story presentation. For the clinician's convenience, the grammatical structures which receive primary and secondary emphasis in the story are also listed.

Clinicians may want to use real objects, three-dimensional doll figures, puppets, and a variety of other visual aids, but we have confined our materials to the simplest possible paper-doll figures and construction-paper cutouts. Many suitable figures of children, parents, firemen, policemen, etc., can be found in paper-doll sets or in children's coloring books. It is important that the visual aids not attract more attention than the verbal presentation of the story. Clinicians must not become overly engaged in making the figures perform every action in the story, nor should they worry about the relative sizes of furniture, houses, animals, and people. A paper figure does not have to sit in a chair or literally walk through a door or get into a car; figures can be placed beside the cutouts appropriate to the action. Sometimes a cutout is withdrawn from the flannel board and another substituted, as when a package cutout is opened and a birthday present appears or when a frosted cake is substituted for an unfrosted one. A store front may serve merely to separate areas on the flannel board, and action within the store simply takes place on the other side of it. Trees, ponds, and hills are paper shapes of the proper color to identify them, and birds, fish, and squirrels will necessarily be out of proportion to their natural surroundings. The flannel board serves merely to keep the items of the story in view and in mind; it is in no way a dramatic playing-out of the narrative.

Within the lesson proper, each target response which the clinician will try to elicit from a child is listed in a separate column, and, by reading the target responses downward, the clinician can see how well they match the grammatical goals of the lesson. Furthermore, each target response has been scored according to the Developmental Sentence Scoring (DSS) procedure, which is reproduced as Chart I on pages 4–5. Numbers representing the weighted scores have been placed directly above the structures to which they refer. Where a grammatical structure includes two words, as in *is bringing*, *can come*, and *to see*, the score has been placed above the space between the two words, as in the following example:

2 1 3
He is bringing two kites.

In regard to the interrogative reversal, there is no one structure to receive the score, so this entry is made as close to the reversed structures as possible, as in the following example:

2 1 1 1
What is it?

In the DSS procedure, every grammatically correct sentence receives an additional sentence point to account for the correctness of structures which are not given their own individual scores. Errors in plurals, possessives, prepositions, etc., require withholding of the sentence point in scoring a child's language sample. However, in these stories, most of the target responses are in correct and complete grammatical form and would receive DSS sentence points, as follows:

TARGET RESPONSE	SENTENCE POINT
2 1 3 He is bringing two kites.	1
2 1 11 What is it?	1

The total DSS score for each target sentence is listed in the last column. Comparison of DSS scores on Level I stories with DSS scores on Level II stories shows that the grammatical load of the target responses increases as training progresses:

	TARGET RESPONSE	SENTENCE POINT	DSS TOTAL
Level I:	2 1 She is catching the ball.	1	4
	1 1 1 It is not dark.	1	4
Level II:	1 1 2 3 I want to buy some food.	1	8
	1 4 2 Yes, you can take him out.	1	8

Clinicians who write their own stories for Interactive Language Development Teaching need not score every target response but should pay attention to the general grammatical load of the sentences they are expecting children to produce. In this way language can be presented to a child at a developmental level that is appropriate to his own expressive ability.

LEVEL I LESSONS

Level I lessons make use of the earliest-developing forms contained in the eight grammatical categories of the DSS. Lessons 1 through 5 emphasize the formulation of simple grammatically correct sentences and provide opportunity to practice the correct word order of subject-predicate combinations.

Pronoun

In the first lessons, nouns are elaborated into short noun phrases and are sometimes replaced by items from the indefinite-pronoun category (*it*, *this*, *some*, *someone*, *something*; *one*, *two*, *all*) or by personal pronouns (*I*, *he*, *his*, *she*, *her*).

Main Verb

Since many children at this early stage of sentence development use uninflected verb forms and tend to delete copular and auxiliary *be*, Level I lessons give considerable emphasis to these items. The clinician may find it necessary at first to accept the reduced *He running* in place of the target sentence *He is running*; but after the child has achieved the *-ing*, the complete *is* + verb + *-ing* should be required.

Negative

Lessons 8 and 9 introduce the first level of negatives in the DSS: *it*, *this*, *that* + *is* + *not*. In this construction, the *is* may be either the copula or the auxiliary, but we have found that children respond more quickly to the copular form. For this reason the combination of *not* with auxiliary *is* is not stressed until Lesson 26. The grammatical goal is to stabilize the location of the negative and to attach it syntactically to the verb. Short sentences of no more than four words are used, and often the target response is reduced to *No, it is not.* Practice with these incomplete targets has been found useful as an introductory step to the production of complete negative forms. In order to limit sentence length to four words, a general sequence of negative expansion would begin with negation with color or possession (*It is not red*, *This is not mine*), negation with locative words (*It is not here*, *It is not inside*), and negation with proper nouns (*This is not Bobby*). The inclusion of a predicate nominative brings the sentence length to five or more words (*This is not my ball*, *It is not a red wagon*) and presents a more difficult formulation task. Lesson 6 includes the negative with the copula as a secondary goal, and Lessons 8 and 9 give it primary emphasis.

In Lessons 24 through 30, additional negative forms are introduced. Negatives with modal and obligatory auxiliaries in the contracted forms (*can't* and *don't*) are stressed. These negatives occur frequently in the spontaneous speech of young children, often in incomplete or stereotyped utterances (*I can't*, *I don't know*). Both *can't* and *don't* are introduced in Level I lessons; *don't* is stressed before *can't* because of its relatively higher frequency of occurrence in children's speech. Imperatives and incomplete and stereotyped utterances are used to introduce these negative forms. Complete sentence formulation and the combination of *can't* and *don't* with a variety of lexical verbs are then developed.

Conjunction

The conjunction *and* occurs frequently in Lessons 1 through 11, but not always in a complete sentence. Since sentence length must be limited in early lessons, *and* is used in noun + noun, verb + verb, adjective + adjective, or adverb + adverb constructions (*Mommy and Daddy*, *cat and dog*, *come and see*, *big and heavy*, *fast and slow*). As the child begins to stabilize his use of *and* at this level, reduced targets can be expanded to complete sentences (*I see Mommy and Daddy*, *The truck is big and heavy*). The introduction of *and* involves the semantic recognition of additivity, thus paving the way for the appearance of plural pronouns and plural verbs (*Mommy and Daddy are here*, *They are here*). The introduction of *and* as a conjunction between sentences is not made until Lesson 12, and; even there, reduced target sentences are used (*He is*, *and she is*, *Bobby is running*, *and Karen is running*). Considerable increase in sentence length is required when *and* joins two complete basic sentences (*Bobby is walking home*, *and Karen is walking to school*). The last two lessons in Level I introduce the conjunction *but*, which is used to join sentences with parallel structure but oppositional meanings. Often negation is required in the second sentence, making this construction more difficult (*The dog is big*, *but the puppy isn't big*). No other conjunctions are introduced in Level I lessons.

Later-Developing Forms

Lessons 12 through 30 introduce three grammatical categories which are variations of the basic sentences used in the earlier lessons: secondary verbs, interrogative reversals, and wh-questions. The first ten lessons lay the groundwork for the introduction of these structures by presenting them receptively within the story contexts, but they do not become lesson goals until the children have stabilized basic sentence structure.

Secondary verbs. Early infinitive forms are contained in Lessons 12 through 20. Normally developing children show early use of infinitives following the lexical verbs *want*, *go*, *got*, and *let*. In conversational speech the infinitive marker is usually elided into *wanna*, *gonna*, and *gotta*, while *let me* and *let us* become *lemme* and *let's*. Four of these early infinitive forms are introduced in Level I lessons; the structure *gotta* is excluded because its correct formulation requires auxiliary *have* (*have got to*), which is a later-developing verb form. It has been our experience that clinical children respond most readily to the conversational elisions *gonna*, *wanna*, *gotta*, *lemme*, and *let's* rather than to their carefully articulated forms *going to*, *want to*, *got to*, *let me*, and *let us*. Since the child may be expected to produce his first infinitives as elisions, clinicians should not feel uncomfortable about presenting them first in that manner. The introduction of infinitives should begin with *wanna*, *lemme*, and *let's*, where self-reference is the subject and where no other verb inflection is required (*I wanna*, *Lemme see*, *Let's play*). Sentence length can be controlled in these early constructions and can be expanded gradually to include inflections of the main verb (*I wanted to*, *He's going to*). When these main-verb elaborations are introduced, the clinician should then emphasize the articulation of *to* as a separate word (*I want to*, *He is going to*), eliminating the early contracted forms (*wanna*, *gonna*). Lesson 23 demonstrates this step.

The infinitive form with *gonna* or *going to* adds an important semantic dimension to a child's speech, since it is usually the first means he has of marking the future in verbs. Children use this form much earlier than they use the modal verb *will*. The concept of future is best presented to clinical children through the use of *gonna*, and Lessons 12, 14, 27, and 28 introduce it with secondary emphasis before assigning it primary emphasis in Lessons 29 and 30.

One other infinitive form is introduced in Level I: the noncomplementing infinitive, which is used with the copula (*He is ready to go*, *This is fun to do*) or to express purpose (*He stopped to play*, *He opened the door to look*). The infinitive of purpose is a precursor of more difficult structures involving dependent clauses, and it lays the semantic groundwork for the conjunction *so* (*He stopped so he could play*, *He opened the door so he could look*). The noncomplementing infinitive is introduced with secondary emphasis in Lesson 17 and with primary emphasis in Lesson 24.

Interrogative reversal. One of the most important early-developing linguistic concepts is that of the question, and questions comprise a large percentage of the spontaneous utterances of young children. Correct formulation of questions depends on reversal of the subject of the sentences and the first auxiliary verb. In Level I lessons the introduction of the interrogative reversal is delayed until the child has had considerable exposure to the copular and auxiliary *is* in declarative statements. The first step in teaching questions is the reversal of the copula (*Is it Timmy?*), which receives primary emphasis in Lessons 18 and 24 and secondary emphasis in Lessons 17, 19, and 23. The reversal of auxiliary *is* (*Is he going to the store?*) is introduced somewhat later, receiving primary emphasis in Lessons 27 and 29 and secondary emphasis in Lessons 26 and 28.

Wh-question. In the wh-question form, the child must learn not only the interrogative reversal but also the appropriate selection of the wh-word.

Adequate receptive preparation is critical to an understanding of the wh-vocabulary. The wh-words develop largely on a semantic basis, *who* and *what* differentiating human from nonhuman characteristics, *where* representing location, etc. *Who* and *what* are introduced first because they can take the subject slot in a sentence and thus do not add to the length of early sentences (*Who is it? What is it?*). *Where* is the second wh-question to be presented, and its use should be restricted to sentences of four words (*Where is the ball? Where is my hat?*). Once a child is able to formulate wh-questions with the copula, reversal of the auxiliary *is* is introduced (*What is he watching? Where is he going?*). A child should have some experience with the interrogative reversal of auxiliary *is* in yes-no questions (*Is he watching TV? Is he going home?*) before the further complication of wh-word selection is introduced. Lessons 18 through 24 and also 28 and 29 emphasize wh-questions.

The Level I lessons which follow have been written to illustrate how the normal setting and sequence of language acquisition can be used as a guideline for clinical treatment. An index is included to help the clinician locate lessons in which particular structures receive either primary or secondary emphasis. The clinician is again reminded not to regard this set of lessons as a workbook or to follow them rigidly with any one child or group of children. They contain suggestions for planning original and creative language lessons and provide an approach to language teaching that will take individual forms in the hands of individual clinicians.

INDEX TO LEVEL I LESSONS

DSS Score	Structure	Lesson Number: Primary Emphasis	Lesson Number: Secondary Emphasis
Indefinite Pronoun or Noun Modifier			
1	*it*	1, 2, 6-10, 12, 13, 15-19, 21-25, 27, 29	3-5, 11, 20, 26, 28
1	*this*	10	3-8, 15, 17, 19, 23, 24, 26, 30
1	*that*	8	19
3	*some*	4	5, 14
3	*more*	5	
3	*one*	16	3, 8, 13, 23, 26, 29
3	*two*		2
3	*four*		5
3	*all*		5
3	*no*		5
Negative			
1	*it is not*	8, 9	6, 26, 27
4	*don't*	26, 27	24, 25
4	*can't*	30	28, 29
7	N *is not*	10, 11	7

DSS Score	Structure	Lesson Number: Primary Emphasis	Lesson Number: Secondary Emphasis
Personal Pronoun			
1	*I*	1, 3, 5, 8, 12, 13, 18-20, 23	4, 7, 9, 14, 16, 21, 24, 25, 27, 30
1	*me*	14, 15	13
1	*my*		8
1	*mine*		10
1	*you*		8, 10, 14
1	*your*		5
2	*he*	2, 4, 6, 11, 17, 21, 26-30	1, 9, 14, 18, 22, 25
2	*his*	2	9, 22
2	*she*	3, 5, 11, 16	1, 7, 14, 15, 29
2	*her*		3
Conjunction			
3	*and*	2, 6, 12, 15, 20, 21, 23, 26	1, 3, 4, 9, 11, 14, 19, 22, 25, 28, 29
5	*but*	30	29

INDEX TO LEVEL I LESSONS (Cont'd.)

DSS Score	Structure	Lesson Number: Primary Emphasis	Lesson Number: Secondary Emphasis
Main Verb			
1	uninflected verb	1, 3-5, 7-9, 14, 22, 25	6, 9, 10, 17, 18, 21, 23, 29
1	copular *is*	1-13, 15-20, 22-30	21
1	*is* + verb + *-ing*	2-7, 12, 14, 17, 19, 21, 22, 25-29	1, 11, 13, 15, 16, 23
4	obligatory *do* + verb	26, 27	24, 25
4	*can* + verb	30	28, 29
Interrogative Reversal			
1	reversal of copular *is*	18, 24	17, 19, 23
4	reversal of auxiliary *is*	27, 29	26, 28

DSS Score	Structure	Lesson Number: Primary Emphasis	Lesson Number: Secondary Emphasis
Secondary Verb			
2	*wanna* + infinitive	12, 13, 18, 20, 23	16
2	*lemme* + infinitive	14, 15	13
2	*let's* + infinitive	16, 17	9, 15
2	*gonna* + infinitive	29, 30	12, 14, 27, 28
3	noncomplementing infinitive	24	17
Wh-Question			
2	*what*	19, 22	18, 20, 28
2	*what . . . do*	29	
2	*who*	21	
2	*where*	24	23

LEVEL I: LESSON 1

CONCEPTS

schools, colors,
hidden objects

VOCABULARY

teacher, school,
red, blue, swinging,
catching, hiding

FLANNEL-BOARD MATERIALS

paper figures: Bobby, Karen, teacher
paper cutouts: school building, red ball, blue box, tree, swings

ELICITED STRUCTURES	DSS VALUE
Primary emphasis	
indefinite pronoun – *it*	1
personal pronoun – *I*	1
main verb – copular *is*	1
– uninflected	1
Secondary emphasis	
personal pronoun – *he, she*	2
main verb – *is . . . -ing*	1
conjunction – *and*	3

FUN AT SCHOOL

NARRATIVE	TARGET RESPONSE	SENTENCE POINT	DSS TOTAL
Our story is about a boy. His name is Bobby. Here he is! This is Bobby. Who is this boy?	1 1 This is Bobby.	1	3
Bobby is outside. He's going somewhere. Today is a school day. Bobby's going to school. Where's Bobby going?	2 1 He's going to school.	1	4
This is Bobby's school. But who is this lady? It's his teacher. This is Bobby's teacher. She is the teacher. Who is the lady?	2 1 She is the teacher.	1	4
Do you go to school? Who is your teacher?	(Elicit responses.) (Elicit responses.)		
The teacher has something. It's a surprise for Bobby. He says: What do you have? Tell me what it is. What is it? What is it? What does Bobby say?	2 111 What is it?	1	6

NARRATIVE	TARGET RESPONSE	SENTENCE POINT	DSS TOTAL
The teacher says: I have something red. See? Here it is. I have a ball. It's a red ball. What color is the ball?	1 1 { It's red. It's a red ball.	1	3
But she has something else. She says: Look at this, Bobby. This is a box. See it? It is blue. It's a blue box. What is it?	1 1 It's a blue box.	1	3
The ball goes in the box. It goes right in here . . . like this. The box is for the ball. What is the box for?	1 The box is for the ball.	1	2
The teacher has two things. Bobby just saw them. One is red. And . . . The other is blue. Who knows what they are? Who can remember?	3 { A ball and a box. A red ball and a blue box.	–	3
Now it's time to go outside. The teacher says: Put the ball away. It goes in the box. Put it back inside. What does she tell him to do?	1 1 Put it back inside.	1	3
Now Bobby wants to go. He says: I did it, teacher! I put the ball away. Can I go out now? I put it back. What does Bobby say?	1 1 1 I put it back.	1	4
Bobby put the ball away. It went right in here! But look. It's gone now! Bobby can't see it. The ball is gone. Where is it?	1 The ball is gone.	1	2

NARRATIVE	TARGET RESPONSE	SENTENCE POINT	DSS TOTAL
The ball is in the box. Bobby can't see it now. Because it's in the box. Why can't he see the ball?	1 1 (Because) it's in the box.	1	3
There goes Bobby. He's going outside now. He's gonna play ball. Look who else is here! It's Karen. This is Karen. Who is this?	1 1 This is Karen.	1	3
Karen's already outside. And look what she's doing. Karen is on the swing. She's swinging. What's she doing?	2 1 She's swinging.	1	4
Karen says: Come on, Bobby. Come and swing. Bobby is swinging. Look! Both of them are on the swings. Bobby and Karen are swinging. Who is swinging?	3 Bobby and Karen.	–	3
Then Bobby says: Karen, look here. Look what I have. I have a blue box. And something's inside. Come and see it! What does Bobby say?	1 3 1 1 Come and see it.	1	7
Karen says: Oh boy! I see a ball. It's a red ball. Come on. Throw it here. I want it. I want it. What does Karen say?	1 1 1 I want it.	1	4
Bobby throws the ball. It goes way up high. Karen's reaching up . . . like this. She's catching it. Karen is catching the ball. What is she doing?	2 1 She is catching the ball.	1	4
Now let's watch Bobby catch it. But where is Bobby? Where is he?			

NARRATIVE	TARGET RESPONSE	SENTENCE POINT	DSS TOTAL
Karen can't find him. Bobby is playing a trick. He's hiding somewhere. What's Bobby doing?	2 1 He's hiding somewhere.	1	4
Karen is looking. She's trying to find him. Oh, look where he is. Bobby's over here . . . by the swing. He is by the swing. Where is he?	2 1 He is by the swing.	1	4
Oh, oh. She sees him! There he is. Karen found him. Karen says: Come out. Come out. I see you, Bobby. I see you. What does Karen say?	1 1 1 I see you.	1	4
Now it's Karen's turn. She goes behind the tree. Karen is behind the tree. Where is she?	2 1 She is behind the tree.	1	4
Bobby can't find her. He says: Come out, Karen. I can't find you. I give up. I give up. What does Bobby say?	1 1 I give up.	1	3
Now it's time to go home. There is the teacher. Bobby says: Here is your ball. I like to play ball. I like this ball. What does Bobby say?	1 1 1 I like this ball.	1	4
The children are leaving now. Karen says: Good-bye, teacher. The teacher says: Good-bye, children. Good-bye, Bobby and Karen. What does the teacher say?	3 Good-bye, Bobby and Karen.	–	3
There they go. They are both going home.			

LEVEL I: LESSON 2

CONCEPTS

height, flying,
windy weather

VOCABULARY

up, up high, kite,
string, wind, blowing

FLANNEL-BOARD MATERIALS

paper figures: Bobby, Timmy
paper cutouts: house, dog, tree, red kite and blue kite with strings attached

ELICITED STRUCTURES		DSS VALUE
Primary emphasis		
indefinite pronoun –	*it*	1
personal pronoun –	*he, his*	2
main verb –	copular *is*	1
–	*is . . . -ing*	1
conjunction –	*and*	3
Secondary emphasis		
indefinite pronoun –	*two*	3

FLYING KITES

NARRATIVE	TARGET RESPONSE	SENTENCE POINT	DSS TOTAL
Here are two boys. One boy is Bobby. The other one is Timmy. The two boys are brothers. Bobby and Timmy are brothers. Who are brothers?	3 Bobby and Timmy.	–	3
This is their house. The boys live here. Bobby is inside. He's in the house. Where is Bobby?	2 1 He's in the house.	1	4
But Timmy isn't. He's not in the house. Timmy is outside. Where is he?	1 Timmy is outside.	1	2
Timmy says: Bobby, come on outside. Come out and play. Come and play with me. What does Timmy say?	1 3 1 1 Come and play with me.	1	7
Bobby says: Okay, I'm coming. And I'm bringing something.			

NARRATIVE	TARGET RESPONSE	SENTENCE POINT	DSS TOTAL
Timmy doesn't know what it is. He says: What are you bringing? What is it? What is it? What does Timmy say?	2 111 What is it?	1	6
Here comes Bobby. He has a surprise. He's holding something. Look what he has! Bobby is bringing two kites. What is he bringing?	2 1 3 He is bringing two kites.	1	7
One kite is red. And the other is blue. This one is red and . . . This one is blue. The kites are red and blue. What color are they?	3 Red and blue.	–	3
The blue kite belongs to Bobby. This is his kite. Bobby's kite is blue. His kite is blue. What color is Bobby's kite?	2 1 His kite is blue.	1	4
The red one is for Timmy. Timmy's kite is red. This one belongs to him. His kite is red. What color is Timmy's kite?	2 1 His kite is red.	1	4
Now they're gonna fly them. See this string? It's a long one. Each kite has a string. Here is one, and here's the other. I see two kites and two strings. What do I see? I see . . .	3 3 3 Two kites and two strings.	–	9
Bobby is holding his string. See. It's in his hand. And look. Timmy's is, too.			

NARRATIVE	TARGET RESPONSE	SENTENCE POINT	DSS TOTAL
Timmy is holding his string, too. What's Timmy doing?	2 1 2 He's holding his string.	1	6
Bobby says: It's windy today. The wind is blowing hard. Watch my kite go up. Look, there it goes! Bobby's kite is going up and up and up. Where's his kite going?	3 3 Up and up and up.	–	6
	1 1 3 3 It's going up and up and up.	1	9
Now look at Timmy's kite. It's going up, too. Just the way Bobby's did! The kite is going up and up. It's going way up high. What's his kite doing?	1 1 It's going way up high.	1	3
Oh, oh. Look now. Here comes a dog. Guess what his name is! Spot. His name is Spot. What is his name?	2 1 His name is Spot.	1	4
Spot belongs to Bobby and Timmy. He is their dog. Who does Spot belong to?	3 Bobby and Timmy.	–	3
Spot sees the kites. He wants to play, too. He wants to play with Bobby and Timmy. So he starts to bark. He is barking and barking. What's Spot doing?	2 1 3 1 He is barking and barking.	1	8
Timmy says: No, Spot. Go away. You can't play with us. Dogs don't fly kites. Silly dog! Go away right now. What does Timmy tell Spot?	1 Go away right now.	1	2
Spot is going away. Because he can't play. Spot goes way over here . . .			

NARRATIVE	TARGET RESPONSE	SENTENCE POINT	DSS TOTAL
And sits by this tree. He's by a tree. Where is Spot now?	2 1 He's by a tree.	1	4
Then something happens! Oh, oh! Look! Bobby dropped his string. Look at his kite. It's flying away. What's happening to his kite?	1 1 It's flying away.	1	3
Bobby says: Timmy, look! There goes my kite. I dropped the string. Now it's gone. My kite is gone. What does Bobby say?	1 1 My kite is gone.	1	3
But look at Spot! He sees Bobby's kite. He's running after it. He's gonna get it. Spot is running fast. What is Spot doing?	1 Spot is running fast.	1	2
Look! He caught it! It's not gone now. Spot has it. And look where it is! It's in his mouth. Where is the kite?	1 1 2 It's in his mouth.	1	5
Bobby is happy now. Here is his blue kite. It's not lost. Because Spot caught it. Bobby says: Spot can play with us. He is a good dog. What does Bobby say?	2 1 He is a good dog.	1	4
Oh look! Bobby's ready now. He's holding on to the string. There goes the kite. And here comes Spot . . . running fast. He's running after the kite. What's he doing?	2 1 He's running after the kite.	1	4
Spot jumps very high. Oh, oh! He missed it.			

NARRATIVE	TARGET RESPONSE	SENTENCE POINT	DSS TOTAL
But Spot's gonna try again.			
There he goes. Watch!			
He's jumping way up high.	2 1	1	4
What's Spot doing?	He's jumping way up high.		
Oh, oh! He missed it again.			
Spot didn't get it.			
Maybe he will next time.			
What do you think?			
Will Spot get it?	(Elicit responses.)		

LEVEL I: LESSON 3

CONCEPTS
train, riding, speed

VOCABULARY
ticket, train, station, window, buying, slow, fast

FLANNEL-BOARD MATERIALS
paper figures: Karen, Mommy, Grandma
paper cutouts: coat, hat, two tickets, train, window, train station, two houses, barn

ELICITED STRUCTURES		DSS VALUE
Primary emphasis		
personal pronoun	– *I*	1
	– *she*	2
main verb	– copular *is*	1
	– uninflected	1
	– *is . . . -ing*	1
Secondary emphasis		
indefinite pronoun	– *it, this*	1
	– *one*	3
personal pronoun	– *her*	2
conjunction	– *and*	3

THE TRAIN RIDE

NARRATIVE	TARGET RESPONSE	SENTENCE POINT	DSS TOTAL
Our story is about two people. This is Karen. Karen is a girl. And this is her mommy. Mommy is a lady. The story is about Karen and her mommy. Who is it about?	Karen (3) and (2) her mommy.	–	5
	It (1) is (1) about Karen and (3) her (2) mommy.	1	8
They are gonna take a trip. They're gonna visit somebody. Mommy says: Let's go to Grandma's house. She wants to see us. Let's go see Grandma today. What does Mommy say?	Let's (1) go (2) see (2) Grandma today.	1	6
Then she says: We can take the train. The train goes to Grandma's. Who wants to come? Do you, Karen?			

NARRATIVE	TARGET RESPONSE	SENTENCE POINT	DSS TOTAL
Karen says: Oh, yes. I do, I do. What does Karen say?	1 I do.	1	2
Mommy says: Okay. Get ready right now. It's cold outside. So wear your coat, Karen. And put on your hat, too. Wear your hat and coat. What does Mommy say?	1 1 3 Wear your hat and coat.	1	6
Karen's getting ready. First, she puts on her coat. Then she puts her hat on. Now she's all ready. What did Karen put on first? Who remembers?	2 1 2 She put on her coat.	1	6
Now they're all ready to go. They're going to the train station. And here it is . . . this building. This is the train station. What is this?	1 1 This is the train station.	1	3
Mommy says: We need some train tickets. I will buy them. Both of us need tickets. Karen needs one and I need one. Mommy says: Karen needs one and . . .	1 1 3 I need one.	1	6
Mommy gets two tickets. Here is one of them. It's Karen's ticket. This one is for Karen. Who is this one for?	1 3 1 This one is for Karen.	1	6
Here is the other ticket. It's not for Karen. No . . .			

NARRATIVE	TARGET RESPONSE	SENTENCE POINT	DSS TOTAL
It's Mommy's ticket. This one is for Mommy. Who is this one for?	1 3 1 This one is for Mommy.	1	6
Now they are waiting. The train will come soon. Oh, oh. Karen sees it! She says: I see it coming. Here is the train. What does Karen say?	1 Here is the train.	1	2
Now they can get on. Watch. Mommy says: Look, here's a window. Who wants to sit here? Karen says: Me! I do. I do. What does she say?	1 I do.	1	2
Karen sits down. Her seat is by the window. Now she can see outside. Because she's sitting by the window. Where is Karen sitting?	2 1 She's sitting by the window.	1	4
Oh, oh. The train is moving. But it's not going fast. The train is going slow. It's going very slow. Is the train going fast?	1 1 No, it's going very slow.	1	3
Now look. Watch the train. It starts to go fast. It's going fast. The train is going fast now. What is the train doing now?	1 The train is going fast.	1	2
Look at Karen by the window. She's looking out. Maybe she sees something. She is looking and looking. What is she doing?	2 1 3 She is looking and 1 looking.	1	8

NARRATIVE	TARGET RESPONSE	SENTENCE POINT	DSS TOTAL
Karen says: Look, Mommy. Look. Look what I see. There is a house. I see a house. What does Karen say?	1 1 I see a house.	1	3
Mommy says: Yes, I see it. But look over there. That is a barn. I see a barn. What does Mommy say?	1 1 I see a barn.	1	3
Karen says: I can see the barn. But look. Look now. I see another house. There is another one. I see another house. What does Karen say?	1 1 3 I see another house.	1	6
Mommy says: I see that house. Do you know who lives there? That is Grandma's house. It is her house. What does Mommy say?	1 1 2 It is her house.	1	5
Now the train is going slow. It's gonna stop . . . Because they're at Grandma's house. The train is stopping. What is the train doing?	1 The train is stopping.	1	2
Karen is looking out the window. She's looking for somebody. Where is Grandma? Karen is looking for her. She is looking for Grandma. Who is she looking for?	2 1 She is looking for Grandma.	1	4
Karen says: There she is! I see her, Mommy. There is Grandma. What does Karen say?	1 There is Grandma.	1	2

NARRATIVE	TARGET RESPONSE	SENTENCE POINT	DSS TOTAL
Karen and Mommy are getting off. They're getting off the train. Grandma is waiting. Look. She's waving at them. She's waving at Karen and Mommy. What is she doing?	2 1 She's waving at Karen 3 and Mommy.	1	7
Karen says: Hi, Grandma. See the train. We rode on it. It went fast. Then it went slow. I like this train. What does Karen say?	1 1 1 I like this train.	1	4
Trains are fun. Karen likes the train. A train is fun to ride. Did you ever ride on a train?	(Elicit responses.)		

LEVEL I: LESSON 4

CONCEPTS	ELICITED STRUCTURES	DSS VALUE
helping, buying, traffic safety	**Primary emphasis**	
	indefinite pronoun – *some*	3
	personal pronoun – *he*	2
VOCABULARY	main verb – copular *is*	1
milk, store, money, street, corner, across, stoplight, red/green, stop/go	– uninflected	1
	– *is . . . -ing*	1
	Secondary emphasis	
	indefinite pronoun – *it, this*	1
FLANNEL-BOARD MATERIALS	personal pronoun – *I*	1
	conjunction – *and*	3
paper figures: Mommy, Timmy, Bobby, storekeeper paper cutouts: refrigerator, dollar bill, street, stoplight, car, store front, milk carton, paper sack		

GOING TO THE STORE

NARRATIVE	TARGET RESPONSE	SENTENCE POINT	DSS TOTAL
This is Bobby. He's a little boy. He is four years old. How old is he?	2 1 3 He is four years old.	1	7
This boy is Timmy. He's not a little boy. He is Bobby's big brother. Who is Timmy?	2 1 He is Bobby's big brother.	1	4
Here is their mommy. Mommy is in the kitchen. She's making dinner. Oh, oh! Something is wrong! Mommy's looking for some milk. What's Mommy looking for?	3 For some milk.	–	3
	2 1 3 She's looking for some milk.	1	7
But she can't find any. There is no more milk. It's all gone.			

NARRATIVE	TARGET RESPONSE	SENTENCE POINT	DSS TOTAL
Mommy says: Bobby and Timmy. Come here. Both of you, come here. I want you. I want you. What does Mommy say?	1 1 1 I want you.	1	4
Here come the boys. They heard Mommy call them. Now Mommy says: I need some milk. Go to the store for me. Go get some milk. What does Mommy say?	1 1 3 Go get some milk.	1	6
Bobby and Timmy are leaving now. They're going to the store. Oh, look! Here comes Mommy. She says: Boys, boys! Stop! Bobby and Timmy, wait a minute. What does Mommy say?	3 1 Bobby and Timmy, wait a minute.	1	5
Mommy tells them: You forgot the money. I have it here. You must pay for the milk. Here's some money. What does Mommy say?	1 3 Here's some money.	1	5
Now the boys are ready. They can buy some milk. Because Timmy has the money. See, Timmy is holding the money. There they go. Who is holding the money?	1 Timmy is holding the money.	1	2
The boys are walking. Look what they come to. Look at this. It's a street.			

NARRATIVE	TARGET RESPONSE	SENTENCE POINT	DSS TOTAL
Here is the street. What is it?	1 1 It's a street.	1	3
Look. Look over here. Here comes a car. The car is in the street. It's going fast. Watch it. The car is going very fast. Is it going slow?	1 1 No, it's going fast.	1	3
Look at the boys. They'd better be careful. Timmy says: Be careful, Bobby. Don't cross the street. The car is going too fast. Stop at the corner. What does Timmy tell Bobby?	1 Stop at the corner.	1	2
Bobby stops right at the corner. He is waiting. Bobby says: Look at what I see! Timmy, look over there. It's a stoplight. I see a stoplight. What does Bobby say?	1 1 I see a stoplight.	1	3
What does a stoplight tell you?	(Elicit responses.)		
Look. The light is red. Red means stop. The boys can't cross. This is a red light. What kind of light is this?	1 1 This is a red light.	1	3
Bobby stops. So does Timmy. They are not walking. The stoplight is red. The boys are waiting. Because the light is red. Why are they waiting?	1 (Because) the light is red.	1	2
Timmy says: Watch the light. Look.			

NARRATIVE	TARGET RESPONSE	SENTENCE POINT	DSS TOTAL
It's gonna change color. Soon it'll be green. We can walk . . . When it's green. When can they walk?	1 1 (When) it's green.	1	3
Red means stop. But green means go. See, now it's green. The light changed. It's a green light now. What color is the light now?	1 1 It's green. 1 1 It's a green light now.	1 1	3 3
Now the boys can go. The light is green. But first, Bobby looks both ways. He looks this way . . . And he looks that way. What does he do? He looks . . .	1 3 1 This way and that way.	–	5
No cars are coming now. So he goes across the street. See how fast he goes. He's running across. What's he doing?	2 1 He's running across.	1	4
Now watch Timmy. He looks both ways, too. But no more cars come. He runs across, too. Just the way Bobby did. He's running across the street. What's he doing?	2 1 He's running across the street.	1	4
Bobby says: Look, Timmy. There's the store. We're here. This is the store. What does Bobby say?	1 1 This is the store.	1	3
Bobby is first to go in. He's inside the store already! Now there goes Timmy. He's going inside, too. What's Timmy doing?	2 1 He's going inside.	1	4

NARRATIVE	TARGET RESPONSE	SENTENCE POINT	DSS TOTAL
Timmy sees a man. It's the store man. Timmy says: Hello, I need some milk. Here's the money. I want some milk, please. What does Timmy say?	1 1 3 I want some milk.	1	6
The store man says: Yes, I have milk. Here it is. And here's something else. It's a sack . . . for the milk. The sack is for the milk. What's the sack for?	1 The sack is for the milk.	1	2
The man puts the milk inside. Then he gives the sack to Timmy. Now the boys can leave. Timmy has the milk. See? He's carrying it. What's he doing?	2 1 He's carrying the milk.	1	4
Bobby and Timmy are going home. Look at the stoplight. It's green. So they can go. No cars are coming. Watch them! They both run across the street. Bobby and Timmy run fast. Who runs fast?	3 Bobby and Timmy.	–	3
What do the boys do?	3 1 Bobby and Timmy run fast.	1	5
Now they see Mommy. She says: Thank you for the milk. Now I can make dinner.			

LEVEL I: LESSON 5

CONCEPTS

age, numbers, quantity differences

VOCABULARY

birthday, candles, cake, frosting, chocolate, present, counting, more, some

FLANNEL-BOARD MATERIALS

paper figures: Karen, Mommy
paper cutouts: unfrosted cake, frosted cake, four candles, package, doll

ELICITED STRUCTURES		DSS VALUE
Primary emphasis		
indefinite pronoun	– *more*	3
personal pronoun	– *I*	1
	– *she*	2
main verb	– copular *is*	1
	– uninflected	1
	– *is . . . -ing*	1
Secondary emphasis		
indefinite pronoun	– *it, this*	1
	– *some, all, no*	3
	– *four*	3
personal pronoun	– *your*	1

THE BIRTHDAY CAKE

NARRATIVE	TARGET RESPONSE	SENTENCE POINT	DSS TOTAL
Our story is about two people. It's about Mommy. And it's about Karen. Here's one of the people. Who is it? Who is this?	1 1 This is Karen.	1	3
And this is her Mommy. Today is a special day. It's Karen's birthday. Karen is four years old. She's four years old today. How old is she?	2 1 3 She's four years old.	1	7
How old are you?	(Elicit responses.)		
Mommy is in the kitchen. She's making a cake. Mommy says: It's your cake, Karen. I'm making it for you. This is your birthday cake. What does Mommy say?	1 1 1 This is your birthday cake.	1	4

NARRATIVE	TARGET RESPONSE	SENTENCE POINT	DSS TOTAL
Here's her birthday cake. But look real close. Something is wrong with it. It needs some frosting. See, there's no frosting on it. What's wrong with the cake?	1 3 1 There's no frosting on it.	1	6
Mommy says: What kind do you want? Chocolate or vanilla? Karen says: Chocolate! I want chocolate! Not vanilla. Only chocolate. I want all chocolate. What does Karen say?	1 1 3 I want all chocolate.	1	6
Mommy is putting the frosting on. She's putting it on the cake. And Karen is helping her. She's putting frosting on, too. What's Karen doing?	2 1 She's putting frosting on.	1	4
She's helping Mommy. Oh, look. It's done now! Karen's birthday cake is done. It's all done. Is the cake done now?	1 1 3 (Yes,) it's all done.	1	6
Oh, look. Mommy has a candle. It's for the cake. It goes right here. The candle is for the cake. What is the candle for?	1 The candle is for the cake.	1	2
Karen is four years old. But here's only one candle. Mommy needs some more. So she's getting some more candles. What's she getting?	3 3 Some more candles.	–	6
	2 1 3 3 She's getting some more candles.	1	10

NARRATIVE	TARGET RESPONSE	SENTENCE POINT	DSS TOTAL
Here they are. Now she has four candles. Karen says: I wanna count them. She's counting: One, two, three, four. What is she doing?	2 1 She's counting.	1	4
Karen counted all the candles. We can do it, too. Let's count them: One, two, three, four. See. There are four candles. How many are there?	3 Four candles.	–	3
Watch! Mommy's putting them on. One, two, three, four candles. All four candles go on the cake. Mommy's putting on the candles. What's she doing?	1 Mommy's putting on the candles.	1	2
Mommy did it. She put them all on. She put on all four candles. What did Mommy do?	2 1 3 3 She put on all four candles.	1	10
Oh, look. The cake is all done. The frosting is on it. And so are the candles. It's ready to eat. The cake is ready now. Is the cake ready to eat?	1 The cake is ready.	1	2
Mommy says: Happy birthday, Karen. Here is your cake. It's all yours. This is your birthday cake. What does Mommy say?	1 1 1 This is your birthday cake.	1	4

NARRATIVE	TARGET RESPONSE	SENTENCE POINT	DSS TOTAL
Karen says: I like my cake. Now let's blow out the candles. I'm gonna blow them out. Watch me do it. Watch me. What does she say?	1 1 Watch me.	1	3
Everybody watch Karen. She takes a deep breath. And . . . She goes whhhhhhhhhh. She's blowing hard. What's she doing?	2 1 She's blowing hard.	1	4
She blows out one candle. Whhhhhhhh. She blows out another one. Whhhhhh. And another. Whhhhhh. But look. Look at this one. It didn't go out. It's still burning. What's wrong with this candle?	1 1 It's still burning.	1	3
Only three went out. See. One, two, three. There's one more left. Did all the candles go out? How many are left?	1 3 3 There's one more left.	1	8
Watch Karen. She's trying again. She goes whhhhhhhhh. And blows out the last candle. Mommy says: Good for you, Karen. Now look here. I have your birthday present. What does Mommy say?	1 1 1 I have your birthday present.	1	4
Karen says: Thank you for my present. And thank you for my cake. Can I open it now? What can it be?			

NARRATIVE	TARGET RESPONSE	SENTENCE POINT	DSS TOTAL
What is it? What is it? What does Karen say?	2 1 1 1 What is it?	1	6
Karen opens her present. Look at this! It's a doll. That's what her present is. Karen says: Thank you, Mommy. I like my present. What does she say?	1 1 1 I like my present.	1	4
Now it's time to eat. Karen says: Let's eat the cake now. I wanna eat it. I want some cake, please. What does she say?	1 1 3 I want some cake.	1	6
Now Karen's eating her cake. Oh, look. It's all gone. Mommy says: Karen, you ate fast. Do you want some more? There's more cake left. What does Mommy say?	1 3 There's more cake left.	1	5
Karen says: Oh, yes, I do. I want some more. I like my birthday cake. I want some more. What does Karen say?	1 1 3 3 I want some more.	1	9
Look. Here's another piece of cake. Karen's eating fast again. Soon the cake will be all gone.			

LEVEL I: LESSON 6

CONCEPTS	ELICITED STRUCTURES		DSS VALUE
fire, burning, flames, safety, size contrasts, color contrasts	**Primary emphasis**		
	indefinite pronoun –	*it*	1
	personal pronoun –	*he*	2
	main verb –	copular *is*	1
	–	*is . . . -ing*	1
VOCABULARY	conjunction –	*and*	3
fireman, fire truck, smoke, fire, hose, red, blue, big, little	**Secondary emphasis**		
	indefinite pronoun –	*this*	1
	main verb –	uninflected	1
FLANNEL-BOARD MATERIALS	negative –	*it is not*	1
paper figures: fireman, Mommy, Daddy, girl paper cutouts: dog, red fire truck, fire station, burning house, house, fire hose			

PUTTING OUT THE FIRE

NARRATIVE	TARGET RESPONSE	SENTENCE POINT	DSS TOTAL
I have something. Look! It's a truck. This is a fire truck. See? It's a fire truck. What is it?	1 1 It's a fire truck.	1	3
The fire truck is red. Fire trucks are always red. They're not blue, are they? No, a fire truck isn't blue. It's red. It's not blue. Is a fire truck blue?	{ 11 1 No, it's not.	1	4
	1 1 1 It is not blue. }	1	4
This is the fire station. The fire truck stays there. Here is a man. See him. He's by the fire truck . . . right here. He is the fireman. Who is he?	2 1 He is the fireman.	1	4

NARRATIVE	TARGET RESPONSE	SENTENCE POINT	DSS TOTAL
And see what else is here. It's a dog. This is the fireman's dog. This is Spot. Who is this?	1 1 This is Spot.	1	3
Spot is black and white. This isn't a red dog, is it? No, it's not. This is a black-and-white dog. Is this dog red?	1 1 1 No, it's not.	1	4
	1 1 1 It is not red.	1	4
Oh, oh! Look! The fireman sees a fire. Look at what's burning. It's a house. The house is on fire. What is on fire?	1 The house is on fire.	1	2
The house is burning. It's on fire! And look at all of this. It's smoke from the fire. This is smoke. What is this?	1 1 This is smoke.	1	3
Look at all the smoke. It's everywhere! There's a lot of it. I see lots of smoke. How much smoke do you see?	1 1 3 I see lots of smoke.	1	6
People live in this house. Now they're running out. Here comes somebody! It's a girl. A girl is running out. Who is running out?	1 A girl is running out.	1	2
Here come some more people. The mommy and daddy are coming. Look. Everybody ran outside. A mommy and daddy and a girl are outside. Who is outside?	3 A mommy and a daddy 3 and a girl.	–	6

NARRATIVE	TARGET RESPONSE	SENTENCE POINT	DSS TOTAL
Everybody is outside. Because their house is burning. The people are waiting. They're waiting for the fire truck. The people need some help. What do the people need?	1 3 The people need some help.	1	5
Daddy says: Hurry up, fire truck. Our house is on fire. Where is the fire truck? When will it get here? Where is it? Where is it? What does Daddy say?	2 1 1 1 Where is it?	1	6
The fire truck is coming. Here it comes. Listen. Hear the siren? Rrrrrrr. That means it's coming. The fire truck is coming. What is coming?	1 The fire truck is coming.	1	2
The girl hears the siren. It makes a big, loud noise. She says: Daddy, look! There's the fire truck. I see it. I see it. What does the girl say?	1 1 1 I see it.	1	4
The fire truck is at the house. First the fireman gets out. Now Spot is getting out. He's barking. He sees the fire. Spot is barking and barking. What is he doing?	2 1 3 He is barking and 1 barking.	1	8
The fireman needs something. He needs a hose. Look. Here it is. This is a hose. What is this?	1 1 This is a hose.	1	3
But he needs a big one. See, this is a big hose.			

NARRATIVE	TARGET RESPONSE	SENTENCE POINT	DSS TOTAL
It's not a little one. No, it's a big hose. It is not little. Is this a little hose?	1 1 1 No, it is not. 1 1 1 It is not little.	1 1	4 4
Now the fireman needs water. Look at the hose. Watch. Watch the water come out. Here it comes out of the hose. The water is coming out. What's happening to the water?	1 1 It's coming out of the hose.	1	3
There goes the water. It goes right on the fire. So the fireman can put it out. See? He's putting out the fire. What's he doing?	2 1 He's putting out the fire.	1	4
Watch the house. Look. The fire is out. The house is not burning. The fireman did it. He put out the fire. What did he do?	2 1 He put out the fire.	1	4
Look at the house now. See, the fire is all gone. And so is the smoke. There is no more smoke. The house is not burning. And the smoke is all gone. What is all gone?	1 3 The smoke is all gone.	1	5
The daddy says: Thank you, fireman. You put out the fire. The fireman says: It was a little fire. You can go back in. The fire is out now. What does the fireman say?	1 The fire is out now.	1	2

NARRATIVE	TARGET RESPONSE	SENTENCE POINT	DSS TOTAL
There go the people. There goes the girl . . . and the mommy . . . and the daddy. The people are all in the house. Everybody went back in. The mommy and the daddy and the girl did. Who went back in?	3 The mommy and the 3 daddy and the girl.	–	6
The fireman says: Come on, Spot. The fire is out now. Get in the truck. But look at Spot! He's already in the truck. Where is Spot?	2 1 He's already in the truck.	1	4
The fireman is getting into the truck. The fire truck is leaving. The fire is out. There it goes. The fireman is driving away. What is he doing?	2 1 He is driving away.	1	4
There they go. The fireman helped the people. He put out the fire.			

LEVEL I: LESSON 7

CONCEPTS	ELICITED STRUCTURES		DSS VALUE
motion, riding, standing still, ownership	**Primary emphasis**		
	main verb	– copular *is*	1
		– uninflected	1
VOCABULARY		– *is . . . -ing*	1
pony, grass, move, eating, riding	**Secondary emphasis**		
	personal pronoun	– *I*	1
		– *she*	2
FLANNEL-BOARD MATERIALS	negative	– N *is not*	7
paper figures: Karen, Mommy, man paper cutouts: pony, grass, tree			

THE PONY RIDE

NARRATIVE	TARGET RESPONSE	SENTENCE POINT	DSS TOTAL
This is Karen. Karen is four years old. She is four years old. How old is she?	2 1 3 She is four years old.	1	7
This is Mommy. She is Karen's mommy. This is her mommy. Who is this?	1 1 2 This is her mommy.	1	5
Karen and Mommy are outside. They are in the park. Karen sees something! She says: Look, Mommy. Look over there. I see something. What does Karen say?	1 1 3 I see something.	1	6
Something is over here. What can it be? Karen is pointing at it. She's looking at something. She is looking over here. What is she doing?	2 1 She is looking over here.	1	4
Karen says: Look what it is. It's a pony. Mommy, I see a pony. See it over there. I see a pony. What does Karen say?	1 1 I see a pony.	1	3

NARRATIVE	TARGET RESPONSE	SENTENCE POINT	DSS TOTAL
Mommy says: You're right, Karen. It is a pony. I can see it now. It's over there. The pony is by the tree. Where is the pony?	1 1 It is by the tree.	1	3
The pony is standing over here. It's a little one. It is not big. See. It is a little pony. The pony is not big: Is the pony big?	1 1 1 No, it's not.	1	4
	1 7 The pony is not big.	1	9
The pony is eating. Here's some grass. Ponies eat grass. See, he's eating it. The pony is eating grass. What is the pony doing?	1 The pony is eating grass.	1	2
Look at the grass. It's green. Grass is green. But the pony's not. It's not green. The pony is brown and white. What color is the pony?	1 3 The pony is brown and white.	1	5
Karen walks over to the tree. She's looking at the pony. The little pony is eating grass. Karen says: This is a nice pony. I like this pony. What does she say?	1 1 1 I like this pony.	1	4
Karen wants to ride it. She says: Can I ride the pony? Can I, Mommy? Can I? I want a ride. I want a pony ride. What does Karen say?	1 1 I want a pony ride.	1	3

NARRATIVE	TARGET RESPONSE	SENTENCE POINT	DSS TOTAL
Mommy says: But the pony isn't yours. It is not your pony. It belongs to this man. It's his. It is not yours. The pony is not yours. What does Mommy say?	1 7 1 The pony is not yours.	1	10
Here is the man. The pony belongs to him. It's his little pony. Look. He's gonna let Karen ride. The man is letting her ride. What is he doing?	2 1 2 5 He is letting her ride.	1	11
Karen is getting on. She's getting on the pony. The pony is standing still. The man is holding it. Karen is getting on. What is she doing?	1 Karen is getting on.	1	2
Look at Karen! She's on the pony. She is ready to ride. Karen says: Look, Mommy. I'm on the pony. Look at me! Look at me! What does she say?	1 1 Look at me!	1	3
Mommy says: I see you. I'm watching you. But be careful. Don't fall off. Be careful. What does Mommy say?	1 Be careful.	1	2
Look. There they go. The pony is walking. And Karen is riding. She is riding the pony. What is she doing?	2 1 She is riding the pony.	1	4
But Karen wants to go faster. She says: Faster! Faster! Go faster, pony.			

NARRATIVE	TARGET RESPONSE	SENTENCE POINT	DSS TOTAL
The pony is going faster. Watch. There it goes. The pony is going faster. What is the pony doing?	1 The pony is going faster.	1	2
Oh, oh! Oh, oh! Watch. Something is happening. The pony is going slower. See. The pony is slowing down. Now look. The pony is stopping. What is the pony doing now?	1 The pony is stopping.	1	2
Oh, oh! The pony stopped. Karen says: Come on, pony. Move! Move! What does she say?	1 1 Come on, pony. Move!	2	4
But the pony is not moving. Look. It's standing still. Karen says: The pony is not moving. It has stopped. The pony is standing still. What does Karen say?	1 The pony is standing still.	1	2
Karen says: Why did it stop? What's wrong? Is it sleepy? Is that why? Is the pony sleepy?	1 7 The pony is not sleepy.	1	9
The man says: The pony is not sleepy. He is hungry. The pony is not sleepy. What does the man say?	1 7 The pony is not sleepy.	1	9
Oh, look. The pony is eating. But the pony is slow. It is eating too slowly. So Karen says: Hurry up, pony.			

NARRATIVE	TARGET RESPONSE	SENTENCE POINT	DSS TOTAL
Hurry up and eat. What does Karen say?	1 3 1 Hurry up and eat.	1	6
Oh, look. Look at the pony. It's not eating now. The pony is walking again. But the ride is over. Now Karen is getting off. What is she doing?	2 1 She is getting off.	1	4
The ride is over now. Karen says: You're a good pony. That was a nice ride.			

LEVEL I: LESSON 8

CONCEPTS

buying shoes, size differences, time contrasts

VOCABULARY

shoe, shoe store, shoe man, need, size, big, little, sunny, dark

FLANNEL-BOARD MATERIALS

paper figures: Bobby, Mommy, shoe salesman
paper cutouts: sun, shoe with hole, store front, baby shoe, man's shoe, boot, pair of new shoes

ELICITED STRUCTURES		DSS VALUE
Primary emphasis		
indefinite pronoun –	*it, that*	1
personal pronoun –	*I*	1
main verb –	copular *is*	1
–	uninflected	1
negative –	*it is not*	1
Secondary emphasis		
indefinite pronoun –	*this*	1
–	*one*	3
personal pronoun –	*my, you*	1

BUYING NEW SHOES

NARRATIVE	TARGET RESPONSE	SENTENCE POINT	DSS TOTAL
Here is Bobby. Bobby is four years old. He's in our story today. This is Bobby. Who is this?	1 1 This is Bobby.	1	3
Here is Mommy. Mommy is in our story, too. There are two people in our story. This one is Bobby. And that one is Mommy. Who is that one?	1 3 1 That one is Mommy.	1	6
It is morning. Bobby just got up. It's time to get up now. Because it's morning. What time is it?	1 1 It's morning.	1	3
See the sun shining! See how light it is. It's not dark outside now.			

NARRATIVE	TARGET RESPONSE	SENTENCE POINT	DSS TOTAL
No, it's sunny out. It's not dark. Is it dark now?	1 1 1 No, it's not. 1 1 1 It is not dark.	1 1	4 4
Bobby is getting dressed. He's dressing all by himself. He's almost done. Mommy is already up. She is downstairs. Where is she?	2 1 She is downstairs.	1	4
Mommy says: Bobby, Bobby. Are you done dressing? I want you to hurry. Hurry up. I want you. What does Mommy say?	1 1 1 I want you.	1	4
Look. Here comes Bobby. He is all dressed. Oh, oh. Oh, oh. Something is wrong. Something is missing. What is wrong?	3 1 Something is missing.	1	5
Look. Bobby has only one shoe. He is not wearing two shoes. He's wearing only one. Bobby has just one shoe on. There's only one shoe. What is wrong?	1 3 There's only one shoe.	1	5
Mommy says: Bobby, where is your shoe? I don't see it. Where is your other shoe? It's not here. What does Mommy say?	1 1 1 It's not here.	1	4
Bobby says: Here it is, Mommy. I have it. But look here. There's a hole in it!			

NARRATIVE	TARGET RESPONSE	SENTENCE POINT	DSS TOTAL
I have a hole in my shoe. What does Bobby say?	1 1 1 I have a hole in my shoe.	1	4
Look at Bobby's shoe. He can't wear it. There's a hole in it. Bobby's shoe is old. Is Bobby's shoe new?	2 1 No, his shoe is old.	1	4
It isn't new. It's all worn out. This shoe is old. It's not new. Is this a new shoe?	1 1 1 No, it's not.	1	4
	1 1 1 It's not new.	1	4
Mommy says: Let's go shopping. You need some new shoes. Let's go buy some. You can't wear old shoes. Bobby, you need new shoes. What does Mommy say?	1 1 You need new shoes.	1	3
Bobby says: Oh boy! Oh boy! Let's go. I wanna go. Let's go shopping. Let's go right now. What does he say?	1 2 Let's go right now.	1	4
Here they go. They're going to the shoe store. Bobby's gonna get new shoes. See what this is! Here's the store. This is the shoe store. What is this?	1 1 This is the shoe store.	1	3
Oh, look. Look now. Here is a man. He is the shoe man. This is the shoe store. And that is the shoe man. Who is that?	1 1 That is the shoe man.	1	3
The shoe man says: Hello. Hello. Can I help you? Bobby says: Yes, you can.			

NARRATIVE	TARGET RESPONSE	SENTENCE POINT	DSS TOTAL
My shoes are old. I need new shoes. I want some new ones. What does Bobby say?	1 1 3 3 I want some new ones.	1	9
A shoe store has lots of new shoes. The shoe man can help Bobby. Look. He's bringing lots of shoes. The shoe man says: Here are some new shoes. Here they are, Bobby. These shoes are for you. I have new shoes for you. What does the shoe man say?	1 1 1 I have new shoes for you.	1	4
Bobby sees all the shoes. He's gonna try some on. Oh, oh. Look at this one. Something is wrong. Is this a shoe? Bobby says: I want new shoes. That is a boot. I don't want that. It's not a shoe. That is not a shoe. What does he say?	1 1 1 That is not a shoe.	1	4
Bobby doesn't want boots. He only wants new shoes. Here is one. Oh, oh. Look. Bobby can't wear this one. Because it's too little. Why can't he wear it?	1 1 (Because) it's too little.	1	3
Bobby says: That is too little. It's a baby's shoe. I need a bigger one. I can't wear a baby shoe.			

NARRATIVE	TARGET RESPONSE	SENTENCE POINT	DSS TOTAL
That's not big enough. What does Bobby say?	1 1 1 That's not big enough.	1	4
That shoe is the wrong size. It's too little for Bobby. Here is another one. Oh, oh. Now what's wrong? It's too big. See? Bobby says: This shoe is too big. It's not the right size. It's too big for me. That's not my size. What does he say?	1 1 1 1 That's not my size.	1	5
The shoe man says: Here's one other shoe. Try it on, Bobby. Maybe it will fit. Bobby is trying it on. Now he's standing up. Mommy says: How does it fit, Bobby? Is it the right size? Is it? Is it okay? What does Mommy say?	1 11 Is it okay?	1	4
Oh, look. The shoe fits him! It's the right size. Bobby says: This shoe fits me. It fits just right. This one is just right. What does he say?	1 3 1 This one is just right.	1	6
Mommy is buying the shoes. They fit Bobby. The new shoes are the right size. Bobby says: Thank you, Mommy. Thank you for the shoes. I like them very much.			

NARRATIVE	TARGET RESPONSE	SENTENCE POINT	DSS TOTAL
I like my new shoes. What does Bobby say?	1 1 1 I like my new shoes.	1	4
Bobby likes his new shoes. He's already wearing them. He is gonna wear them home. He needed new shoes.			

LEVEL I: LESSON 9

CONCEPTS

zoo, animal, similarities and differences

VOCABULARY

elephant, monkey, animal, long, short, rough, soft, big, little

FLANNEL-BOARD MATERIALS

paper figures: Bobby, Daddy
paper cutouts: elephant made of sandpaper, monkey made of felt, two cages

ELICITED STRUCTURES		DSS VALUE
Primary emphasis		
indefinite pronoun –	*it*	1
main verb –	copular *is*	1
negative –	*it is not*	1
Secondary emphasis		
personal pronoun –	*I*	1
–	*he, his*	2
main verb –	uninflected	1
conjunction –	*and*	3
secondary verb –	early-developing infinitives	2

FUN AT THE ZOO

NARRATIVE	TARGET RESPONSE	SENTENCE POINT	DSS TOTAL
Our story is about two people. This is a little boy. This one is Bobby. The little boy is Bobby. Who is the little boy?	1 The little boy is Bobby.	1	2
This is a big man. This one is Daddy. The big man is Daddy. Who is the big man?	1 The big man is Daddy.	1	2
Daddy is going to the zoo. He says: Who wants to go? Do you wanna go, Bobby? Bobby says: Yes, I do. I wanna go. I like the zoo. What does Bobby say?	1 1 I like the zoo.	1	3
Bobby wants to see the animals. The animals are at the zoo. They stay there. The animals live at the zoo.			

NARRATIVE	TARGET RESPONSE	SENTENCE POINT	DSS TOTAL
Where do the animals live?	1 The animals live at the zoo.	1	2
Look! Here it is. This is the zoo. Daddy says: The animals are inside. Let's go find them. Let's find the animals. What does Daddy say?	1 2 Let's find the animals.	1	4
Bobby sees a big animal! Look, it's an elephant. Look how big it is. The big animal is an elephant. What is the big animal?	1 The big animal is an elephant.	1	2
Bobby says: Look, Daddy. Look. There's a great big elephant. Let's go see it. I wanna go see it. What does Bobby say?	1 1 2 2 1 I wanna go see it.	1	8
They are looking at the elephant. He's in a cage. See. That's where he lives. The elephant stays there. He is in his cage. Where is he?	2 1 2 He is in his cage.	1	6
Bobby likes the elephant. He wants to touch him. Bobby says: Lemme touch the elephant. Can I, Daddy? Can I? Lemme touch him. What does Bobby say?	1 1 2 2 Lemme touch him.	1	7
Daddy lets him. He's letting Bobby touch him. Watch. Bobby is touching him. He's touching the elephant. What's he doing?	2 1 He's touching the elephant.	1	4

NARRATIVE	TARGET RESPONSE	SENTENCE POINT	DSS TOTAL
Now everybody touches the elephant. An elephant feels rough. Feel this. An elephant is not soft. It is a rough animal. It's not soft. Is an elephant soft?	1 1 1 No, it's not.	1	4
	1 1 1 It's not soft.	1	4
Bobby says: Look at this. This is his trunk. See how long it is. An elephant's trunk is long. What does Bobby say?	1 An elephant's trunk is long.	1	2
Daddy says: Yes, it is long. His trunk is not short. See, it's not a short one. The elephant's trunk is long. It is not short. Is the elephant's trunk short?	1 1 1 No, it is not.	1	4
	1 1 1 It is not short.	1	4
Bobby likes the elephant. It's a great big animal. It is big, and it is rough. An elephant is two things. It is big and rough. What is an elephant?	1 1 3 It is big and rough.	1	6
Now Bobby sees something else. It is another animal. Here it is. Look. Look. It's a monkey. This animal is a monkey. Is this an elephant?	1 1 1 No, it's not.	1	4
	1 1 1 It's not an elephant.	1	4
See how little it is. The monkey is not big. It is little. Bobby sees a little animal. The little animal is a monkey. What is the little animal?	1 The little animal is a monkey.	1	2

NARRATIVE	TARGET RESPONSE	SENTENCE POINT	DSS TOTAL
The monkey is in his cage. He lives in a cage, too. Just like the elephant. He is in his cage. Where is the monkey?	2 1 2 He is in his cage.	1	6
Watch. The monkey can climb. He's climbing up his cage. He can go high. Watch him climb. He's climbing up his cage. What's the monkey doing?	2 1 2 He's climbing up his cage.	1	6
Bobby says: Look at the little monkey. He's climbing his cage. Let's go watch him. Come on, Daddy. Let's go. Let's go to the monkey cage. What does Bobby say?	1 2 Let's go to the monkey cage.	1	4
There they go. This is the monkey cage. Look, everybody! Look at his tail. This is his tail. What is this?	1 1 2 This is his tail.	1	5
The monkey has a long tail. It's not a short one. It is long. It is not short. Is the monkey's tail short?	1 1 1 No, it is not.	1	4
	1 1 1 It is not short.	1	4
Look. Bobby's touching him. Now, everybody, touch the monkey. A monkey feels soft. Feel this. A monkey is not rough. It is a soft animal. It's not rough. Is the monkey rough?	1 1 1 No, it's not.	1	4
	1 1 1 It is not rough.	1	4

NARRATIVE	TARGET RESPONSE	SENTENCE POINT	DSS TOTAL
Bobby likes the monkey. It is a little animal. It is little, and it is soft. A monkey is not rough. It is very soft. A monkey is little and soft. What is a monkey?	1 1 3 It is little and soft.	1	6
Bobby says: I like the zoo. Today I saw two animals. I saw an elephant and a monkey. I like those animals. I like the elephant and monkey. What does Bobby say?	1 1 3 I like the elephant and monkey.	1	6
Daddy says: I like them, too. But it's time to go. Let's go home now. It's time to go. What does Daddy say?	1 1 3 It's time to go.	1	6
The zoo was lots of fun. But now they will go home.			

LEVEL I: LESSON 10

CONCEPTS	ELICITED STRUCTURES		DSS VALUE
Halloween, disguise, contrasts	**Primary emphasis**		
	indefinite pronoun –	*it, this*	1
	main verb –	copular *is*	1
	negative –	N *is not*	7
VOCABULARY			
mask, clown, witch, funny, scary, surprise, Halloween	**Secondary emphasis**		
	personal pronoun –	*you, mine*	1
	main verb –	uninflected	1

FLANNEL-BOARD MATERIALS

paper figures: Bobby, Karen, Mommy, Daddy
paper cutouts: house, clown's mask and witch's mask to fit faces of figures

HALLOWEEN MASKS

NARRATIVE	TARGET RESPONSE	SENTENCE POINT	DSS TOTAL
Here are two children. They are brother and sister. The boy is Bobby. Bobby is the brother. Who is Bobby?	1 Bobby is the brother.	1	2
The girl is Karen. Karen is Bobby's sister. She is the sister. Who is Karen?	1 Karen is the sister.	1	2
Bobby and Karen are in school. They're having lots of fun. They are making something. It's something for Halloween. Look! Look what it is! It is a mask. It's a Halloween mask. What is it?	1 1 It's a Halloween mask.	1	3
What are you gonna be on Halloween?	(Elicit responses.)		

NARRATIVE	TARGET RESPONSE	SENTENCE POINT	DSS TOTAL
Look. Here is Bobby's. His mask is funny. See the clown's face. It's a funny face. Funny clown! It has blue hair! See it? What kind is he making?	2 1 He is making a funny mask.	1	4
Look, now. This one is Karen's. Her mask is scary. Look. This witch's face is scary. See it? It's not a funny one. This is a scary face. Karen's mask is not funny. Is her mask funny?	1 1 1 No, it's not.	1	4
	2 1 7 Her mask is not funny.	1	11
Their masks are all finished now. Look. Karen's is all done. And so is Bobby's! They're ready for Halloween. It's tonight. Tonight is Halloween. When is Halloween?	1 Tonight is Halloween.	1	2
Now they can take them home. Maybe they will wear them! School is over now. It's time to go home. What time is it?	1 1 3 It's time to go home.	1	6
Bobby says: I like your mask, Karen. But I like mine, too. My mask is funny. It has a funny face and blue hair. Mine is a funny one. What does Bobby say?	1 1 3 Mine is a funny one.	1	6
Karen says: Mine is scary. I like my witch's mask.			

NARRATIVE	TARGET RESPONSE	SENTENCE POINT	DSS TOTAL
'Cause it's a scary one. It's not funny like yours. Mine is not a funny one. What does Karen say?	1 1 7 3 Mine is not a funny one.	1	13
Oh, look. Bobby and Karen are home. Here is their house. And here is their Mommy. She is at home . . . right here. Where is Mommy?	2 1 She is at home.	1	4
But where is Daddy? Daddy is not at home. He's still working. That's where he is. Daddy is not home yet. Is Daddy home now?	2 1 7 No, he's not.	1	11
	1 7 Daddy is not home.	1	9
Karen says: Let's play a trick. When Daddy comes home . . . Let's put our masks on. Daddy won't know us. Let's play a trick. Okay? What does Karen say?	1 2 Let's play a trick.	1	4
Bobby says: Okay, let's surprise Daddy. We'll wear our masks. And he won't know us. I'll wear my mask. And you wear yours. I'll wear my mask and . . .	1 1 1 You wear yours.	1	4
There's gonna be a surprise. Bobby is gonna be a clown! Karen will be a witch! Daddy won't know them. It's a surprise. What is it?	1 1 It's a surprise.	1	3

NARRATIVE	TARGET RESPONSE	SENTENCE POINT	DSS TOTAL
Oh, oh. Here he comes. He's gonna be surprised. Here is Daddy. He is coming home. Who is coming home?	1 Daddy is coming home.	1	2
Bobby and Karen are getting ready. They are putting on their masks. Bobby says: Karen, you look like a witch. You don't look like my sister. You look scary. What does Bobby say?	1 1 You look scary.	1	3
Karen says: Bobby, is that you? Are you my brother? I don't know you. You look like a clown. You look funny, Bobby. What does Karen say?	1 1 You look funny.	1	3
Here comes Karen. She has on her witch's mask. Daddy sees her. Daddy says: Who is this witch? I don't know you. Who is this? Who is it? What does Daddy say?	2 1 1 1 Who is it?	1	6
Now here comes Bobby. Here comes the clown. Daddy says: Who is this clown? I don't know you. Who is this? What does Daddy say?	2 1 1 1 Who is this?	1	6
Daddy doesn't know them. He says: This is a clown. He is funny. But Bobby's not a clown. This clown is not Bobby. What does Daddy say?	1 1 7 This clown is not Bobby.	1	10

NARRATIVE	TARGET RESPONSE	SENTENCE POINT	DSS TOTAL
Now Daddy is looking at Karen. He says: This is a witch. It's not Karen. Where is she? This witch is not Karen. What does he say?	1 1 7 This witch is not Karen.	1	10
Daddy says: Where are my children? Where are Karen and Bobby? I can't find them. Is this a trick? What does Daddy say?	1 1 1 Is this a trick?	1	4
Karen takes off her mask. She says: I'm not a witch. See. This is a mask. I made a mask at school. Mine is a witch's mask. What does Karen say?	1 1 Mine is a witch's mask.	1	3
Now Bobby takes off his mask. He says: I am Bobby. I'm not a clown. I had a mask on. It's for Halloween. I have a clown's mask. What does he say?	1 1 I have a clown's mask.	1	3
Bobby says: This is a surprise. We fooled you, Daddy. We played a trick. This is a surprise. What does Bobby say?	1 1 This is a surprise.	1	3
Daddy says: You fooled me. I didn't know you. This was a surprise.			

LEVEL I: LESSON 11

CONCEPTS	ELICITED STRUCTURES	DSS VALUE
hiding, searching, spatial relations, age and location contrasts	**Primary emphasis**	
	personal pronoun – *he, she*	2
	main verb – copular *is*	1
	negative – N *is not*	7
VOCABULARY	**Secondary emphasis**	
hide-and-seek, looking, by, in, under, behind	indefinite pronoun – *it*	1
	main verb – *is . . . -ing*	1
	conjunction – *and*	3

FLANNEL-BOARD MATERIALS

paper figures: Bobby, Karen
paper cutouts: table, TV set, couch, chair, closet door

PLAYING HIDE-AND-SEEK

NARRATIVE	TARGET RESPONSE	SENTENCE POINT	DSS TOTAL
Here are two children. The boy is Bobby. And the girl is Karen. Our story is about them. It's about Bobby and Karen.			
Who is the story about?	3 Bobby and Karen.	–	3
	1 1 3 It's about Bobby and Karen.	1	6
Bobby is five years old. But Karen isn't. Karen is four years old. She's not five years old. Who is five years old?	1 3 Bobby is five years old.	1	5
Bobby is older. He is five. Karen is four years old. She's not five. No, she's not. Bobby is older than Karen. Is Karen five years old?	2 1 7 No, she's not.	1	11
	2 1 7 3 She's not five.	1	14
Do you have a brother? Is he older than you?	(Elicit responses.)		

NARRATIVE	TARGET RESPONSE	SENTENCE POINT	DSS TOTAL
Karen and Bobby are inside. They can't go out. They have to stay in. Because it's raining outside. Why can't they go out?	1 1 (Because) it's raining outside.	1	3
Karen says: We can't go outside. Because it's raining. So let's do something. Let's play a game. What does Karen say?	1 2 Let's play a game.	1	4
Bobby says: Okay. I know a game. How about hide-and-seek? That's a good game. I wanna play hide-and-seek. What does Bobby say?	1 1 2 I wanna play 3 hide-and-seek.	1	8
Karen says: Let's go into the living room. We can hide in there. Bobby says: But who will be first? Is it gonna be you, Karen? Is it? Is it you? What does Bobby say?	1 11 1 Is it you?	1	5
Karen says: Yes, I'm first. I wanna be first. Bobby says: Okay. You can hide first. But I'll find you, Karen. Go and hide right now. What does Bobby say?	1 3 1 Go and hide right now.	1	6
Karen is looking. She's looking for a hiding place. Oh, oh. She sees a good place. Look what it is! It's the table. What is Karen's hiding place?	1 1 It's the table.	1	3

NARRATIVE	TARGET RESPONSE	SENTENCE POINT	DSS TOTAL
Karen's getting under the table. There she goes. Watch! Now you can't see her. Karen is hiding. She is under the table. Where is she?	2 1 She is under the table.	1	4
Now Bobby's gonna find Karen. He says: Watch out, Karen! Ready or not. I'm coming. Here I come. Here I come. What does Bobby say?	1 1 Here I come.	1	3
Bobby starts to look. He looks this way . . . and that way. He's looking for Karen. He is looking and looking. What is he doing?	2 1 3 He is looking and 1 looking.	1	8
First, he goes to the TV set. But he doesn't see Karen. Because she's not there. That's not the right place. Karen is not there. Is Karen by the TV?	2 1 7 No, she's not.	1	11
	2 1 7 She's not there.	1	11
Next, Bobby walks to the closet. Maybe Karen is in there. He opens the door . . . . But Karen's not there either. She's not in the closet. Is Karen in the closet?	2 1 7 No, she's not.	1	11
	2 1 7 She's not in the closet.	1	11
Bobby can't find Karen. Oh, oh. Oh, oh. Look now! He's walking to the table. That's where he's gonna look!			

NARRATIVE	TARGET RESPONSE	SENTENCE POINT	DSS TOTAL
Here he comes. Over to the table. Bobby is walking to the table. What is he doing?	2 1 He is walking to the table.	1	4
Oh, oh. Bobby sees someone. Look who it is! It's Karen! Bobby sees her. He found Karen. Bobby says: Come out, Karen. I see you. What does Bobby say?	1 1 1 I see you.	1	4
Karen says: You found me. I was under the table. Now you go and hide. It's your turn. What does Karen say?	1 1 1 It's your turn.	1	4
Bobby is looking now. He's looking for his hiding place. Oh, he sees a good one . . . over here. It is the couch. What is Bobby's hiding place?	1 1 It is the couch.	1	3
Look what he's doing. He's going behind it. Bobby is hiding behind the couch. You can't see him. He's hiding. Bobby is behind the couch. Where is he?	2 1 He is behind the couch.	1	4
Karen says: Here I come. Ready or not! Here I come, Bobby. Now Karen starts to look. She's looking for Bobby. Who is she looking for?	2 1 She's looking for Bobby.	1	4
Where could he be? Karen doesn't know. She's trying to find him.			

NARRATIVE	TARGET RESPONSE	SENTENCE POINT	DSS TOTAL
She's looking everywhere. Karen is gonna find him. What is she gonna do?	2 1 2 2 She is gonna find him.	1	8
First she goes to the table. He might be under it. Karen looks under the table. But that's not where he is. That's the wrong place! Bobby's not there. Is he there?	2 1 7 No, he's not.	1	11
	2 1 7 He's not there.	1	11
Next she walks to the chair. Maybe that's where he is. Karen is looking by the chair. But Bobby's not there either. That's not the right place. Is the chair the right place?	1 1 1 No, it's not.	1	4
	1 1 1 It's not the right place.	1	4
That was another wrong place. Bobby's not hiding by the chair. No, he isn't. He is not by the chair. Is Bobby by the chair?	2 1 7 No, he is not.	1	11
	2 1 7 He is not by the chair.	1	11
Oh, oh. She's looking at the couch. There's Bobby! There he is! Karen sees Bobby. She's looking right at him. What's she doing?	2 1 She's looking right at 2 him.	1	6
Bobby says: You found me fast, Karen. Karen says: Yes, I did. You can't fool me.			

LEVEL I: LESSON 12

CONCEPTS	ELICITED STRUCTURES		DSS VALUE
bright, hard, round	**Primary emphasis**		
	indefinite pronoun –	*it*	1
VOCABULARY	personal pronoun –	*I*	1
shiny, penny, sun, new, hard, turtle, round, shell	main verb –	copular *is*	1
	–	*is . . . -ing*	1
	secondary verb –	*wanna* + infinitive	2
FLANNEL-BOARD MATERIALS	conjunction –	*and*	3
paper figures: Bobby, Karen	**Secondary emphasis**		
paper cutouts: sun, turtle, penny	secondary verb –	*gonna* + infinitive	2

GOING FOR A WALK

NARRATIVE	TARGET RESPONSE	SENTENCE POINT	DSS TOTAL
This is Bobby. This is Karen. They are brother and sister. Bobby is the brother. Karen is the sister. Who is the brother?	1 Bobby is the brother.	1	2
Who is the sister?	1 Karen is the sister.	1	2
Karen says: Today is Saturday, Bobby. Let's do something. Let's go for a walk. I wanna take a walk. What does Karen say?	1 1 2 I wanna take a walk.	1	5
Bobby says: Oh, boy. I wanna do that. Let's take a walk. I wanna go too. I wanna go with you. What does Bobby say?	1 1 2 1 I wanna go with you.	1	6
They are going now. Here they go. Karen says: See the sun. Look, Bobby. It is so sunny today. See the sun shining. It is very sunny. What does Karen say?	1 1 It is very sunny.	1	3

NARRATIVE	TARGET RESPONSE	SENTENCE POINT	DSS TOTAL
Look, everybody. Look at the sun. It is big. The sun is big. It's round, too. See, it is round. The sun is big, and it's round. It is big and round. What does the sun look like?	1 1 3 It is big and round.	1	6
Watch. Watch now. Bobby is walking. And Karen is walking, too. They are both walking. Bobby is walking, and Karen is walking. Who is walking?	3 Bobby is, and Karen is.	1	4
	1 3 Bobby is walking, and 1 Karen is walking.	1	6
Oh, oh. Karen stops walking. Because she sees something. It's lying on the ground. Something is on the ground. What is on the ground?	3 1 Something is on the ground.	1	5
Karen is looking at it. She says: Bobby, what is this? I see something. What is it? What is it? What does Karen say?	2 111 What is it?	1	6
Now Bobby is looking. He says: I know. I know what it is. It's a green turtle. It is a little green turtle. What does Bobby say?	1 1 It is a little green turtle.	1	3
Karen says: It's so little. The turtle isn't big. I wanna touch it. I wanna touch it. What does Karen say?	1 1 2 1 I wanna touch it.	1	6
This is his shell. It is hard.			

NARRATIVE	TARGET RESPONSE	SENTENCE POINT	DSS TOTAL
It's round, too. The shell is round and hard. What is it?	1 1 3 It is round and hard.	1	6
Oh, oh. There goes the turtle. It's walking away. Karen says: Look at the turtle. It's going away. Stop it! The turtle is going away. What is happening?	1 The turtle is going away.	1	2
Watch Bobby! He starts to run. He says: Watch me, Karen. I'm gonna get the turtle. I'm gonna get it. Bobby is gonna get it. What is he gonna do?	2 1 2 1 He is gonna get it.	1	7
But Bobby stops. He's looking for the turtle. He can't find it. It's not there. The turtle is gone. Where is the turtle?	1 The turtle is gone.	1	2
Karen says: Let's both look for it. I'll help you look. Lemme look too. I wanna help you. What does Karen say?	1 1 2 1 I wanna help you.	1	6
Then Karen sees it. She says: Bobby, Bobby. I found it. Here it is. The turtle is right here. What does Karen say?	1 The turtle is right here.	1	2
Look. Karen is gonna get it. See what she does. She's gonna pick up the turtle.			

NARRATIVE	TARGET RESPONSE	SENTENCE POINT	DSS TOTAL
Watch. Karen is gonna pick it up. What is she gonna do?	2 1 2 She is gonna pick 1 it up.	1	7
Look. Karen has the turtle. Now Bobby sees something. It is on the ground. He says: I see something. But what is this? What is it? What is it? What does Bobby say?	2 111 What is it?	1	6
Karen says: I know, Bobby. I know what it is. That's a penny. See how shiny it is. It's a new penny. What is it?	1 1 It's a new penny.	1	3
Bobby says: You have the turtle. I want the penny. I wanna get it. I wanna pick it up. What does Bobby say?	1 1 2 1 I wanna pick it up.	1	6
Look, everybody. Look at the penny. It's a brand new one. See how shiny it is. Look, it's round too. The penny is round and shiny. What is it?	1 The penny is round 3 and shiny.	1	5
Bobby gets the penny. He is holding it now. But look. Oh, oh. He let go. Bobby dropped the penny. It is rolling away. What is it doing?	1 1 It is rolling away.	1	3
There goes Bobby. He is running. He's trying to get the penny. He's gonna get it. Watch. He is gonna get it. What is he gonna do?	2 1 2 1 He is gonna get it.	1	7

NARRATIVE	TARGET RESPONSE	SENTENCE POINT	DSS TOTAL
Bobby gets the penny. He is holding it now. But look. Oh, oh. He let go again. Bobby dropped the penny. It is rolling away. What is it doing?	1 1 It is rolling away.	1	3
There goes Bobby. He is running. He's trying to get the penny. He's gonna get it. Watch. He is gonna get it. What is he gonna do?	2 1 2 1 He is gonna get it.	1	7
Look, Bobby got it. He has the penny. Now they're both holding something. See? Bobby is holding the penny. And Karen is holding the turtle. What are they holding?	3 A turtle and a penny.	–	3
	1 Karen is holding the 3 turtle and Bobby 1 is holding the penny.	1	6
Bobby and Karen are happy. They had fun on their walk.			

LEVEL I: LESSON 13

CONCEPTS

weather, fall, colors

VOCABULARY

jacket, sweater, leaf, brown, yellow, nut, squirrel

FLANNEL-BOARD MATERIALS

paper figures: Bobby, Karen
paper cutouts: sweater, jacket, squirrel, nut, tree, several yellow and brown leaves detachable from the tree

ELICITED STRUCTURES		DSS VALUE
Primary emphasis		
indefinite pronoun –	*it*	1
personal pronoun –	*I*	1
main verb –	copular *is*	1
secondary verb –	*wanna* + infinitive	2
Secondary emphasis		
indefinite pronoun –	*one*	3
personal pronoun –	*me*	1
main verb –	*is . . . -ing*	1
secondary verb –	*lemme* + infinitive	2

THE SQUIRREL

NARRATIVE	TARGET RESPONSE	SENTENCE POINT	DSS TOTAL
Our story is about two children. One is a boy. This is Bobby. He is the boy. Who is the boy?	Bobby is the boy. (1)	1	2
The other one is a girl. Here is Karen. She is the girl. Who is the girl?	Karen is the girl. (1)	1	2
Who is the boy, and who is the girl?	Bobby (1) is the boy and (3) Karen is (1) the girl.	1	6
Karen and Bobby are in the house. Karen says: I'm going outside. Do you wanna come? Bobby says: Yes, I do. I wanna come with you. What does Bobby say?	I (1) wanna (1, 2) come with you (1).	1	6

NARRATIVE	TARGET RESPONSE	SENTENCE POINT	DSS TOTAL
Karen says: Get your jacket, Bobby. It's pretty cool outside. Summer is over. It is not hot now. What does she say?	1 1 1 It is not hot now.	1	4
Here is Bobby's jacket. It's a brown one. Bobby says: It's not hot any more. I need my jacket. What does he say?	1 1 1 I need my jacket.	1	4
But Karen isn't wearing a jacket. She says: Here's my sweater. I'm not wearing a jacket. I wanna wear my sweater. What does Karen say?	1 1 2 1 I wanna wear my sweater.	1	6
Karen is wearing a sweater. But Bobby's not. He's wearing a jacket. Karen's wearing a sweater. And Bobby's wearing a jacket. What are Bobby and Karen wearing?	1 Bobby's wearing a jacket, 3 1 and Karen's wearing a sweater.	1	6
Bobby sees something. Look at this. It's a tree. See how big it is. This is a great big tree. What is this?	1 1 This is a great big tree.	1	3
Bobby says: Look at this tree. It's a great big one. Let's go closer. I wanna see it up close. What does he say?	1 1 2 1 I wanna see it up close.	1	6

NARRATIVE	TARGET RESPONSE	SENTENCE POINT	DSS TOTAL
Everybody, look at the big tree. See all the leaves. Karen says: The tree has lots of leaves. There are so many. I see lots of leaves. What does she say?	1 1 3 I see lots of leaves.	1	6
Oh, look. One is falling down. Watch! Here it comes. It falls very, very slowly. One of the leaves is falling down. What is happening?	{ 3 One of the leaves 1 is falling down.	1	5
	1 A leaf is falling down. }	1	2
Look. A leaf is on the ground. It fell off the tree. Let's look at it. It is brown. It is a brown leaf. What color leaf is it?	1 1 It is a brown leaf.	1	3
Now another leaf is falling down. Here it comes . . . very slowly. This one is yellow. A yellow leaf is falling down. What is falling down?	1 A yellow leaf is falling down.	1	2
This leaf is yellow. It is not brown. It's not like this one. It's not the same. It is different. Is this leaf the same as this?	1 1 No, it is different.	1	3
Oh, oh. Guess what? Something is in the tree. And look what it is. It's a squirrel. What is it?	1 1 It's a squirrel.	1	3
Karen says: A squirrel's up there. But I can't see it. Show it to me, Bobby.			

NARRATIVE	TARGET RESPONSE	SENTENCE POINT	DSS TOTAL
Lemme see it. What does she say?	1 1 2 1 Lemme see it.	1	6
Bobby says: Shhh, be quiet. Don't make any noise. Don't scare it away. I wanna see it first. Lemme look first. What does he say?	1 1 2 Lemme look first.	1	5
It's very quiet. There it is! And the squirrel has something. He has a nut. The squirrel is holding a nut. What is the squirrel holding?	1 The squirrel is holding a nut.	1	2
It's still very quiet. Bobby and Karen are watching. Aa-choo. Aa-choo. Bobby sneezed! Oh, oh. The sneeze is too loud. What is wrong?	1 The sneeze is too loud.	1	2
The squirrel heard it. It made a big noise. The noise scared him away. The squirrel is gone. Where is the squirrel?	1 The squirrel is gone.	1	2
Bobby says: The squirrel is gone. I scared him away. He will not come back. He is hiding somewhere. What does Bobby say?	2 1 He is hiding somewhere.	1	4
Karen says: Oh, wait a minute. Look at all the leaves. I want one, Bobby. I wanna take one home. What does she say?	1 1 2 3 I wanna take one home.	1	8

NARRATIVE	TARGET RESPONSE	SENTENCE POINT	DSS TOTAL
Karen wants the yellow leaf. But Bobby takes it. Karen says: That's my leaf. I saw it first. Lemme have it. What does she say?	1 1 2 1 Lemme have it.	1	6
Bobby gives it to her. He's getting another one. Bobby says: I want this one. I wanna take the brown leaf. What does he say?	1 1 2 I wanna take the brown leaf.	1	5
Now they're going home. They each have a leaf. Bobby has one, and so does Karen.			

LEVEL I: LESSON 14

CONCEPTS	ELICITED STRUCTURES	DSS VALUE
growing, planting, garden	**Primary emphasis**	
	personal pronoun – *me*	1
VOCABULARY	main verb – uninflected	1
seed, flower, hoe, tomato, corn, digging, watering, planting	– *is . . . -ing*	1
	secondary verb – *lemme* + infinitive	2
FLANNEL-BOARD MATERIALS	**Secondary emphasis**	
paper figures: Bobby, Karen, Daddy	indefinite pronoun – *some*	3
paper cutouts: corn, tomato, and flower plants, package of seeds, hose, hoe	personal pronoun – *I, you*	1
	– *he, she*	2
	secondary verb – *gonna* + infinitive	2
	conjunction – *and*	3

PLANTING FLOWERS

NARRATIVE	TARGET RESPONSE	SENTENCE POINT	DSS TOTAL
Here is Daddy. He's looking for somebody. He can't find Karen. And he can't find Bobby. Daddy is looking for Karen and Bobby. What is he doing?	2 1 He is looking for Karen 3 and Bobby.	1	7
Here they are! Daddy found them. He says: Hey, Bobby, Hey, Karen. I need your help. Come here, both of you. Come and help me. What does Daddy say?	1 3 1 1 Come and help me.	1	7
See what Daddy has. These are flower seeds. They need to be planted. And Daddy is gonna do it. He is gonna plant the seeds. What is Daddy gonna do?	2 1 2 He is gonna plant the seeds.	1	6

NARRATIVE	TARGET RESPONSE	SENTENCE POINT	DSS TOTAL
Daddy says: I'm ready to plant. Who wants to help me? Bobby says: I do. I wanna help. Please, Daddy. Lemme help. Lemme help you. What does he say?	1 1 2 1 Lemme help you.	1	6
Daddy says: Okay. You can help. How about you, Karen? Do you wanna help? I need lots of help. What does he say?	1 1 3 I need lots of help.	1	6
Karen says: Oh, yes. I wanna help. I like to plant seeds. Lemme help too. Lemme plant some seeds. What does Karen say?	1 1 2 3 Lemme plant some seeds.	1	8
Daddy says: You can bring the hoe. The hoe is for digging. Here it is. You need it. You dig with it. What do you do with a hoe?	1 1 1 You dig with it.	1	4
Daddy gives Karen the hoe. She can carry it. She's gonna take it. Karen is gonna carry the hoe. What is she gonna do?	2 1 2 She is gonna carry the hoe.	1	6
But Bobby doesn't have anything. He says: I wanna carry the seeds. Lemme carry them. Lemme take the seeds. What does Bobby say?	1 1 2 Lemme take the seeds.	1	5

NARRATIVE	TARGET RESPONSE	SENTENCE POINT	DSS TOTAL
Now they both have something. Karen has the hoe. And Bobby has the seeds. Look, look. Here it is. This is the garden. What is this?	1 1 This is the garden.	1	3
Karen says: Here are the tomatoes. And here is the corn. I see two plants. I see tomatoes and corn. What does Karen say?	1 1 3 I see tomatoes and corn.	1	6
Bobby says: Look at the plants. Plants come from seeds. They grow from little seeds. Now I wanna plant some. I wanna plant the seeds. What does he say?	1 1 2 I wanna plant the seeds.	1	5
Karen says: I wanna help plant, too. What kind of seed is this? Is it a tomato seed? Or is it a corn seed? What is it? What is it? What does Karen say?	2 111 What is it?	1	6
Daddy says: This is a flower seed. You can plant it. But first, we need some holes. You do that. Dig some holes. What does he say?	1 3 Dig some holes.	1	5
Watch Karen. She's digging. Karen is using the hoe. She's digging in the ground.			

NARRATIVE	TARGET RESPONSE	SENTENCE POINT	DSS TOTAL
The seeds go in the ground. Where do the seeds go?	1 The seeds go in the ground.	1	2
Karen's making some holes. The seeds go into the holes. Karen is digging holes. What is she doing?	2 1 She is digging holes.	1	4
Look. See the holes. The holes are for the seeds. Bobby takes some seeds. He is gonna plant them. Bobby is gonna plant the seeds. What is he gonna do?	2 1 2 He is gonna plant the seeds.	1	6
Daddy has some more seeds. He says: I have more seeds. Who wants them? I have some more seeds. What does Daddy say?	1 1 3 3 I have some more seeds.	1	9
Karen says: I want them. I wanna plant the seeds. Lemme have them. Lemme have the seeds. What does she say?	1 1 2 Lemme have the seeds.	1	5
Now Karen is planting her seeds. She puts them in the holes. They go in the ground, too. She's planting the seeds in the ground. What's she doing?	2 1 She's planting the seeds in the ground.	1	4
Look. All the seeds are planted. Karen and Bobby did it. Now they have to water them. The seeds need water. What do the seeds need?	1 The seeds need water.	1	2

NARRATIVE	TARGET RESPONSE	SENTENCE POINT	DSS TOTAL
Daddy says: Here is the hose. We have to water the seeds. The seeds need water. Water makes them grow. Let's water the seeds. What does he say?	1 2 Let's water the seeds.	1	4
Karen holds the hose. Here comes the water. The water is coming out. Karen is watering the seeds. What is she doing?	2 1 She is watering the seeds.	1	4
Bobby sees something. He says: Look over here, Karen. Here are some other flowers. Let's take some to Mommy. Bobby is gonna pick the flowers. What is he gonna do?	2 1 2 He is gonna pick the flowers.	1	6
Karen wants to pick some too. She says: Wait a minute, Bobby. I wanna help. Lemme help you. What does Karen say?	1 1 2 1 Lemme help you.	1	6
Bobby and Karen are picking them. The flowers are for Mommy. She will like them.			

LEVEL I: LESSON 15

CONCEPTS	ELICITED STRUCTURES		DSS VALUE
baking, mixing, shape and tactile contrasts	**Primary emphasis**		
	indefinite pronoun –	*it*	1
	personal pronoun –	*me*	1
VOCABULARY	main verb –	copular *is*	1
cookies, oven, stirring, spoon, baking, dough, soft, hard, round, star	secondary verb –	*lemme* + infinitive	2
	conjunction –	*and*	3
FLANNEL-BOARD MATERIALS	**Secondary emphasis**		
	indefinite pronoun –	*this*	1
	personal pronoun –	*she*	2
paper figures: Karen, Susan, Mommy	main verb –	*is . . . -ing*	1
paper cutouts: bowl of cookie dough, spoon, rolling pin, two cookie cutters, oven, round cookie, star cookie	secondary verb –	*let's* + infinitive	2

BAKING COOKIES

NARRATIVE	TARGET RESPONSE	SENTENCE POINT	DSS TOTAL
Here are two girls. This is Karen. And this is Susan. They are both in our story. Who are the two girls?	3 Karen and Susan.	–	3
This is Mommy. She is in the story too. Today's story is about three people. Karen and Susan and Mommy are in it. Who are the three people?	3 3 Karen and Susan and Mommy.	–	6
Mommy is in the kitchen. She's making cookies. Here come the girls. Susan says: Mommy, I wanna help. I wanna bake cookies. What does she say?	1 1 2 I wanna bake cookies.	1	5

NARRATIVE	TARGET RESPONSE	SENTENCE POINT	DSS TOTAL
Karen says: Me too, Mommy. I like to bake cookies, too. Lemme help you. What does she say?	1 1 2 1 Lemme help you.	1	6
Mommy says: Yes, you can help me. Baking cookies is fun. Come to the kitchen. Let's make them right now. What does she say?	1 2 3 Let's make them right now.	1	7
Mommy says: I'm gonna make the dough. Cookies are made from dough. I'll make the dough. But first I need a bowl. What does she say?	1 1 I need a bowl.	1	3
Here is the bowl. Mommy puts some things in it. Because she's making the dough. Mommy is making cookie dough. What is she doing?	2 1 She is making cookie dough.	1	4
This is a big spoon. It is for stirring. Mommy stirs the dough. Susan says: Lemme try, Mommy. Lemme stir the dough. What does she say?	1 1 2 Lemme stir the dough.	1	5
Mommy gives her the spoon. Look, Susan is stirring. She is making the dough. She's helping Mommy. What's she doing?	2 1 She's helping Mommy.	1	4
Now Karen wants to do it.			

NARRATIVE	TARGET RESPONSE	SENTENCE POINT	DSS TOTAL
Karen says: It's my turn now. I wanna stir the dough. Lemme have a turn. What does Karen say?	1 1 2 Lemme have a turn.	1	5
Karen is stirring the dough. Mommy says: Look at the dough. It is very soft now. That means it's ready. The cookie dough is done. What does Mommy say?	1 The cookie dough is done.	1	2
Cookie dough isn't hard. It isn't hard. This is very soft. Is this hard?	1 1 No, this is very soft.	1	3
Susan wants to touch it. She says: I wanna touch it. Give it to me. Lemme touch it. What does Susan say?	1 1 2 1 Lemme touch it.	1	6
The dough is round, like a ball. But it has to be flat. Mommy has a rolling pin. She's making the dough flat. She is rolling it flat. What is Mommy doing?	2 1 1 She is rolling it flat.	1	5
Karen says: Cookie dough is very soft. It's easy to roll flat. Because it's so soft. Now I wanna try it. Lemme make it flat. What does she say?	1 1 2 1 Lemme make it flat.	1	6
Look how flat the dough is. Karen and Mommy did it. The dough is flat now. And it is soft.			

NARRATIVE	TARGET RESPONSE	SENTENCE POINT	DSS TOTAL
Cookie dough is soft and flat. What is it?	1 1 3 It is soft and flat.	1	6
Here are some cookie cutters. Karen is cutting out cookies. And so is Susan. Susan is cutting out cookies, too. What is she doing?	2 1 She is cutting out cookies.	1	4
There are two kinds of cookies. This one is round. This one looks like a star. This cookie is a star. And this is a round cookie. What kind is this?	1 1 This is a round cookie.	1	3
What kind is that one?	1 3 1 That one is a star.	1	6
Mommy says: I'm gonna bake them. Let's put them in the oven. The oven is for baking. The cookies go in the oven. Let's bake them. What does Mommy say?	1 2 3 Let's bake them.	1	7
Here is the oven. The cookies are inside. They are baking. Cookies bake in an oven. Where do cookies bake?	1 Cookies bake in an oven.	1	2
Susan says: Are they done yet? Mommy says: Let's find out. They might be done. Let's look and see. What does she say?	1 2 3 2 Let's look and see.	1	9
Oh, look. Look at the cookies.			

NARRATIVE	TARGET RESPONSE	SENTENCE POINT	DSS TOTAL
The cookies are baked. The oven baked the dough. The cookies are done. Are the cookies done?	2 Yes, the cookies are done.	1	3
All the cookies are hard. The oven baked them. The round cookie is hard now. Is the round cookie soft?	1 The round cookie is hard.	1	2
See the star cookie. It is baked. It's hard too. See, it's not soft now. The star cookie is hard. Is the star cookie soft?	1 The star cookie is hard.	1	2
All the cookies are done. They're ready to eat now. Karen and Susan will eat them.			

LEVEL I: LESSON 16

CONCEPTS

friend, playing, caution, colors

VOCABULARY

friend, park, swing, slide, balloon, red, yellow, green, blue

FLANNEL-BOARD MATERIALS

paper figures: Karen, Susan, balloon man
paper cutouts: blue swing, green swing, slide, red balloon, yellow balloon

ELICITED STRUCTURES		DSS VALUE
Primary emphasis		
indefinite pronoun –	*it*	1
–	*one*	3
personal pronoun –	*she*	2
main verb –	copular *is*	1
secondary verb –	*let's* + infinitive	2
Secondary emphasis		
personal pronoun –	*I*	1
main verb –	*is . . . -ing*	1
secondary verb –	*wanna* + infinitive	2

PLAYING IN THE PARK

NARRATIVE	TARGET RESPONSE	SENTENCE POINT	DSS TOTAL
Here are two girls. This is Karen. And this is Susan. The story is about them. It is about two girls. Who is the story about?	1 1 3 It is about two girls.	1	6
Karen and Susan are friends. They have fun playing. Susan is Karen's best friend. Her best friend is Susan. Who is her best friend?	2 1 Her best friend is Susan.	1	4
Karen and Susan are playing. And look where they are. They're in the park. Karen and Susan are playing in the park. Karen is in the park, and Susan is in the park. Where are Karen and Susan?	1 3 Karen is in the park, and 1 Susan is in the park.	1	6

NARRATIVE	TARGET RESPONSE	SENTENCE POINT	DSS TOTAL
They like the park. Look what they can do. They can come down the slide. This is a slide. What is this?	1 1 This is a slide.	1	3
Or they can play on the swing. This is a swing. Karen likes the swing best. It is fun to swing. What is it fun to do?	1 1 3 It is fun to swing.	1	6
Karen says: I wanna swing. I'm gonna go way up high. Come on, Susan. Let's swing. Let's swing way up high. What does she say?	1 2 Let's swing way up high.	1	4
Susan says: Wait for me. I'm coming, Karen. I want to swing, too. I wanna swing. What does Susan say?	1 1 2 I wanna swing.	1	5
Look. There are two swings. Here is a blue swing. That is Karen's swing. She is swinging on the blue one. What is Karen doing?	2 1 She is swinging on the 3 blue one.	1	7
Here is a green swing. Susan's on that one. It is Susan's swing. She is on the green one. Which one is Susan on?	2 1 3 She is on the green one.	1	7
Look at Karen and Susan. They are swinging high. Watch Karen. Look at the blue swing. See how high it is. It is too high. What is wrong with the swing?	1 1 It is too high.	1	3

NARRATIVE	TARGET RESPONSE	SENTENCE POINT	DSS TOTAL
Karen might fall off. She'd better be careful. Her swing is too high. Karen is swinging too high. What is she doing?	2 1 She is swinging too high.	1	4
Susan says: Be careful, Karen. You might fall off. You're going too high. Don't fall! Don't fall off! What does she say?	4 4 Don't fall off.	1	9
Karen says: My swing is too high. You are right. I'm gonna get off now. I don't wanna fall. I wanna get off right now. What does Karen say?	1 1 2 I wanna get off right now.	1	5
Karen is getting off. She didn't fall. Now Susan is getting off. She's looking at the slide. What's she doing?	2 1 She's looking at the slide.	1	4
She says: I wanna go slide. There's the slide. Let's go over there, Karen. Let's play on the slide now. What does Susan say?	1 2 Let's play on the slide now.	1	4
There they go. Here's the slide. Now they're gonna slide. Susan is first. She is gonna slide down. What is Susan gonna do?	2 1 2 She is gonna slide down.	1	6
Susan says: Come on, Karen. Come on. Let's slide. I like to slide down. Let's go down the slide. What does she say?	1 2 Let's go down the slide.	1	4

NARRATIVE	TARGET RESPONSE	SENTENCE POINT	DSS TOTAL
Look. Susan is sliding. She is sliding down. Here she comes. She did it! Now it's Karen's turn. Whose turn is it?	1 1 It's Karen's turn.	1	3
Karen says: Watch me, Susan. I wanna slide now. It's my turn to slide. I wanna slide. What does Karen say?	1 1 2 I wanna slide.	1	5
Oh, look at Karen. She is sliding down. It's fun to slide. Look! Karen sees someone. It is a man. Who is it?	1 1 It is a man.	1	3
The man has something. Look! He has balloons. He has lots of balloons. He is the balloon man. Who is he?	2 1 He is the balloon man.	1	4
Karen says: Let's get a balloon. I want a red one. This is the one I want. I wanna get a red one. Let's get a red balloon. What does she say?	1 2 Let's get a red balloon.	1	4
Susan says: I don't want red. Let's get a yellow one. I want a yellow balloon. I don't want a red one. Let's get a yellow one. What does she say?	1 2 3 Let's get a yellow one.	1	7
The balloon man has two balloons. He has a red one. And here is a yellow one.			

NARRATIVE	TARGET RESPONSE	SENTENCE POINT	DSS TOTAL
The man says: I have both kinds. One is red, and one is yellow. What does he say?	3 1 3 3 1 One is red, and one is yellow.	1	12
Look. He gives balloons to both girls. See? Karen gets the red one. And Susan is getting the yellow one. Which one is Susan getting?	2 1 She is getting the 3 yellow one.	1	7
The girls are happy. They both have balloons. The balloon man gave them a balloon.			

LEVEL I: LESSON 17

CONCEPTS	ELICITED STRUCTURES		DSS VALUE
airport, size contrasts, flying	**Primary emphasis**		
	indefinite pronoun –	*it*	1
	personal pronoun –	*he*	2
VOCABULARY	main verb –	copular *is*	1
airplane, airport, different, big, little, fly	–	*is . . . -ing*	1
	secondary verb –	*let's* + infinitive	2
FLANNEL-BOARD MATERIALS	**Secondary emphasis**		
	indefinite pronoun –	*this*	1
	main verb –	uninflected	1
paper figures: Bobby, Mommy, Daddy	secondary verb –	noncomplementing infinitive	3
paper cutouts: bed, car, several airplanes	interrogative –	copular *is* reversal	1

GOING TO THE AIRPORT

NARRATIVE	TARGET RESPONSE	SENTENCE POINT	DSS TOTAL
Here is Bobby. Look, he's in bed. He is sleeping. See? He's sleeping in his bed. Bobby is in bed. Where is he?	2 1 He is in bed.	1	4
Look. Watch Bobby. He is waking up. First he opens his eyes. Now he is yawning. Now what is he doing?	2 1 He is yawning.	1	4
Show me how you yawn.	(Elicit responses.)		
Now he is stretching his arms. Bobby is gonna get up. He is waking up. What is he doing?	2 1 He is waking up.	1	4
Today is special. Something is gonna happen. Bobby's going somewhere. Today is a special day. What kind of day is it?	1 Today is a special day.	1	2
Bobby's going to the airport.			

NARRATIVE	TARGET RESPONSE	SENTENCE POINT	DSS TOTAL
Because Daddy is coming home. He is at the airport. Bobby is going to the airport. Where is he going?	2 1 He is going to the airport.	1	4
Here is Mommy. She says: Hurry up. Let's go. It's time to leave. Let's go to the airport. What does Mommy say?	1 2 Let's go to the airport.	1	4
Bobby is wide awake now. He's coming. He is all ready. He wants to go. He is ready to go. Is Bobby ready to go?	2 1 3 He is ready to go.	1	7
Bobby says: I am coming, Mommy. Is it time to go now? Is it? I am all ready. Is it time to go? What does he say?	1 11 3 Is it time to go?	1	7
Mommy says: Yes, let's go right now. We will drive to the airport. I am gonna drive. Let's go in the car. What does she say?	1 2 Let's go in the car.	1	4
Here is their car. Mommy is getting in first. She is gonna drive. Now Bobby is getting in. He's sitting in the front seat. Where is Bobby sitting?	2 1 He's sitting in the front seat.	1	4
There they go. Look at Mommy. She is driving. Not Bobby. Mommy is driving the car. Who is driving?	1 Mommy is driving the car.	1	2

NARRATIVE	TARGET RESPONSE	SENTENCE POINT	DSS TOTAL
Look. Here is the airport. Mommy says: Here we are, Bobby. Look at all the planes. Let's look at them. Let's get out and look. What does she say?	1 2 3 2 Let's get out and look.	1	9
Mommy gets out of the car. Bobby is getting out, too. He says: See all the planes. There are lots and lots. I see a lot of planes. What does Bobby say?	1 1 3 I see a lot of planes.	1	6
Oh, look. Here's a big one. Bobby says: Come on, Mommy. Look at this plane. Let's go see it. What does he say?	1 2 2 1 Let's go see it.	1	7
They are looking at the plane. See how big it is. It's a white airplane. Look, it is big and white. The airplane is big and white. What kind is it?	1 1 3 It is big and white.	1	6
Now Mommy sees another plane. This is a different plane. It is not big. And it's not white. Mommy sees a different plane. This plane is different. What kind is this one?	1 1 This plane is different.	1	3
Bobby says: This is a different one. What kind is it? It's not a big one. Is it little? Is it a little plane? What does he say?	1 1 1 Is it a little plane?	1	4

NARRATIVE	TARGET RESPONSE	SENTENCE POINT	DSS TOTAL
Bobby guessed it. It is a little plane. It's not big and white. See how it's different. It is little and red. How is it different?	1 1 3 It is little and red.	1	6
An airport has lots of planes. Bobby says: This kind is big. And this one is little. I see a big one and a little one. What kind is this plane?	1 1 This plane is big.	1	3
What kind is this one?	1 3 1 This one is little.	1	6
Look, somebody is coming. He's waving at Bobby. It is Daddy. Daddy is coming. Who is coming?	1 Daddy is coming.	1	2
Here comes Daddy. He was in the airplane. Daddy was flying in the plane. But now he is back home. Where is Daddy now?	2 1 He is back home now.	1	4
Bobby says: I saw lots of planes. Is flying lots of fun? Tell me, Daddy. Is it fun? Is it fun to fly? What does he say?	1 11 3 Is it fun to fly?	1	7
Daddy says: Yes, it is fun. Flying is lots of fun. But now I wanna go home. Let's get in the car. Let's go home now. What does he say?	1 2 Let's go home now.	1	4
There they go. Everybody is leaving. They are going home now.			

LEVEL I: LESSON 18

CONCEPTS	ELICITED STRUCTURES		DSS VALUE
surprise, guessing	**Primary emphasis**		
	indefinite pronoun –	*it*	1
VOCABULARY	personal pronoun –	*I*	1
kite, rock, ball, time	main verb –	copular *is*	1
	secondary verb –	*wanna* + infinitive	2
FLANNEL-BOARD MATERIALS	interrogative –	copular *is* reversal	1
paper figures: Bobby, Timmy, Mommy	**Secondary emphasis**		
paper cutouts: ball, box, window	personal pronoun –	*he*	2
	main verb –	uninflected	1
	wh-question –	*what*	2

THE SURPRISE

NARRATIVE	TARGET RESPONSE	SENTENCE POINT	DSS TOTAL
Here is Bobby. And there is Mommy. They are in our story today. Look, here is their house. Bobby is in the house, and Mommy is in the house. Where are Bobby and Mommy?	Bobby (1) is in the house, and (3) Mommy is (1) in the house.	1	6
Mommy is looking outside. She says: It's a nice day. Look up. See the sun. The sun is shining. What does she say?	The sun is (1) shining.	1	2
Bobby says: I wanna play outside. Can I, Mommy? Can I go? I wanna go outside. What does he say?	I (1) wanna (1) go (2) outside.	1	5
Mommy says: Yes, you can. You can go out.			

NARRATIVE	TARGET RESPONSE	SENTENCE POINT	DSS TOTAL
Oh, oh. Mommy sees somebody. Somebody is outside the house. Who is outside?	3 1 Somebody is outside the house.	1	5
Mommy sees a boy. She says: I see a boy outside. Who is it, Bobby? Is it your friend Timmy? Is it? Is it Timmy? What does Mommy say?	1 1 1 Is it Timmy?	1	4
Bobby says: Yes, it is. It is my friend Timmy. He came to play. He is gonna play with me. What does he say?	2 1 2 He is gonna play 1 with me.	1	7
There goes Bobby. He is going outside. Oh, look. Timmy has something. It is a surprise. What is it?	1 1 It is a surprise.	1	3
Bobby says: Timmy, what is it? You have a surprise. What do you have? What is it? What is it? What does he say?	2 1 1 1 What is it?	1	6
But Timmy won't tell him. The surprise is in here. The surprise is in this box. Where is the surprise?	1 1 The surprise is in this box.	1	3
Bobby has to guess it. Timmy says: I'm not gonna tell you. You guess what it is. Try to guess, Bobby. Try and guess the surprise. What does he say?	1 3 1 Try and guess the surprise.	1	6

NARRATIVE	TARGET RESPONSE	SENTENCE POINT	DSS TOTAL
Bobby says: Maybe it is a kite. Is that what it is? Is it a kite, Timmy? Is it? Is it a kite? What does he say?	1 1 1 Is it a kite?	1	4
The surprise is not a kite. Timmy says: You are wrong, Bobby. I don't have a kite. Take another guess. It's something else. What does Timmy say?	1 1 3 It's something else.	1	6
Bobby says: It's not a kite. But maybe it's a rock. Is that your surprise? Is it? Is it a rock? What does Bobby say?	1 1 1 Is it a rock?	1	4
But Bobby guessed wrong. It's not a rock. And it's not a kite. Bobby is wrong again. Is he right this time?	2 1 No, he is wrong again.	1	4
Timmy says: You are wrong, Bobby. My surprise isn't a rock. And it's not a kite. Try again, Bobby. You have one more guess. What does he say?	1 1 3 3 You have one more guess.	1	9
Bobby says: I can't guess it. I give up now. I can't guess any more. What is it? What is it? What does he say?	2 1 1 1 What is it?	1	6
Timmy is gonna tell him. He says: I have a ball.			

NARRATIVE	TARGET RESPONSE	SENTENCE POINT	DSS TOTAL
See, it isn't a rock. And it isn't a kite. My surprise is a ball. What does Timmy say?	1 1 My surprise is a ball.	1	3
Bobby says: That's a good surprise. Let's play now. Let's play with it. I wanna play ball. What does he say?	1 1 2 I wanna play ball.	1	5
Timmy says: I wanna throw first. Get ready, Bobby. Get ready to catch it. I wanna throw right now. What does he say?	1 1 2 I wanna throw right now.	1	5
Bobby is ready. He's gonna catch it. Timmy throws the ball. Bobby is gonna catch it. What is he gonna do?	2 1 2 1 He is gonna catch it.	1	7
Watch the ball. It's a long one. Bobby is running. He caught it. Bobby says: Now, it's my turn. Get ready, Timmy. I wanna throw it now. What does he say?	1 1 2 1 I wanna throw it now.	1	6
Oh, oh. Watch the ball. Bobby is throwing it. It's another long one. What kind is it?	1 1 3 3 It's another long one.	1	9
Oh, oh. He dropped it. Timmy dropped the ball. He says: Throw it again, Bobby. I wanna try again. What does Timmy say?	1 1 2 I wanna try again.	1	5
Bobby throws the ball again.			

NARRATIVE	TARGET RESPONSE	SENTENCE POINT	DSS TOTAL
But watch Timmy this time. He catches it. Look at him. He didn't drop it. Timmy's holding the ball. What's he doing?	2 1 He's holding the ball.	1	4
Timmy says: I'd better go now. What time is it, Bobby? Bobby says: I don't know. I'll ask Mommy. What time is it, Mommy? What time is it? What does Bobby say?	2 1 1 1 What time is it?	1	6
Mommy says: It's getting late now. It's time to go home. Timmy can come back tomorrow.			

LEVEL I: LESSON 19

CONCEPTS	ELICITED STRUCTURES		DSS VALUE
helping, cleaning, guessing	**Primary emphasis**		
	indefinite pronoun –	*it*	1
	personal pronoun –	*I*	1
VOCABULARY	main verb –	copular *is*	1
washing, brush, clean, car, ice cream, cone, chocolate	–	*is . . . -ing*	1
	secondary verb –	*wanna* + infinitive	2
	wh-question –	*what*	2
FLANNEL-BOARD MATERIALS	**Secondary emphasis**		
paper figures: Bobby, Karen, Mommy	indefinite pronoun –	*this, that*	1
paper cutouts: kitchen sink, house front with large window, car, two brushes, bucket, ice-cream truck, two chocolate ice-cream cones	conjunction –	*and*	3
	interrogative –	copular *is* reversal	1

THE ICE-CREAM MAN

NARRATIVE	TARGET RESPONSE	SENTENCE POINT	DSS TOTAL
This is Bobby. And this is Karen. Our story is about them. It is about two children. Who is the story about?	1 1 3 It is about two children.	1	6
Look. Here are their parents. Here are Mommy and Daddy. They are in our story, too. This is Mommy, and this is Daddy. Who are these people?	1 1 3 This is Mommy, and 1 1 this is Daddy.	1	8
Mommy is in the house. She's in the kitchen. She is washing the dishes. What is Mommy doing?	2 1 She is washing the dishes.	1	4
Daddy isn't in the house. He is outside.			

NARRATIVE	TARGET RESPONSE	SENTENCE POINT	DSS TOTAL
Look what he's doing. He is washing the car. What is Daddy doing?	2 1 He is washing the car.	1	4
What are Mommy and Daddy doing?	1 Mommy is washing the 3 dishes, and Daddy 1 is washing the car.	1	6
Bobby wants to help Daddy. He says: I wanna help wash. Please let me, Daddy. I wanna help you. What does Bobby say?	1 1 2 1 I wanna help you.	1	6
Daddy says: Okay. You can help. The car needs washing. And I need a helper. The car is very dirty. What does he say?	1 The car is very dirty.	1	2
Bobby is getting something. He needs a bucket. Here it is. This is a bucket. What is this?	1 1 This is a bucket.	1	3
Oh, oh. Bobby touches something. He says: I touched something. Something is in the bucket. What is it, Daddy? What is it? What does Bobby say?	2 1 1 1 What is it?	1	6
Daddy says: You know what it is. That is a brush. It's for the tires. It's a brush for the tires. What is it?	1 1 It's a brush for the tires.	1	3
Bobby says: The tires are very dirty. Can I wash them?			

NARRATIVE	TARGET RESPONSE	SENTENCE POINT	DSS TOTAL
This brush will clean them. I wanna wash the tires. What does Bobby say?	1 1 2 I wanna wash the tires.	1	5
Oh, look. Here comes Karen. She is holding something. Bobby says: What do you have? What is it, Karen? What is it? What does he say?	2 1 1 1 What is it?	1	6
See what it is. Karen has another brush. Now there are two brushes. It is another brush. What is it?	1 1 3 It is another brush.	1	6
Karen says: I have a brush, too. Now I can help. I wanna clean the tires. I wanna help you. What does she say?	1 1 2 1 I wanna help you.	1	6
Now Daddy has two helpers. Bobby is helping him. And Karen is helping. Bobby says: Listen, everybody. I hear something. What does he say?	1 1 3 I hear something.	1	6
Karen says: I hear it, too. It's a noise. What is it, Daddy? What is that noise? What does she say?	2 1 1 1 What is that noise?	1	6
Daddy is listening. Ding! Ding! Ding! Ding! The noise is getting louder. Look. It's a truck making noise. It's the ice-cream truck. What is it?	1 1 It's the ice-cream truck.	1	3

NARRATIVE	TARGET RESPONSE	SENTENCE POINT	DSS TOTAL
Bobby says: Look, Karen. Look. It's the ice-cream man. Look who's coming. The ice-cream man is coming. Who is coming?	The ice-cream man 1 is coming.	1	2
Karen says: Oh, boy. I want some. Let's get some ice cream. Can we, Daddy? Can we? I wanna get some ice cream. What does Karen say?	1 1 2 3 I wanna get some ice cream.	1	8
Bobby says: Me, too. Me, too. I like ice cream. I wanna get a cone. Please let us, Daddy. I wanna get chocolate. What does he say?	1 1 2 I wanna get chocolate.	1	5
Daddy says: You can have some ice cream. Because you were good helpers. There goes Karen. Watch her. She is going to the truck. Where is she going?	2 1 She is going to the truck.	1	4
Look at all the ice cream. There are lots of kinds. Karen says: You have lots of ice cream. What is that one? What is that kind? What does she say?	2 11 1 What is that kind?	1	6
The man says: That is chocolate. Do you want that kind? Karen says: Yes, that's what I want.			

NARRATIVE	TARGET RESPONSE	SENTENCE POINT	DSS TOTAL
I wanna get that kind. Lemme have chocolate. What does Karen say?	1 1 2 Lemme have chocolate.	1	5
Karen likes chocolate ice cream. And Bobby wants chocolate. He wants a cone, too. They both want chocolate. Karen and Bobby like chocolate best. What do Karen and Bobby like?	3 1 Karen and Bobby like chocolate best.	1	5
Bobby says: I want an ice-cream cone. Do you have more chocolate? Is that one chocolate, too? Is it? What is that one? What does he say?	2 11 1 3 What is that one?	1	9
The man says: These are both chocolate. Here is your ice cream. Karen and Bobby both have chocolate cones. Karen is eating chocolate, and so is Bobby. He's eating a chocolate cone, too. What's he eating?	2 1 He's eating a chocolate cone.	1	4
What are they both doing?	1 Karen is eating a chocolate cone, 3 and Bobby 1 is eating a chocolate cone.	1	6
Karen and Bobby helped Daddy. They were good helpers. Now they can eat their ice cream.			

LEVEL I: LESSON 20

CONCEPTS	ELICITED STRUCTURES	DSS VALUE
animals, colors, height	**Primary emphasis**	
	personal pronoun – *I*	1
	main verb – copular *is*	1
VOCABULARY	secondary verb – *wanna* + infinitive	2
cat, dog, brown, white, climbing, chasing, top, bottom	conjunction – *and*	3
	Secondary emphasis	
	indefinite pronoun – *it*	1
FLANNEL-BOARD MATERIALS	wh-question – *what*	2
paper figures: Bobby, Timmy paper cutouts: cat, dog, door, two bowls, tree, ladder		

THE ANIMAL STORY

NARRATIVE	TARGET RESPONSE	SENTENCE POINT	DSS TOTAL
Our story is about two animals. One animal is a dog. The other is a cat. The story is about a cat and a dog. What is it about?	1 1 3 It is about a cat and a dog.	1	6
Here is one animal. This is Spot. Spot is a dog. What is Spot?	1 Spot is a dog.	1	2
This is the other animal. This is Puff. Puff is a cat. What is Puff?	1 Puff is a cat.	1	2
Spot is brown and white. See. This is brown. And here is white. There are two colors. Spot is a brown-and-white dog. What is Spot?	1 3 Spot is a brown-and-white dog.	1	5

NARRATIVE	TARGET RESPONSE	SENTENCE POINT	DSS TOTAL
Now look at Puff. Puff is only one color. She is white. See. Puff is a white cat. What is Puff?	1 Puff is a white cat.	1	2
Spot and Puff stay here. They stay in this house. This is Bobby's house. And here is Bobby. Who is this?	1 1 This is Bobby.	1	3
The animals are hungry. They wanna eat. The dog is hungry. And the cat is hungry. Spot and Puff wanna eat. What do they wanna do?	3 1 2 Spot and Puff wanna eat.	1	7
Bobby is gonna feed them. Oh, oh. He hears something. Knock-knock. Knock-knock. Someone is at the door. Who is at the door?	3 1 Someone is at the door.	1	5
Bobby doesn't know who it is. He says: Who is it? Who is at the door? Who is it? What does Bobby say?	2 1 1 1 Who is it?	1	6
Look who it is. It is Timmy. He came over to play. Timmy is here to play. Why is he here?	2 1 3 He is here to play.	1	7
Timmy says: Hi, Bobby. I came to play. Let's go outside. I wanna play outside. What does he say?	1 1 2 I wanna play outside.	1	5
Bobby says: Okay, but wait a minute. Spot and Puff are hungry. They wanna eat now.			

NARRATIVE	TARGET RESPONSE	SENTENCE POINT	DSS TOTAL
It's time for them to eat. What does he say?	1 1 3 It's time for them 5 to eat.	1	11
Timmy says: Spot and Puff? I don't know who Spot is. Who is Spot, Bobby? Who is Spot? What does Timmy say?	2 11 Who is Spot?	1	5
Bobby says: Spot is my dog. Timmy says: Oh, I know him. But who is Puff? Is Puff a dog, too? Who is Puff? What does he say?	2 11 Who is Puff?	1	5
Bobby says: Puff is my cat. And Spot is my dog. I'm gonna feed them. Timmy says: Okay, but hurry up. I wanna go outside. What does he say?	1 1 2 I wanna go outside.	1	5
Here is Spot's food. And here is Puff's food. The two animals wanna eat. Look, it's ready now. The food is ready to eat. Is the food ready?	1 3 The food is ready to eat.	1	5
Timmy says: They're eating fast. They must be hungry. I like to watch them. I like your animals. What does he say?	1 1 1 I like your animals.	1	4
Bobby says: Spot and Puff are finished. They are through eating. Let's take them with us.			

NARRATIVE	TARGET RESPONSE	SENTENCE POINT	DSS TOTAL
I wanna take Spot and Puff. What does Bobby say?	1 1 2 I wanna take Spot 3 and Puff.	1	8
Oh, look. Look at Spot and Puff. They are running fast. Spot wants to chase Puff. See, Spot is chasing Puff. What is he doing?	1 Spot is chasing Puff.	1	2
Oh, oh. Oh, oh. Watch Puff. She is running faster. She runs to this tree. Puff is climbing up and up. What is Puff doing?	1 3 Puff is climbing up and up.	1	5
Look at Puff. Look where she is. She is way up high. Puff is at the top of the tree. Where is Puff?	1 Puff is at the top of the tree.	1	2
Look where Spot is. He's way down here. He's not up high. Spot is at the bottom of the tree. Where is Spot?	1 Spot is at the bottom of the tree.	1	2
Oh, oh. Something is wrong. Puff is stuck. Look. She can't get down. Puff is stuck up in the tree. What is wrong?	1 Puff is stuck up in the tree.	1	2
Oh, oh. Puff needs help. She needs help to get down. Bobby says: I'll help Puff. I wanna do it. I wanna help Puff. What does he say?	1 1 2 I wanna help Puff.	1	5

NARRATIVE	TARGET RESPONSE	SENTENCE POINT	DSS TOTAL
Bobby gets the ladder.			
Now he's climbing the tree.			
He has Puff. Bobby got her.			
Puff is not stuck any more.			
Now she is safe.	2 1	1	4
Is Puff stuck now?	No, she is safe now.		
Bobby says: Puff is safe now. She is all right. She isn't stuck any more.			

LEVEL I: LESSON 21

CONCEPTS	ELICITED STRUCTURES	DSS VALUE
beach, swimming, summer	**Primary emphasis**	
	indefinite pronoun – *it*	1
	personal pronoun – *he*	2
VOCABULARY	main verb – *is . . . -ing*	1
beach, towels, ball, dry, wet, swimming, wading, watch	conjunction – *and*	3
	wh-question – *who*	2
	Secondary emphasis	
FLANNEL-BOARD MATERIALS	personal pronoun – *I*	1
	main verb – copular *is*	1
	– uninflected	1
paper figures: Bobby, Karen, Daddy		
paper cutouts: two beach towels, beach ball, lake		

GOING TO THE BEACH

NARRATIVE	TARGET RESPONSE	SENTENCE POINT	DSS TOTAL
This story is about three people. Here is Daddy. And here are the children. They are Bobby and Karen. The story is about Daddy and two children. Who is it about?	1 1 3 It is about Daddy and 3 two children.	1	9
Today is a special day. Daddy is gonna go somewhere. It's somewhere special. He is going to the beach. Where is he going?	2 1 He is going to the beach.	1	4
Daddy says: It is so hot outside. I'm gonna go to the beach. Who is coming with me? Who is coming? What does he say?	2 1 Who is coming?	1	4

NARRATIVE	TARGET RESPONSE	SENTENCE POINT	DSS TOTAL
Bobby says: I am! I am! I wanna go. Karen says: Me, too! Wait for me. I wanna go with you. What does she say?	1 1 2 1 I wanna go with you.	1	6
Bobby and Karen like the beach. They like to swim in the water. Bobby's going to the beach and so is Karen. Bobby is going, and Karen is going. Who is going to the beach?	1 3 Bobby is going, and 1 Karen is going.	1	6
Everybody is gonna go. Daddy says: We must take two things. I need some help. I need two helpers. What does he say?	1 1 3 I need two helpers.	1	6
Daddy says: We need beach towels. Here they are. Who is carrying them? Who is taking the towels? What does Daddy say?	2 1 Who is taking the towels?	1	4
Karen wants the towels. Daddy says: Karen has the towels. But here's the beach ball. Who is taking the ball? Who is taking it? What does he say?	2 1 1 Who is taking it?	1	5
Bobby says: I wanna help Daddy.			

NARRATIVE	TARGET RESPONSE	SENTENCE POINT	DSS TOTAL
I'll take the beach ball. Lemme have it. I wanna carry the beach ball. What does Bobby say?	1 1 2 I wanna carry the beach ball.	1	5
Now they are both helping Daddy. Karen is taking the towels. And Bobby's taking the beach ball. What are Karen and Bobby taking?	1 Karen is taking the 3 towels, and Bobby 1 is taking the beach ball.	1	6
Everybody is ready to go. They are all going to the beach. Here it is. Look at all the water. This is the beach. What is this?	1 1 This is the beach.	1	3
And look now. See what this is? This is the sun. The sun is shining. It is a very hot day. It's hot because the sun is shining. Why is it hot?	(Because) the sun 1 is shining.	1	2
Daddy says: It is hot out here. I'm going into the water. Who is coming with me? Who is going in? What does he say?	2 1 Who is going in?	1	4
Bobby says: I am! I am! Karen says: Me, too! Me, too! But look at Daddy. He's in already.			

NARRATIVE	TARGET RESPONSE	SENTENCE POINT	DSS TOTAL
Daddy is swimming in the water. What is he doing?	2 1 He is swimming in the water.	1	4
Karen and Bobby are standing up. They are wading. They are not swimming. Only Daddy is swimming. Karen and Bobby are wading. Who is wading?	3 Karen and Bobby 2 are wading.	1	6
Now Bobby gets the beach ball. He is gonna throw it. He's all ready now. He is gonna throw it. What is he gonna do?	2 1 2 1 He is gonna throw it.	1	7
Bobby says: Daddy, Karen. Look here. I'm ready to throw. Somebody look at me. Who is looking at me? Who is looking? What does he say?	2 1 Who is looking?	1	4
Karen says: I'm ready, Bobby. I am looking at you. Throw the beach ball to me. What does she say?	1 Throw the beach ball 1 to me.	1	3
Bobby throws it to Karen. Look. She caught it. Now it's Daddy's turn. Oh, oh. He missed it. The ball is in the water. Where is the beach ball?	1 1 It is in the water.	1	3
Daddy didn't catch it. Now he's gonna throw it.			

NARRATIVE	TARGET RESPONSE	SENTENCE POINT	DSS TOTAL
There it goes. Watch. He's throwing it over to Bobby. What's Daddy doing?	2 1 1 He's throwing it over to Bobby.	1	5
And look! Bobby caught it. Now Bobby's throwing it to Daddy. There it goes. Daddy is ready. Bobby is throwing it back to Daddy. What is he doing?	2 1 1 He is throwing it back to Daddy.	1	5
Daddy caught it, too. Everybody caught the ball. Now Daddy is getting out. He's getting out of the water. What's he doing?	2 1 He's getting out of the water.	1	4
Daddy gets his towel. He's all wet. He needs to dry off. He is gonna dry off. What is Daddy gonna do?	2 1 2 He is gonna dry off.	1	6
Daddy says: Come on, Bobby and Karen. It's time to leave. Get out of the water. Come and get your towels. What does he say?	1 3 1 1 Come and get your towels.	1	7
They're getting out now. Bobby and Karen get their towels. They must get dry. It's time to leave. What time is it?	1 1 3 It's time to leave.	1	6
They liked the beach. They will come back another day.			

LEVEL I: LESSON 22

CONCEPTS	ELICITED STRUCTURES	DSS VALUE
winter, weather, body parts	**Primary emphasis**	
	indefinite pronoun – *it*	1
VOCABULARY	main verb – copular *is*	1
cold, winter, snowing, snowball, eyes, nose, mouth, big, bigger, biggest	– uninflected	1
	– *is . . . -ing*	1
	wh-question – *what*	2
	Secondary emphasis	
	personal pronoun – *he, his*	2
	conjunction – *and*	3

FLANNEL-BOARD MATERIALS

paper figures: Bobby, Timmy, Karen
paper cutouts: two large snowballs, two small snowballs, paper "rocks" for eyes, nose, and mouth

MAKING A SNOWMAN

NARRATIVE	TARGET RESPONSE	SENTENCE POINT	DSS TOTAL
This is a story about Bobby. And here he is. Bobby is outside. And look! It is snowing. What is happening outside?	1 1 It is snowing.	1	3
It's wintertime now. It's very cold out. See all the snow. The weather is very, very cold. Because it's winter. Why is it so cold?	1 1 (Because) it's winter.	1	3
Listen. Everybody listen. Bobby hears something. He hears a noise. It's a loud noise. What is it?	1 1 It's a loud noise.	1	3
Bobby says: I hear a noise. What can it be? What is making that noise? What is making it? What does he say?	2 1 1 What is making it?	1	5

NARRATIVE	TARGET RESPONSE	SENTENCE POINT	DSS TOTAL
Bobby is standing still. He's very quiet. Shhhh. He's not moving. He is listening. What is he doing?	2 1 He is listening.	1	4
The noise is coming closer. Bobby says: Something is coming. But what is it? What is coming? What does he say?	2 1 What is coming?	1	4
Guess what the noise is! It is a snowball fight. Some children are throwing snowballs. And they're making a lot of noise. The noise is from a snowball fight. What is the noise from?	1 The noise is from a snowball fight.	1	2
Here come the children. Look who is here. This is Timmy. And this is Karen. Timmy and Karen are the children. Who are they?	3 2 Timmy and Karen are the children.	1	6
Look at their snow-balls. There are two of them. See how big they are. They have two big snowballs. What do they have?	3 1 3 They have two big snowballs.	1	8
Timmy says: Hi, Bobby. Watch out. You'd better duck. Here comes a snowball. Oh, oh. Timmy is throwing it. What is he doing?	2 1 1 He is throwing it.	1	5

NARRATIVE	TARGET RESPONSE	SENTENCE POINT	DSS TOTAL
Look. Bobby didn't get hit. He moved out of the way. The snowball missed him. See, it's on the ground. Where is the snowball?	1 1 It's on the ground.	1	3
Now Karen says: Hey, Bobby. Look out. Something is coming. Bobby says: What is it, Karen? What is coming? What does he say?	2 1 What is coming?	1	4
Guess what it is . . . another snowball. Here it comes. Oh, she got him. Karen hit Bobby's leg. She hit his leg. What did she do?	2 1 2 She hit his leg.	1	6
Look at Bobby. He is ready. It's his turn now. Karen had better watch out. Bobby is gonna throw a snowball. What is he gonna do?	2 1 2 He is gonna throw a snowball.	1	6
Bobby is throwing it. But Karen is running fast. Oh, oh. He got her. The snowball hit Karen's arm. Where did it hit?	1 1 It hit Karen's arm.	1	3
Karen says: Good throw, Bobby. Now let's make a snowman. . . . a great big one. Let's make a big snowman. What does she say?	1 2 Let's make a big snowman.	1	4
The snowball fight is over. Now they're gonna make something.			

NARRATIVE	TARGET RESPONSE	SENTENCE POINT	DSS TOTAL
Everybody is gonna make a snowman. They need three snowballs. How many do they need?	3 1 3 They need three snowballs.	1	8
Bobby is gonna make a big one. And Timmy will make a bigger one. But Karen's making the biggest one. Which one is Karen making?	2 1 She is making the 3 biggest one.	1	7
Let's see what she does. First she takes a little snowball. Then she rolls it in the snow. Look! It is getting bigger and bigger. What is happening to the snowball?	1 1 3 It is getting bigger and bigger.	1	6
Now her snowball is done. Here are all the snowballs. See, there are three of them. It's time to make the snowman. What's it time to do?	1 1 3 It's time to make the snowman.	1	6
Karen says: Mine is the biggest. It goes on the bottom. Timmy's goes in the middle. And Bobby's goes on top. This one is the head. What is this one?	1 3 1 This one is the head.	1	6
Timmy says: Oh, oh. Something is missing. Bobby says: What's missing, Timmy?			

NARRATIVE	TARGET RESPONSE	SENTENCE POINT	DSS TOTAL
What is it? What is missing? What does Bobby say?	2 1 What is missing?	1	4
Karen says: His eyes are missing. We need two eyes. Here are two rocks. They can be the eyes. Rocks make good eyes. What does she say?	1 Rocks make good eyes.	1	2
Karen says: Now the snowman has eyes. But he needs something else. Timmy says: What is it, Karen? What else does he need? What else is missing? What does Timmy say?	2 1 What else is missing?	1	4
Look, his nose is missing. And so is his mouth. Here are some more rocks. Watch what Timmy does. He is making his mouth and his nose. What is Timmy doing?	2 1 2 He is making his mouth 3 2 and his nose.	1	11
Look, the snowman is all done. This is his body. And he has two eyes, a nose, and a mouth. Bobby and Timmy and Karen made him. The snowman is all done now. Is the snowman done?	1 3 The snowman is all done.	1	5
Everybody likes the big snowman. But now they have to leave. Everybody is gonna go home now.			

LEVEL I: LESSON 23

CONCEPTS

animals, pets

VOCABULARY

fish, bird, puppy, cat, animal, pet store, fishbowl, birdcage

FLANNEL-BOARD MATERIALS

paper figures: Bobby, Karen, Daddy, storekeeper
paper cutouts: store front, dog, cat, kitten, puppy, two birds, fish, birdcage, fishbowl

ELICITED STRUCTURES		DSS VALUE
Primary emphasis		
indefinite pronoun –	*it*	1
personal pronoun –	*I*	1
main verb –	copular *is*	1
secondary verb –	*want to* + infinitive	2
conjunction –	*and*	3
Secondary emphasis		
indefinite pronoun –	*this*	1
–	*one*	3
main verb –	uninflected	1
–	*is . . . -ing*	1
wh-question –	*where*	2
interrogative –	copular *is* reversal	1

THE PET STORE

NARRATIVE	TARGET RESPONSE	SENTENCE POINT	DSS TOTAL
Three people are in the story. Here is one. This is Daddy. Here are the other two. This is Bobby and Karen. Who is this?	1 1 3 This is Bobby and Karen.	1	6
The story is about three people. Let's count them. One, two, three. Three people. How many people is the story about?	1 1 3 It is about three people.	1	6
Daddy has a surprise. The surprise is for Bobby and Karen. Daddy says: We're going someplace special. Get ready to go somewhere. What does he say?	1 3 Get ready to go somewhere.	1	5

NARRATIVE	TARGET RESPONSE	SENTENCE POINT	DSS TOTAL
Bobby says: Oh, boy! I am ready. But where are we going? Where is the special place? Where is it? Where is it? What does he say?	2 1 1 1 Where is it?	1	6
Daddy says: Listen. I'll tell you. We're going to a pet store. That's where we're going. The pet store is the special place. What is the special place?	1 The pet store is the special place.	1	2
Lots of animals stay there. A pet store has many animals. It has dogs and cats. And there are birds and fish. What kinds of animals are there?	3 Dogs and cats.	–	3
	3 Birds and fish.	–	3
Karen says: Oh boy! Let's go. I wanna see the animals. I want to go right now. What does she say?	1 1 2 I want to go right now.	1	5
Bobby says: Me too. I am ready. I want to see them. There they go. Everybody is going. Here it is. This is the pet store. What is this?	1 1 This is the pet store.	1	3
The animals are all inside. You can't see them. The children wanna see them.			

NARRATIVE	TARGET RESPONSE	SENTENCE POINT	DSS TOTAL
Bobby and Karen want to go inside. What do Bobby and Karen want to do?	3 1 Bobby and Karen want 2 to go inside.	1	7
Now they're going inside. Oh, look at all the animals. There are so many. The animals are everywhere. Where are the animals?	3 The animals are everywhere.	1	4
Bobby says: There are dogs and cats. And little kittens and puppies. And birds and fish. I see lots and lots of animals. What does he say?	1 1 3 3 3 I see lots and lots of animals.	1	12
Karen says: I wanna see a fish. A great big one. Where are the fish? I want to see a big fish. What does she say?	1 1 2 I want to see a big fish.	1	5
Daddy says: I see one, Karen. It is over here. It's in the fishbowl. Where is it?	1 1 It is in the fishbowl.	1	3
Look at this. It's a big fish. This is not a little fish. No, it's a great big one. Is this a little fish?	1 1 3 It's a great big one.	1	6
There is water in the fishbowl. And look at the fish. It's swimming. The big fish is swimming in the fishbowl. Where is the big fish swimming?	1 The big fish is swimming in the fishbowl.	1	2

NARRATIVE	TARGET RESPONSE	SENTENCE POINT	DSS TOTAL
Bobby says: I wanna see a bird. But where are they? Where are the birds? I want to see a bird. What does he say?	1 1 2 I want to see a bird.	1	5
Daddy sees some birds. He says: Here's a big one and a little one. They are both yellow. See them? This one is big, and that one is little. What does Daddy say?	1 3 1 3 1 This one is big, and that 3 1 one is little.	1	14
And look at this! This is a birdcage. This is where they live. The birds live in a cage. Where do the birds live?	1 The birds live in a cage.	1	2
Now Daddy's looking for something. It isn't a fish. And it isn't a bird. He's looking for something else. Is he looking for a bird?	2 1 No, he's looking for 3 something else.	1	7
Daddy says: I wanna see the puppies. But I can't find them. Where are they? I want to find the puppies. What does he say?	1 1 2 I want to find the puppies.	1	5
Karen wants to see them, too. She is looking everywhere. She's trying to find a puppy. Karen is looking everywhere. What is she doing?	2 1 She is looking everywhere.	1	4

NARRATIVE	TARGET RESPONSE	SENTENCE POINT	DSS TOTAL
Karen says: I'm looking for a puppy. But I don't see one. Where can it be? Where is it? Where is it? What does she say?	2 1 1 1 Where is it?	1	6
Bobby found a puppy. And here it is. He found a little brown one. It is a little brown puppy. What is it?	1 1 It is a little brown puppy.	1	3
Daddy says: I have another surprise. You can have a pet. A fish, a bird, or a puppy. What do you want? What does he say?	2 6 1 4 What do you want?	1	14
Bobby says: We want this puppy. Daddy says: Okay. You can have it. Now let's find the store man. Where is he? Where is he? What does Daddy say?	2 1 1 2 Where is he?	1	7
Here is the store man. He says: You can have this puppy. He will be your pet. You can take him home now.			

LEVEL I: LESSON 24

CONCEPTS	ELICITED STRUCTURES		DSS VALUE
travel, farm, animals	**Primary emphasis**		
	indefinite pronoun –	*it*	1
	main verb –	copular *is*	1
VOCABULARY	secondary verb –	noncomplementing infinitive	3
Grandma, family, purse, cow, horse, barn animal	wh-question –	*where*	2
	interrogative	copular *is* reversal	1
FLANNEL-BOARD MATERIALS	**Secondary emphasis**		
paper figures: Bobby, Karen, Mommy, Daddy, Grandma	indefinite pronoun –	*this*	1
	personal pronoun –	*I*	1
paper cutouts: table, purse, car, barn, cow, horse, two houses	negative –	*don't*	4
	main verb –	obligatory *do* + verb	4

A TRIP TO THE FARM

NARRATIVE	TARGET RESPONSE	SENTENCE POINT	DSS TOTAL
Look, everybody is in the car. Mommy and Daddy are in the car. And so are Bobby and Karen. The family is ready to leave. What is the family ready to do?	The family (1) is ready to leave (3).	1	5
Everybody is going to Grandma's. Bobby says: Where does she live? Is it far away? Or is it close? Where is it? Where is it? What does he say?	Where (2) is (1 1) it (1)?	1	6
Daddy says: Grandma lives far away. It isn't close. We have to drive. Because it's not close. Why do they have to drive?	(Because) it's (1 1) not (1) close.	1	4

NARRATIVE	TARGET RESPONSE	SENTENCE POINT	DSS TOTAL
Look, Mommy got out of the car. She says: I forgot my purse. Don't leave yet. I don't have my purse. What does Mommy say?	1 4 4 1 I don't have my purse.	1	11
Mommy goes back into the house. She is looking for it. But something is wrong. Mommy can't find her purse. What is wrong?	4 4 Mommy can't find 2 her purse.	1	11
Mommy says: I've lost my purse. Can somebody help me? Where is it? Where is my purse? What does she say?	2 11 1 Where is my purse?	1	6
Karen knows where it is. She says: It's on the table. Don't you see it? It is on the table. Where is the purse?	1 1 It is on the table.	1	3
Oh, look. Mommy found it. See, she has it. She's ready. They can leave now. Because Mommy is ready to go. Why can they leave now?	1 (Because) Mommy is 3 ready to go.	1	5
Watch the car. It's moving. Everybody is leaving now. They're going to Grandma's house. It's time to go to Grandma's house. What's it time to do?	1 1 3 It's time to go to Grandma's house.	1	6

NARRATIVE	TARGET RESPONSE	SENTENCE POINT	DSS TOTAL
Oh, look. Here it is. This is Grandma's house. And here she is. It's Grandma. Grandma lives on a farm. Where does she live?	2 2 She lives on a farm.	1	5
Bobby says: Do you have a cow? I wanna see it. Where is it, Grandma? Where is the cow? What does he say?	2 11 Where is the cow?	1	5
Oh, look. Here is the cow. It is black and white. But look. Now it's leaving. The cow is going somewhere. What is the cow doing?	1 The cow is going somewhere.	1	2
The cow is gone. Nobody can see it. Because it's not here. The cow went away. What did the cow do?	2 The cow went away.	1	3
Here comes Karen. She says: Where is the cow? I don't see it now. Where can it be? I don't see the cow. What does Karen say?	1 4 4 I don't see the cow.	1	10
Here comes Grandma. Maybe she knows. Grandma says: I can tell you. Look at this. This is a red barn. What is this?	1 1 This is a red barn.	1	3
Guess where the cow went. The cow went inside. That's where it is now. The cow is in the red barn. Where is the cow?	1 The cow is in the red barn.	1	2

NARRATIVE	TARGET RESPONSE	SENTENCE POINT	DSS TOTAL
Let's look in the barn. Here it is. Here is the cow. And something else is here. There is another animal in the barn. What else is in the barn?	1 3 There is another animal in the barn.	1	5
See what it is. It's a horse. There are two animals in here. This animal is a cow. And this animal is a horse. What are the two animals?	1 1 3 This animal is a cow, and 1 1 this animal is a horse.	1	8
Oh, oh. Bobby hears a noise. Karen hears it too. "Bobby . . . Karen. Bobby . . . Karen." Somebody is calling them. Who is calling them?	3 1 Somebody is calling 3 them.	1	8
It's Mommy. Mommy is calling. Mommy says: Where are you two? Where is Bobby? Where is Karen? What does she say?	2 11 Where is Bobby? 2 11 Where is Karen?	1 1	5 5
Mommy can't find them. Karen says: Here we are, Mommy. We're looking at the animals. We are in the barn. What does she say?	3 2 We are in the barn.	1	6
Here they are. Mommy sees them. She says: Come on, now. Let's go.			

NARRATIVE	TARGET RESPONSE	SENTENCE POINT	DSS TOTAL
Dinner is ready. It is time to eat. What does Mommy say?	1 1 3 It is time to eat.	1	6
Karen is gonna go and eat. But Bobby doesn't want to. He wants to stay in the barn. He's not ready to eat. Is Bobby ready to eat?	2 1 7 3 He's not ready to eat.	1	14
Bobby says: I wanna stay here. Just for a few minutes. I don't wanna leave now. I don't wanna go yet. What does he say?	1 4 4 2 I don't wanna go yet.	1	12
Bobby is gonna stay there. He's gonna stay for a few minutes. Then he will go and eat.			

LEVEL I: LESSON 25

CONCEPTS	ELICITED STRUCTURES		DSS VALUE
helping, raking leaves	**Primary emphasis**		
	indefinite pronoun –	*it*	1
VOCABULARY	main verb –	copular *is*	1
rake, leaves, back yard, basket, squirrel, nut	–	uninflected	1
	–	*is . . . -ing*	1
FLANNEL-BOARD MATERIALS	**Secondary emphasis**		
paper figures: Bobby, Karen, Daddy	personal pronoun –	*I*	1
paper cutouts: house, two rakes, pile of leaves, several trees, squirrel, nuts, two baskets	–	*he*	2
	negative –	*don't*	4
	conjunction –	*and*	3
	main verb –	obligatory *do* + verb	4

RAKING LEAVES

NARRATIVE	TARGET RESPONSE	SENTENCE POINT	DSS TOTAL
Here are a boy and a girl. The boy's name is Bobby. The girl's name is Karen. They are both in our story. The story is about Bobby and Karen. Who is it about?	1 1 3 It is about Bobby and Karen.	1	6
Here is their house. Bobby and Karen are inside. But let's see what's outside. Oh, look. This is the back yard. What is this?	1 1 This is the back yard.	1	3
See all the trees! And look at all the leaves. The leaves are everywhere. The back yard is full of leaves. What is the back yard full of?	1 1 It is full of leaves.	1	3

NARRATIVE	TARGET RESPONSE	SENTENCE POINT	DSS TOTAL
Do you have a back yard?	(Elicit responses.)		
Here is Daddy. He has a rake. Daddy is working hard. He is raking all the leaves. What is he doing?	2 1 3 He is raking all the leaves.	1	7
Here comes Bobby. He says: Look at all the leaves. They are everywhere. I see lots and lots of leaves. What does Bobby say?	1 1 3 3 3 I see lots and lots of leaves.	1	12
Look at this. It's another rake. Bobby says: Here's another rake. What's it doing here? What is it for? What does he say?	2 1 1 1 What is it for?	1	6
Daddy says: It is for you, Bobby. I want you to help me. Stay out here now. Don't go back inside. What does he say?	4 4 Don't go back inside.	1	9
Bobby says: Okay, I'll help. I'll use my rake. I like to rake leaves. I wanna help you. What does he say?	1 1 2 1 I wanna help you.	1	6
Now Bobby is helping Daddy. Watch him. He's raking leaves too. Daddy and Bobby are both raking. Daddy is raking leaves, and Bobby is too. Who is raking leaves?	1 Daddy is raking leaves, 3 1 and Bobby is raking leaves.	1	6
Oh, look. Here comes Karen.			

NARRATIVE	TARGET RESPONSE	SENTENCE POINT	DSS TOTAL
Bobby says: Hi, Karen. I am raking leaves. Come and help me. What does he say?	1 3 1 1 Come and help me.	1	7
Karen says: No, you can do it. I just wanna watch. I don't wanna rake. I don't want to. What does she say?	1 4 4 I don't want to.	1	10
Karen is not raking. Daddy says: Karen, see that basket? I need it. Go get it. Bring me the basket. What does he say?	1 1 Bring me the basket.	1	3
Karen gets the basket. She says: Here is the basket. But why do you want it? What's the basket for? What is it for? What does Karen say?	2 1 1 1 What is it for?	1	6
Daddy says: The basket is for the leaves. You put leaves in it. Everybody–watch Daddy. He is putting leaves in the basket. What is he doing?	2 1 He is putting leaves in the basket.	1	4
He puts in some more. And a few more. Now look! The basket is full. It is full of leaves. How does the basket look?	1 1 It is full of leaves.	1	3
Now Karen sees another basket. She says: I see another one. Do you want it, Bobby?			

NARRATIVE	TARGET RESPONSE	SENTENCE POINT	DSS TOTAL
Here is another basket. What does Karen say?	1 3 Here is another basket.	1	5
Bobby says: Not now, Karen. I don't need one. I'm not ready for it. I don't need a basket. What does he say?	1 4 4 I don't need a basket.	1	10
Oh, oh. Karen hears something. She hears a noise. Shhhh. Karen is very quiet. She is listening. What is she doing?	2 1 She is listening.	1	4
Something is under the leaves. There it is. It's a squirrel. Look. The squirrel is running. It is running over to this tree. What is it doing?	1 1 It is running over to 1 this tree.	1	4
The squirrel went up the tree. He is gone. But look. Look at this tree . . . right here. There's a hole in it. What's in the tree?	1 1 There's a hole in it.	1	3
Karen says: The squirrel puts nuts there. The hole is for nuts. He drops them down in. The squirrel keeps nuts there. What does she say?	2 The squirrel keeps nuts there.	1	3
Now the squirrel is coming out. He is looking for something. Oh, look. He found a nut. It's a nut. What is it?	1 1 It's a nut.	1	3

NARRATIVE	TARGET RESPONSE	SENTENCE POINT	DSS TOTAL
He's gonna drop it in the hole. Watch him. The squirrel is dropping it. He is dropping the nut in the hole. What is he doing?	2 1 He is dropping the nut in the hole.	1	4
The squirrel needs more nuts. There he goes. He is gone. He went under the leaves. He is looking for more nuts. What is he doing?	2 1 3 He is looking for more nuts.	1	7
Karen is waiting for the squirrel. Soon he will come out. Maybe he'll have another nut.			

LEVEL I: LESSON 26

CONCEPTS	ELICITED STRUCTURES		DSS VALUE
rain, rainclothes	**Primary emphasis**		
	personal pronoun –	*he*	2
VOCABULARY	main verb –	copular *is*	1
raining, umbrella, raincoat, rainhat, boots, mud puddle	–	*is . . . -ing*	1
	–	obligatory *do* + verb	4
	negative –	*don't*	4
	conjunction –	*and*	3
FLANNEL-BOARD MATERIALS	**Secondary emphasis**		
paper figures: Bobby, Timmy, Mommy	indefinite pronoun –	*it, this*	1
	–	*one*	3
paper cutouts: boots, yellow raincoats and hats, umbrella, dog, mud puddle, house	negative –	*it is not*	1
	interrogative –	auxiliary *is* reversal	4

THE RAINY DAY

NARRATIVE	TARGET RESPONSE	SENTENCE POINT	DSS TOTAL
Our story is about two boys. This is Bobby. That is Timmy. This one is Bobby, and that one is Timmy. Who is this one, and who is that one?	This (1) one (3) is (1) Bobby, and (3) that (1) one (3) is (1) Timmy.	1	14
Here is their house. The two boys are in the house. They wanna go out and play. Bobby is looking out the window. What is he doing?	He (2) is (1) looking out the window.	1	4
Oh, oh. There is no sun. Bobby can't find it. The sun isn't shining today. It is not shining. Is the sun shining today?	No, it (1) is (1) not (1) shining.	1	4

NARRATIVE	TARGET RESPONSE	SENTENCE POINT	DSS TOTAL
Bobby says: Come here, Timmy. Come and look outside. The sun's not shining. We can't go out. What does he say?	3 4 4 We can't go out.	1	12
Timmy says: Why not? Why can't we? Is it raining? Is it raining outside? What does he say?	41 1 Is it raining outside?	1	7
Bobby says: Yes, it's raining. But not too hard. I'll go ask Mommy. This is Bobby's mommy. Who is this?	1 1 This is Bobby's mommy.	1	3
Bobby says: Mommy, we wanna go out. Please let us go. It's raining, but not hard. It's not raining hard. What does he say?	1 1 1 It's not raining hard.	1	4
Mommy says: Yes, you can go. It's not raining hard. Get your raincoats and boots. You need your raincoats and your boots. What does she say?	1 1 1 You need your raincoats 3 1 and your boots.	1	8
Timmy says: You forgot something. We need something else. We need our rainhats. Don't forget the rainhats. What does he say?	4 4 Don't forget the rainhats.	1	9

NARRATIVE	TARGET RESPONSE	SENTENCE POINT	DSS TOTAL
The boys are getting their raincoats. This one is Bobby's. And that one is Timmy's. They are both yellow. What color are they?	3 2 They are yellow.	1	6
The boys both have yellow raincoats. This one is for Bobby. And that one is for Timmy. Who are this one and that one for?	1 3 1 This one is for Bobby, 3 1 3 1 and that one is for Timmy.	1	14
Here are their boots. This pair is for Bobby. And these are Timmy's. They are black boots. What color are they?	3 2 They are black boots.	1	6
These are their rainhats. They are yellow, too. Here are their raincoats and boots. They are all ready now. The boys have raincoats, rainhats, and boots. What do the boys have?	1 The boys have raincoats, 3 rainhats, and boots.	1	5
Bobby says: Wait a minute. I don't have something. Where's the umbrella? I don't have an umbrella. What does he say?	1 4 4 I don't have an umbrella.	1	10
Here it is. See? Here is the umbrella. It is a big one. This is a big umbrella. What is this?	1 1 This is a big umbrella.	1	3
Mommy says: Be careful, boys. Don't get soaked. Watch out for mud puddles.			

NARRATIVE	TARGET RESPONSE	SENTENCE POINT	DSS TOTAL
And remember, don't fall down. What does she say?	4 4 Don't fall down.	1	9
Here they go. They are leaving the house. The boys are going outside. Bobby is holding the umbrella. What is he doing?	2 1 He is holding the umbrella.	1	4
Oh, oh. Here comes Spot. Timmy says: Oh, look. Here is Spot. Is Spot coming with us? Is he going outside? What does he say?	4 2 1 Is he going outside?	1	8
Bobby says: Yes, let him come. Spot can go with us. Oh, look. Look at this. Here is a mud puddle. It's a big mud puddle. What is it?	1 1 It's a big mud puddle.	1	3
Oh, oh. There goes Spot. Timmy says: Don't go in the puddle. Come back here, Spot. Don't go in the mud puddle. What does he say?	4 4 Don't go in the mud puddle.	1	9
But Spot is getting closer. He's almost there. Look how close he is. Spot is going closer and closer. What is he doing?	1 Spot is going closer 3 and closer.	1	5
Bobby says: Timmy, look at Spot. What's he gonna do?			

NARRATIVE	TARGET RESPONSE	SENTENCE POINT	DSS TOTAL
Is he going to stop? Is he going in the water? What does he say?	4 2 1 Is he going in the water?	1	8
The boys are watching. What will Spot do? Oh, look. He isn't going in. He is going around the puddle. What is Spot doing?	2 1 He is going around the puddle.	1	4
Timmy says: Hey, Bobby. Guess what? It stopped raining. It isn't raining now. It is not raining. What does he say?	1 1 1 It is not raining.	1	4
Bobby says: You're right. It stopped. I can put the umbrella down. I don't need it any more. Now I don't need it. What does Bobby say?	1 4 4 1 I don't need it.	1	11
The rain has stopped. Here comes the sun. The sun is shining. Now the boys can play.			

LEVEL I: LESSON 27

CONCEPTS	ELICITED STRUCTURES		DSS VALUE
circus, animals	**Primary emphasis**		
	indefinite pronoun –	*it*	1
VOCABULARY	personal pronoun –	*he*	2
tent, circus, clown, elephant, horse, bear, climbing, chasing, tricks	main verb –	copular *is*	1
	–	*is . . . -ing*	1
	–	obligatory *do* + verb	4
	negative –	*don't*	4
FLANNEL-BOARD MATERIALS	interrogative –	auxiliary *is* reversal	4
paper figures: Bobby, Karen, Mommy, Daddy, clown	**Secondary emphasis**		
	personal pronoun –	*I*	1
paper cutouts: elephant, two horses, bear, circus tent	secondary verb –	*gonna* + infinitive	2
	negative –	*it is not*	1

FUN AT THE CIRCUS

NARRATIVE	TARGET RESPONSE	SENTENCE POINT	DSS TOTAL
Our story is about a special place. Everybody is going to the circus. Here are Bobby and Karen. And here is Mommy. They are going to the circus. Where are they going?	3 2 They are going to the circus.	1	6
But where is Daddy? He isn't here. Bobby says: Isn't Daddy coming? Is Daddy going to the circus? Is he? Is he going? What does he say?	4 2 1 Is he going?	1	8
Oh, here is Daddy. He is going to the circus. And look. Here is the tent. This is the big circus tent. What is this?	1 1 This is the big circus tent.	1	3

NARRATIVE	TARGET RESPONSE	SENTENCE POINT	DSS TOTAL
The circus is inside. Daddy says: Here is the big tent. Let's all go in. Let's go see the circus. What does he say?	1 2 2 Let's go see the circus.	1	6
Mommy says: Be careful, Karen. Be careful, Bobby. Don't get lost. Stay close to us. Don't get lost. What does she say?	4 7 Don't get lost.	1	12
Daddy is going inside. And here goes Bobby. He is gonna go inside. What is Bobby gonna do?	2 1 2 He is gonna go inside.	1	6
Everybody is going into the tent. Oh, look at this. Here is a clown. See his great big smile. This is a clown. What is this?	1 1 This is a clown.	1	3
Look at his funny clothes. Funny clown. He's upside down. He's not standing up. The clown is upside down. Is he standing up?	2 1 No, he is upside down.	1	4
Karen says: The clown is funny. He's upside down. Why's he doing that? Is he playing a trick? What does she say?	4 2 1 Is he playing a trick?	1	8
Let's find out. Oh, oh. See what this is. It's an elephant. See how big it is. It is a very big elephant. What is it?	1 1 It is a very big elephant.	1	3
Oh, oh. Watch the elephant. It is not moving. See. The elephant is standing still.			

NARRATIVE	TARGET RESPONSE	SENTENCE POINT	DSS TOTAL
It is not moving. Is the elephant moving?	1 1 1 It is not moving.	1	4
Oh, oh. Now it's moving. Karen says: Look, everybody. The elephant is moving. But where's it going? Is it going away? What does she say?	4 1 1 Is it going away?	1	7
Watch. Watch the funny clown. He's gonna do a trick. He is climbing on the elephant. The clown is gonna do a trick. What is he gonna do?	2 1 2 He is gonna do a trick.	1	6
He is gonna ride the elephant. Bobby says: Be careful. Don't fall. The elephant is very big. Don't fall off. What does he say?	4 4 Don't fall off.	1	9
Look at the funny clown. He is riding the big elephant. Now here come the horses. The horses are coming. What is coming?	2 The horses are coming.	1	3
Bobby doesn't see them. He says: I don't see any. Where are they, Daddy? I don't see the horses. What does Bobby say?	1 4 4 I don't see the horses.	1	10
Here they are. There are two horses. Oh, oh. Look at this horse. It's not moving. Is this horse moving?	1 1 1 No, it's not moving.	1	4

NARRATIVE	TARGET RESPONSE	SENTENCE POINT	DSS TOTAL
This horse is standing still. But not this one. Look. It's not standing still. This horse is moving fast. It is not standing still. Is this horse standing still?	1 1 1 It is not standing still.	1	4
The horse is moving faster. It is gonna chase the elephant. Oh, oh. There goes the horse. It is gonna chase the elephant. What is the horse gonna do?	1 1 2 It is gonna chase the elephant.	1	5
The clown starts to wave. Karen says: What's the horse doing? It's chasing the elephant away. And there goes the clown. Is it playing a trick? What does she say?	4 1 1 Is it playing a trick?	1	7
The horse did play a trick. The elephant went away. The horse chased it away. The elephant is gone. Where is the elephant?	1 The elephant is gone.	1	2
Karen says: I don't like that trick. I want the elephant back. I want it to come back. I don't like that trick. What does she say?	1 4 4 1 I don't like that trick.	1	11
Oh, look. Here comes the elephant. And look what else is coming. It's a bear. Look at this.			

NARRATIVE	TARGET RESPONSE	SENTENCE POINT	DSS TOTAL
The elephant is bringing a bear. What is he doing?	2 1 He is bringing a bear.	1	4
Bobby says: The bear is chasing something. What is it? What's it chasing? Is it the horse? Is it chasing the horse? What does he say?	4 1 1 Is it chasing the horse?	1	7
The bear is chasing the horse. Look. The horse is too slow. The bear caught it. Because the horse was too slow. Why did he catch the horse?	2 (Because) the horse was too slow.	1	3
Daddy says: It's time to leave. Karen says: I don't wanna leave. I like the circus. I don't wanna go home. What does she say?	1 4 4 2 I don't wanna go home.	1	12
But they have to leave now. Maybe they will come back soon.			

LEVEL I: LESSON 28

CONCEPTS

building, height, strength, tools, halves

VOCABULARY

doghouse, tall, strong, hammer, saw, nails, wood

FLANNEL-BOARD MATERIALS

paper figures: Daddy, Bobby, Karen
paper cutouts: dog, hammer, saw, nails, wood

ELICITED STRUCTURES		DSS VALUE
Primary emphasis		
personal pronoun –	*he*	2
main verb –	copular *is*	1
–	*is . . . -ing*	1
Secondary emphasis		
indefinite pronoun –	*it*	1
secondary verb –	*gonna* + infinitive	2
negative –	*can't*	4
conjunction –	*and*	3
wh-question –	*what*	2
main verb –	*can* + verb	4
interrogative –	auxiliary *is* reversal	4

BUILDING A DOGHOUSE

NARRATIVE	TARGET RESPONSE	SENTENCE POINT	DSS TOTAL
Our story is about three people. And it's about a dog, too. Here are the people. Daddy, Bobby, and Karen are the people. Who are the people?	3 Daddy, Bobby, and 2 Karen are the people.	1	6
This is Spot. He's the dog. Look who's in our story. Daddy, Bobby, Karen, and Spot. It is about three people and a dog. Who is the story about?	1 1 3 It is about three people 3 and a dog.	1	9
Bobby and Karen are watching Daddy. Because Daddy is making something. It's a surprise. It's something special. The surprise is something special. What is it?	1 1 3 It is something special.	1	6

NARRATIVE	TARGET RESPONSE	SENTENCE POINT	DSS TOTAL
Look. Here are some tools. Here are a hammer and a saw. Daddy needs his tools. Because . . . He is gonna make the surprise. What is Daddy gonna do?	2 1 2 He is gonna make the surprise.	1	6
Karen says: Look at Daddy's tools. He is making something. But what is it? What is he making? What does she say?	2 4 2 1 What is he making?	1	10
Bobby says: I know, Karen. I know what it is. It's a doghouse. What is it?	1 1 It's a doghouse.	1	3
Daddy is making something for Spot. And you know what it is. It's gonna be a doghouse. The doghouse is gonna be for Spot. Who is it gonna be for?	1 1 2 It is gonna be for Spot.	1	5
Daddy has his tools. Now he needs some nails. Karen will get them. Here they are. Karen's getting them. What is she doing?	2 1 She's getting the nails.	1	4
Look. They're up too high. Karen can't reach them. She is too little. Karen can't get the nails. Can she get the nails?	2 4 No, she can't.	1	7
	2 4 4 She can't get the nails.	1	11
Here comes Daddy. He is tall. Daddy is bigger than Karen. He can reach the nails. Because he is tall. Why can Daddy get them?	2 1 (Because) he is tall.	1	4

NARRATIVE	TARGET RESPONSE	SENTENCE POINT	DSS TOTAL
Now he needs some wood. There goes Bobby. Look. Bobby is gonna get it. He is gonna get some wood. What is he gonna do?	2 1 2 3 He is gonna get some wood.	1	9
Here is the wood. But look. Something is wrong. Bobby can't lift it. The wood is too heavy. What is wrong?	1 The wood is too heavy.	1	2
Bobby needs some help. The wood is too heavy. He can't carry it by himself. Bobby can't carry the wood. Can he carry the wood?	2 4 No, he can't.	1	7
	2 4 4 He can't carry the wood.	1	11
Here comes Daddy. He is strong. Daddy can carry the wood. Because he is a strong man. Why can Daddy carry it?	2 1 (Because) he is a strong man.	1	4
Now everything is ready. Daddy picks up the saw. Karen says: Daddy has the saw. What's he doing with it? What is he gonna do? What does she say?	2 4 2 1 2 What is he gonna do?	1	12
Bobby says: He's gonna saw the wood. He needs two pieces. So he will saw it in half. Look. Daddy is sawing the wood in half. What is he doing?	2 1 He is sawing the wood in half.	1	4
See the two pieces. Daddy sawed the big piece in half. He made two little pieces of wood.			

NARRATIVE	TARGET RESPONSE	SENTENCE POINT	DSS TOTAL
There are two pieces now. How many pieces are there?	2 3 There are two pieces.	1	6
Now he gets the hammer. Karen says: Look, Bobby. Look now. Daddy has the hammer. What's he doing? What is he doing now? What does she say?	2 4 2 1 What is he doing?	1	10
Watch. He puts two pieces of wood here. Then he hammers them together. Like this. Now he takes two more pieces. And he hammers them together. Now he puts everything together. And what is this?	1 1 This is the doghouse.	1	3
But something is missing. Karen says: The roof is missing. Where is it? Where is the roof? What does she say?	2 1 1 Where is the roof?	1	5
Daddy says: You're right, Karen. It needs a roof. I didn't forget it. Here it is. This is the roof. What is this?	1 1 This is the roof.	1	3
Daddy is putting the roof on. And now Spot has a doghouse. Spot is so happy. He is barking and barking. What is he doing?	2 1 3 1 He is barking and barking.	1	8
Bobby says: Hey, Spot. Go inside.			

NARRATIVE	TARGET RESPONSE	SENTENCE POINT	DSS TOTAL
Go in your new doghouse. Oh, look at Spot. There he goes. He's going in his new doghouse. What's he doing?	2 1 2 He's going in his new doghouse.	1	6
Oh, oh. Where did Spot go? You can't see him now. Spot is inside the doghouse. You can't see him. Can you see Spot now?	1 4 No, you can't.	1	6
	1 4 4 2 You can't see him.	1	12
Now it's time to clean up. Daddy says: Let's clean up. The tools go back inside. Let's put the tools away. What does he say?	1 2 Let's put the tools away.	1	4
Here comes Spot. Now you can see him. He likes his new doghouse.			

LEVEL I: LESSON 29

CONCEPTS	ELICITED STRUCTURES		DSS VALUE
fishing, bait, digging, contrasts	**Primary emphasis**		
	indefinite pronoun –	*it*	1
	personal pronoun –	*he*	2
VOCABULARY	main verb –	copular *is*	1
fishing pole, worm, shovel, digging, frog, string, hopping, can	–	*is . . . -ing*	1
	secondary verb –	*gonna* + infinitive	2
	wh-question –	*what . . . do*	2
FLANNEL-BOARD MATERIALS	interrogative –	auxiliary *is* reversal	4
paper figures: Bobby, Karen, Daddy	**Secondary emphasis**		
paper cutouts: two fishing poles, shovel, worms, two cans, frog, fish, pond	indefinite pronoun –	*one*	3
	personal pronoun –	*she*	2
	main verb –	uninflected	1
	–	*can* + verb	4
	negative –	*can't*	4
	conjunction –	*and*	3
	–	*but*	5

THE FISHING TRIP

NARRATIVE	TARGET RESPONSE	SENTENCE POINT	DSS TOTAL
Today's story is about a trip. It's about a fishing trip. Bobby is going, and so is Daddy. They are both gonna go. Bobby is gonna go, and Daddy is gonna go. Who is gonna go?	Bobby[1] is gonna[2] go, and[3] Daddy is[1] gonna[2] go.	1	10
Here's what they're taking. They need two things. And here they are. They have two fishing poles. What do they have?	They[3] have[1] two fishing[3] poles.	1	8
This is a big one. It's Daddy's. This is a little fishing pole. It is for Bobby. One pole is big, and one is little.			

NARRATIVE	TARGET RESPONSE	SENTENCE POINT	DSS TOTAL
What do the two poles look like?	3 1 3 3 1 One is big, and one is little.	1	12
Bobby says: We have two fishing poles. Daddy's is big. But not mine. It's little. Daddy's is big, but mine is little. What does he say?	1 5 1 1 Daddy's is big, but mine is little.	1	9
They are both ready to go. Oh, oh. Here comes Karen. Karen says: Please let me come. I want to go with you. What does she say?	1 1 2 1 I want to go with you.	1	6
Daddy says: Okay. You can come. Look how happy Karen is. She is happy because . . . She can go fishing too. Karen is gonna go too. Why is she happy?	2 1 2 (Because) she is gonna go.	1	6
Now look. See what Daddy has. This is a shovel. Daddy is digging . . . like this. He is digging for something. What is Daddy doing?	2 1 He is digging for 3 something.	1	7
Karen says: Look. Daddy has a shovel. He is digging with it. Why is he doing that? What is he digging for? What does she say?	2 4 2 1 What is he digging for?	1	10
Bobby says: He's digging for worms.			

NARRATIVE	TARGET RESPONSE	SENTENCE POINT	DSS TOTAL
We need worms for fishing. Oh, look. Daddy found some. Here's a can. It is for the worms. What is the can for?	1 1 It is for the worms.	1	3
Daddy puts them in the can. His can is full. Look. Now Bobby is gonna look for worms. Watch Bobby. Look, everybody. Bobby is gonna dig for worms. What is he gonna do?	2 1 2 He is gonna dig for worms.	1	6
Look. Bobby found some. And here is another can. Bobby puts the worms in. But look. His can is not full. Is his can full?	1 1 1 No, it is not full.	1	4
Karen says: See the two cans. This one is full. But not that one. This one is full, but that one is not. What does she say?	1 3 1 5 1 This one is full, but that 3 1 1 one is not.	1	17
There they go. They're going to the lake. That's where they fish. This is the lake. What is this?	1 1 This is the lake.	1	3
Watch Daddy. He is holding a worm. Karen says: Daddy has a worm. Why does he have it? What is he doing? What does she say?	2 4 2 1 What is he doing?	1	10
Look, everybody. Watch Daddy.			

NARRATIVE	TARGET RESPONSE	SENTENCE POINT	DSS TOTAL
See this string . . . right here? The string is on the fishing pole. Daddy's putting a worm on the string. What's he doing?	2 1 He's putting a worm on the string.	1	4
Now Bobby is gonna try it. But he can't do it. The worm won't stay on. He can't do it. Can Bobby do it?	2 4 No, he can't.	1	7
	2 4 4 1 He can't do it.	1	12
Daddy is helping him. Now Bobby throws the string and . . . Splash! The worm goes in the water. He can fish now. The worm is in the water. Where is the worm?	1 The worm is in the water.	1	2
Now Bobby and Daddy are fishing. But Karen's not fishing. Bobby says: Daddy, look at Karen. What is she doing? Why isn't she fishing? What is she doing? What does he say?	2 4 2 1 What is she doing?	1	10
Karen sees something over here. She is looking at something. Daddy says: What does Karen see? What is it? What is she looking at? What does he say?	2 4 2 1 What is she looking at?	1	10
Oh, look. It's a frog. That's what Karen sees. It is right by the water. It's a little green frog. What is it?	1 1 It's a little green frog.	1	3

NARRATIVE	TARGET RESPONSE	SENTENCE POINT	DSS TOTAL
Oh, oh. The frog starts to move. Bobby says: What's it doing? Is it going away? What is the frog doing? What does he say?	2 4 1 What is the frog doing?	1	8
Frogs like to hop. That's what it's doing. See, the frog is hopping. It is hopping up and down. What is the frog doing?	1 1 3 It is hopping up and down.	1	6
But it's going away. Karen is chasing it. But she can't find it. The frog is too fast. Karen can't catch it. Can Karen catch the frog?	2 4 No, she can't.	1	7
	2 4 4 1 She can't catch it.	1	12
Oh, look. She got it. Karen has the frog. Oh, oh. Look at Bobby's pole. Something is pulling on it. What's happening to his pole?	3 1 Something is pulling 1 on it.	1	6
It's a fish. See it? It's a great big one. Bobby is gonna catch it. What is he gonna do?	2 1 2 1 He is gonna catch it.	1	7
He caught it. Look! Bobby says: I caught a fish. You have a frog, Karen. But look what I have. You have a frog, but I have a fish. What does he say?	1 1 5 1 You have a frog, but I 1 have a fish.	1	10

LEVEL I: LESSON 30

CONCEPTS

size, color, and action contrasts

VOCABULARY

bike, wagon, big, little, red, green, riding, walking, lost, found

FLANNEL-BOARD MATERIALS

paper figures: Bobby, Timmy
paper cutouts: dog, red wagon, green bike, tree, house front

ELICITED STRUCTURES		DSS VALUE
Primary emphasis		
personal pronoun –	*he*	2
main verb –	copular *is*	1
–	*can* + verb	4
secondary verb –	*gonna* + infinitive	2
negative –	*can't*	4
conjunction –	*but*	5
Secondary emphasis		
indefinite pronoun –	*this*	1
personal pronoun –	*I*	1

THE BIG RACE

NARRATIVE	TARGET RESPONSE	SENTENCE POINT	DSS TOTAL
Two boys are in our story. This boy is Bobby. And this one is Timmy. The two boys are Bobby and Timmy. Who are the two boys?	The two boys (3) are (2) Bobby and (3) Timmy.	1	9
Bobby is a big boy. But Timmy isn't. He is a little boy. Bobby is big, but Timmy is little. What do they look like?	Bobby is (1) big, but (5) Timmy is (1) little.	1	8
See what Bobby has. It's a wagon. See, it's a red one. Bobby has a red wagon. What does he have?	He (2) has (2) a red wagon.	1	5
Timmy has something else. He has this. Look, it's a green bike.			

NARRATIVE	TARGET RESPONSE	SENTENCE POINT	DSS TOTAL
Timmy has a green bike. What does he have?	2 2 He has a green bike.	1	5
The boys have two different things. This is a wagon, but this isn't. This is something different. It's a bike. This is a wagon, but this is a bike. What is the difference?	1 1 5 1 This is a wagon, but this 1 is a bike.	1	10
Bobby says: We have a bike and a wagon. They are different things. But something else is different. The colors are different. What else is different?	2 The colors are different.	1	3
Timmy says: You are right, Bobby. Your wagon is red. But my bike is green. Yours is red, but mine is green. What does he say?	1 1 5 1 1 Yours is red, but mine is green.	1	10
They're going for a ride now. Timmy is sitting here. But Bobby is sitting on the back of the bike. Bobby is behind Timmy. Where is Bobby?	1 Bobby is behind Timmy.	1	2
They are taking the wagon, too. They're gonna pull it. The bike is gonna pull the wagon. What is the bike gonna do?	1 2 The bike is gonna pull the wagon.	1	4
There they go. They're riding down the street. Oh, oh. The boys fell off! Timmy's bike is on the ground. Where is the bike?	1 The bike is on the ground.	1	2

NARRATIVE	TARGET RESPONSE	SENTENCE POINT	DSS TOTAL
Timmy says: This won't work, Bobby. You can't ride with me. It's too hard with two people. It's too hard to ride. What does he say?	1 1 3 It's too hard to ride.	1	6
One boy had better walk. Bobby is going to. But not Timmy. He's riding. Bobby is gonna walk, but Timmy is gonna ride. What are the boys gonna do?	1 2 5 Bobby is gonna walk but 1 2 Timmy is gonna ride.	1	12
Timmy is riding his bike. But Bobby is walking. Oh, look. Who is this? This is their dog, Spot. Who is this?	1 1 3 This is their dog, Spot.	1	6
Bobby says: Get in the wagon. I'll pull you. Watch Spot. He's jumping in. Spot is gonna ride in the wagon. What is he gonna do?	2 1 2 He is gonna ride in the wagon.	1	6
Timmy sees a tree way over here. He wants to race to it. He says: I'll race you, Bobby. Let's race to the tree. What does Timmy say?	1 2 Let's race to the tree.	1	4
There they go. Oh, oh. Look who's ahead. It's Timmy. He's gonna win the race. Look how fast he's going. Timmy is gonna win. Who is gonna win?	1 2 Timmy is gonna win.	1	4

NARRATIVE	TARGET RESPONSE	SENTENCE POINT	DSS TOTAL
Look. He did. Timmy won. Timmy says: I beat you, Bobby. I am faster. I beat you to the tree. What does he say?	1 1 1 I beat you to the tree.	1	4
Bobby says: You aren't faster. I just can't go fast. Because I'm pulling Spot. Spot is too heavy. So I can't go fast. What does he say?	1 4 4 I can't go fast.	1	10
See what Bobby's doing. He's taking Spot out. Now Bobby is gonna race. He can go fast now. What can he do now?	2 4 He can go fast now.	1	7
There they go. But look. Timmy is ahead again. He's leading. Bobby is behind. Look. Timmy won again. Bobby just can't beat Timmy. Can Bobby beat Timmy?	{ 2 4 No, he can't.	1	7
	2 4 4 He can't beat Timmy. }	1	11
Oh, oh. Something is wrong. The boys went too far. They went too far from home. Bobby is lost. Bobby says: Where are we? I can't see my house. Where is it? Where is it? I can't find it. What does he say?	1 4 4 1 I can't find it.	1	11
Timmy starts to look. He looks over here.			

NARRATIVE	TARGET RESPONSE	SENTENCE POINT	DSS TOTAL
And then he looks over there. Timmy is looking for Bobby's house. What is he doing?	2 1 He is looking for Bobby's house.	1	4
Timmy says: I can't find your house. I am lost, too. The boys are both lost. Bobby and Timmy can't find the house. What is wrong?	3 Bobby and Timmy 4 4 can't find the house.	1	12
Oh, look at Spot. Spot is barking and barking. Maybe he knows where it is. There he goes. Spot is running somewhere. What is he doing?	1 Spot is running somewhere.	1	2
And there go Bobby and Timmy. Everybody is running. But the boys can't keep up. They can't run as fast as Spot. The boys run fast, but Spot is faster. Do the boys run as fast as Spot?	1 5 The boys run fast, but 1 Spot is faster.	1	8
Oh, look. Here is the house. The boys are home. Spot found it. They are not lost now.			

LEVEL II LESSONS

Level II lessons emphasize the intermediate structures contained in the eight grammatical categories of the DSS, which is reproduced as Chart I, pages 4–5. Lessons at this level also emphasize combinations of structures at all the DSS levels. Considerable emphasis is given to plural pronouns and to elaborations of the main verb: copular and auxiliary *is*, *am*, *are*, *was*, and *were*; *-s* and *-ed* tense markers; irregular past tense; modal verbs *can* and *will*; and obligatory *do*. In Level II lessons the emphasis is no longer primarily on word order or simple sentence formulation but on expanding the child's repertoire of language structures and giving him a variety of ways for expressing his ideas. Compound and complex sentences — and, with them, increasing sentence length — take on importance at this stage of teaching.

Indefinite Pronoun

The indefinite pronouns *some*, *all*, *somebody*, *someone*, *something*, and *another*, which were merely introduced in Level I, now receive primary emphasis in Lessons 2 through 4. This use of indefinite pronouns and quantifying words sets the stage for the introduction of the negative pronouns (*nothing*, *nobody*, *none*, *no one*), which give the child a new way of making a negative statement. At Level I, only the negation of verbs appeared; now the child is taught to negate the pronoun. At this point the child begins to learn the rule governing negation in standard English: that only one negative word negates the entire sentence. He is taught to use a negative pronoun in sentences where the verb is not negated (*Nobody was home*). The common error of the double negative inevitably arises, and children often try to negate both the pronoun and verb (*Nobody wasn't home*). Children can be helped to discover the underlying negative rule by repeatedly contrasting examples of both forms (*He had no more cookies. He didn't have any more cookies*).

The negative pronouns inevitably lead to the introduction of the indefinite words *any*, *anyone*, and *anything*, and these forms are stressed in Lessons 17 and 18. *Any* and *anything* are stressed with verb negations such as *isn't*, *can't*, and *won't*, and it is best to introduce these forms in sentences where they occur as the last word (*I don't have any. I can't see anything*). The other indefinite words, *every* and *everything*, are introduced after the establishment of the *nothing* and *anything* forms.

Personal Pronoun

Groundwork was laid for the introduction of plural pronouns in Level I, where *and* was used as the conjunction between two nouns. Level I forms, such as *Mommy and Daddy* and *the dog and the cat*, are presented in Level II with the appropriate plurals (*we*, *us*, *our*, *they*, *them*, *their*). The use of plural pronouns inevitably leads to further verb elaborations and the problems of subject-verb agreement; thus, plural pronouns and additional verb forms must be taught simultaneously. If the child has stabilized the use of the copular and auxiliary *is*, then the shift to *am* and *are* is not too difficult and can be accomplished by stressing the number and person characteristics of the subject and linking these with the appropriate verb forms. Learning may be facilitated by contrasting singulars and plurals within the same story (*He is*, *They are*).

Reflexive pronouns are introduced in Lesson 16. The most common usage of reflexives in children's language is in sentences such as *I did it by myself* and *He went all by himself.* In such a construction, the child is learning even more than the use of a reflexive pronoun; he is also learning the preposition *by* as the marker of an agent, the initiator of action. This form will be used at a much later time in the development of passive sentences, such as *He was hit by a car.* The clinician may facilitate the later learning of this very mature structure, the passive, by introducing the reflexive in the form *by myself.*

Main Verb

Modal verbs *can* and *will* and the obligatory *do* are introduced in Lesson 1. These auxiliaries take the same privilege of occurrence in verb elaborations and are taught together. *Will* is introduced as a replacement for the earlier form, *is gonna*, and its meaning will be made more clear to the child if the two future forms are presented interchangeably. *Can* and *do* usually appear first in their negative forms, *can't* and *don't*, in normal language development, and this sequence should be observed also in clinical teaching. When a child has had some success with *can't* and *don't*, then sentences with *can* and *do* may be presented. Tense markers on auxiliary verbs are first introduced with modals in Lesson 18, then with obligatory *do* in Lesson 26, and they are used in negative and interrogative sentences in both lessons.

The final primary-verb elaborations stressed in Level II are the use of the auxiliary *have* (*have eaten*), the modal *must* (*must go*), and the use of more than one auxiliary (*he might have been*). These forms are seen very late in the normal development of syntax and often are omitted entirely from a clinical teaching program. Were it not for its critical role in the common verb form *have got*, *have* might not be introduced at all in these lessons. These late-developing verb elaborations are presented for illustration in

Lessons 23, 28, and 29, where they are used with both negatives and questions.

Secondary Verb

Whereas the secondary verbs in Level I were largely the early-developing infinitives, Level II introduces another secondary verb, the participle, in Lessons 5 and 6. Participles are verb forms which fulfill an adjectival function and can be considered as one means of joining two basic sentences. Present participles are introduced first and are placed as the last word in the sentence (*He sees the house burning*). The participial form can be increased in difficulty by placing it prior to the noun (*He sees the burning house*) or by expanding the participial phrase (*I see a dog playing in the yard*).

Infinitival complements are introduced in Lessons 10 and 11. These are not the early infinitives of Level I but are complements of other lexical verbs (*try to*, *have to*, *like to*, *ought to*, etc.). These infinitives provide still other ways for children to combine basic sentences, and the sentences which result are much shorter than sentences joined with conjunctions. Further steps in the development of infinitives involve the use of subjects other than the subject of the main verb (*I want you to come*) and a wh-word followed by an infinitive (*I know how to swim*). These forms should be reserved for fairly advanced language-development groups.

The gerund is a verb form used as a noun and, like participles and infinitives, combines the information contained in two basic sentences. Gerunds are infrequent in the speech of young children and, when they do occur, are apt to be used with *go* (*go fishing*, *go swimming*) or in a wh-question form (*How about going with me?*). Lesson 26 contains some examples of the gerund with *go*, and Lesson 22 introduces it with *How about . . . ?*

Negative

Lessons 7 through 9 introduce the negative contractions *isn't* and *won't*. The use of *is not* with *it*, *this*, and *that* as subjects was introduced early in Level I but never in a contracted form. *Isn't* is a difficult word to articulate, and its introduction should be delayed until the clinician is sure that the child has stabilized the use of *is* and understands the concept of negation. *Won't* can be introduced once the concept of future has been established, first through *gonna* and then through *will*. In Lesson 20, uncontracted negatives receive emphasis with such forms as *cannot*, *do not*, and *will not*. Since the normal pattern of language development shows the early appearance of negative contractions, the clinician should delay the use of uncontracted negatives until the child has shown considerable success with the common contractions. Lessons 23 and 29 introduce the latest-appearing negative form, the negation of auxiliary *have*.

Conjunction

The early conjunction *and* was introduced at Level I but is necessarily reintroduced in the Level II lessons which stress plural pronouns and verb forms. Compound subjects (*Tommy and Betty*, *you and I*) develop into plural forms (*they are*, *we were*) and are used to clarify and explain them. More mature conjunctions (*if*, *so*, *or*) are introduced into the stories in the last half of Level II. These conjunctions involve greater sentence length and must therefore be used cautiously. Moreover, the semantic relations which these conjunctions express must be made very clear in the story context; their meanings must be motivated by situational events. The conjunction *if* introduces the concept of conditionality and allows the child to express ideas not founded on actual experience. *If* is important in the expression of imagination, hopes, and wishes, an important semantic step in language usage. The conjunction *so* introduces the concept of purpose, which has already been presented in the noncomplementing infinitive (*He opened the door to look. He opened the door so he could see*). The conjunction *so* is also used to express resulting events (*I got into the wagon, so now Daddy can push it*). The conjunction *or* presents a situation where there is a choice, and a child must understand the concept of alternatives if he is to use this word. *Or* can initially be presented as a conjunction between two nouns (*Karen or Bobby will go*, *We can go on the swings or the slide*) in order to keep sentence length to manageable proportions. The simultaneous teaching of the wh-word *which*, at least at the receptive level, appears to facilitate the learning of *or* (*Which do you want*, *the red or the green*?).

The conjunction *because* embodies one of the most semantically powerful concepts which children encounter, since cultural patterns of causality, purpose, and motivation are often revealed to them in this form. Prior to the use of *because* between clauses, a child is taught to respond to why-questions with only the dependent clause and the starter word *because* (*Why did he go*? *Because he was hungry*). Once the relationship of *why* to *because* is firmly established, the two-clause sentence is expected in the target response (*Why did he go*? *He went because he was hungry*).

Interrogative Reversal

Simple reversals of the copula and auxiliary *is* were first presented in Level I, but Level II stories contain more mature interrogative forms. The reversal of modal verbs and obligatory-*do* forms are given primary emphasis in Lessons 12 through 15 and again in the last two lessons. The children's target responses are limited to the obligatory-*do* form (*Do you want to ride?*), but the narrative presents reversals of obligatory *does* and *did* as well (*Does Bobby want to ride? Did he do it?*). These more difficult forms could be used as target responses by a clinician who thought that tense markers on these auxiliaries would not create too difficult a formulation task. The most mature interrogative reversals are with the auxiliary *have* (*Have you seen him?*) and with two or more auxiliaries (*Can Mommy still be sleeping?*), and they are not presented until Lessons 28 and 29.

Wh-Question

Late-developing wh-words are not introduced until the interrogative reversal of most auxiliary verb forms has been established. Understanding of the semantic features of wh-words like *why*, *how come*, *what if*, *how about*, *whose*, *which*, and *which one* must precede expressive usage. Understanding is judged through the child's ability to respond appropriately to the various wh-question forms which elicit target sentences. For example, expressive use of *why* would never be taught until a child was able to respond appropriately to questions like *Why was he late*? When wh-words are included in the target sentences, they are usually presented as the direct quotation of bits of dialogue, as in the following example:

NARRATIVE	TARGET RESPONSE
Daddy said:	
Why are you late?	
What did Daddy say?	Why are you late?

Lessons 13 and 32 present wh-questions with *how* and *when*; Lessons 21 and 22 emphasize *why* and *what if*; Lesson 30 uses *whose* and *which* in target responses.

The clinician is allowed some flexibility in laying out the specific order of grammatical goals once basic sentence structure has been established. An index is included to help the clinician locate lessons in which particular structures receive either primary or secondary emphasis. Level II should be regarded, not as a rigid program to be followed precisely, but merely as one type of possible sequence in which grammatical structures can be effectively presented to children. As long as the developmental levels of the DSS chart (Chart I, pages 4–5) are followed fairly closely, the clinician can select, among many structures, those which would be appropriate lesson goals. The Level II lessons are designed to give guidelines and suggestions to clinicians who will do their own prescriptive planning with their own clinical children.

INDEX TO LEVEL II LESSONS

Indefinite Pronoun or Noun Modifier

DSS Score	Structure	Lesson Number: Primary Emphasis	Lesson Number: Secondary Emphasis
3	*another*	3, 17	19
3	*more*		24
3	*all*	17	1, 16, 25
3	*one, two,* etc.	14, 15	1, 6, 7, 19, 25
3	*some, somebody, something*	2, 3, 14, 15, 17	1, 4, 6, 7, 9, 19, 24
4	*none, nobody, nothing*	4, 12	
7	*any, anything*	17, 18	
7	*everything, everyone*	18	

Personal Pronoun

DSS Score	Structure	Lesson Number: Primary Emphasis	Lesson Number: Secondary Emphasis
2	*he, him, his*	1, 5-14, 18-22, 24-26, 28-32	2, 17, 23, 32
2	*she, her*	1, 9-11, 13, 18, 19, 21, 24-26, 28-32	23, 32
3	*we, us, our*	1, 3, 6, 10, 11, 13, 15, 16, 18, 19, 22-27, 30, 31	2, 9, 28
3	*they, them, their*	1, 3, 6, 10, 11, 13, 15, 16, 18, 19, 22-31	2, 4, 9, 21, 28
3	*these, those*	24, 25	
5	*myself, themselves*	16	
6	*what*		16

Interrogative Reversal

DSS Score	Structure	Lesson Number: Primary Emphasis	Lesson Number: Secondary Emphasis
6	reversal of modal verb	12-15, 27, 31, 32	11, 16, 17, 26
6	reversal of obligatory *do*	12-15, 30-32	11, 16, 17
8	reversal of auxiliary *have*	28, 29	
8	reversal with two or more auxiliaries	28, 29	

Wh-Question

DSS Score	Structure	Lesson Number: Primary Emphasis	Lesson Number: Secondary Emphasis
2	*what, what kind, how many*		3
2	*what . . . do*		12
2	*where*		12
5	*how, how* + adjective	13, 32	
5	*when*	13, 32	
7	*why*	21	
7	*how come, what if, how about*	21, 22	
8	*whose, which, which* + noun	30	

INDEX TO LEVEL II LESSONS (Cont'd.)

DSS Score	Structure	Lesson Number: Primary Emphasis	Lesson Number: Secondary Emphasis
Main Verb			
2	*-s, -ed,* irregular past	1, 2, 5, 6, 9-12, 14, 15, 18, 20-22, 24-27, 30	4, 7, 16, 19, 23, 31
2	copular *am, are*	1-3, 6, 9-15, 18, 21, 22, 24-27, 30, 32	4, 16, 17, 19, 23, 31
2	auxiliary *am, are*	1-3, 5, 6, 9-15, 18, 20-22, 24-27, 30, 32	4, 7, 16, 17, 19, 23, 31
2	copular *was, were*	5, 32	
4	*can, will* + verb	1, 6, 9, 11-17, 20, 23-26, 30-32	5, 7, 18, 21, 27, 28
4	obligatory *do*	1, 9, 11-17, 23, 26, 30-32	3, 7, 18, 21
4	emphatic *do*		27
6	*could, would, should, might,* + verb	18, 26, 27	30
6	obligatory *does, did*	26	19, 30, 31
7	*have* + verb + *-en*	23, 29	28
7	*have got*		28
7	*must* + verb	29	
7	passive with *get*		9
7	passive with *be*		9

DSS Score	Structure	Lesson Number: Primary Emphasis	Lesson Number: Secondary Emphasis
Secondary Verb			
2	early infinitive	1, 2, 8, 10, 15-19, 21, 23-25, 30-32	3, 7, 9, 12, 22, 27
3	noncomplementing infinitive	12	
4	participle	5, 6	
5	later infinitival complement	10, 11, 16	1, 23, 26
5	infinitive with wh-word	11, 16	23, 30
8	gerund	26	22
Negative			
4	*can't, don't*	12	9, 16, 17, 31
5	*isn't, won't*	7-9, 17, 31	
7	N + *is not*	19, 23	
7	uncontracted negatives	20, 26, 29	
7	*doesn't*	19, 26	
7	*couldn't*	26	
7	*have not*	23, 29	
Conjunction			
3	*and*	10, 18, 19	1, 6, 9, 12, 14, 15, 21, 31
5	*if, so*	24, 25	
5	*or*	27	
6	*because*	16, 20, 26	30

LEVEL II: LESSON 1

CONCEPTS

shoveling snow,
warm and cold,
surprise

VOCABULARY

shovel, sweep, cocoa,
driveway, broom, garage

FLANNEL-BOARD MATERIALS

paper figures: Daddy, Mommy, Bobby, Karen
paper cutouts: house, garage, driveway, two shovels, broom, table
additional materials: cotton balls to resemble snow

ELICITED STRUCTURES		DSS VALUE
Primary emphasis		
personal pronoun –	*he, him, his, she*	2
–	*we, they, their*	3
main verb –	*-s,* copular *am, are,* auxiliary *are*	2
–	*can, will* + verb, obligatory *do* + verb	4
secondary verb –	early-developing infinitives	2
Secondary emphasis		
indefinite pronoun –	*some, all, six, five*	3
secondary verb –	later infinitival complements, obligatory deletions	5
conjunction –	*and*	3

SHOVELING THE SNOW

NARRATIVE	TARGET RESPONSE	SENTENCE POINT	DSS TOTAL
This is Bobby. Bobby is six. He is six years old. How old is Bobby?	1 3 Bobby is six years old.	1	5
This is Karen. Karen is five. She is five years old. How old is Karen?	1 3 Karen is five years old.	1	5
Karen is Bobby's sister. She is Bobby's sister. She is his sister. Is she Bobby's sister?	2 1 Yes, she is Bobby's sister.	1	4
This is Mommy. This is Bobby's and Karen's mommy. This is their mommy. Who is this?	1 1 3 This is their mommy.	1	6

NARRATIVE	TARGET RESPONSE	SENTENCE POINT	DSS TOTAL
This is Daddy. This is Bobby's and Karen's daddy. This is their daddy. Who is this?	1 1 3 This is their daddy.	1	6
Mommy says: Look, it is snowing outside. It is snowing very hard. It is snowing hard. It is snowing very hard. What does Mommy say?	1 1 It is snowing very hard.	1	3
Daddy says: We will have to clean the driveway. We will have to clean the snow off the driveway. Who wants to help me? Who wants to help clean the driveway? Who wants to help me? What does Daddy say?	2 2 2 1 Who wants to help me?	1	8
Bobby says: I will help. It will be fun. I like to shovel snow. I will help shovel the snow. What does Bobby say?	1 4 5 I will help shovel the snow.	1	11
Karen says: I will help, too. I like to shovel snow. I like to clean. I will help clean the driveway. What does Karen say?	1 4 5 I will help clean the driveway.	1	11
Bobby and Karen and Daddy go outside. They go outside in the snow. It is cold. The wind is blowing. Bobby and Karen and Daddy are outside in the snow. They are outside. They are outside in the snow.			

NARRATIVE	TARGET RESPONSE	SENTENCE POINT	DSS TOTAL
Who is outside in the snow?	3 3 Bobby and Karen and 2 Daddy are outside (in the snow).	1	9
Daddy says: We need shovels. We need shovels for the snow. They're in the garage. The shovels are in the garage. Where are the shovels?	2 The shovels are in the garage.	1	3
Daddy is giving a shovel to Bobby. He is giving a shovel to Bobby. Bobby says: The shovel is heavy. It is heavy. It is very heavy. Is the shovel heavy?	1 Yes, the shovel is very heavy.	1	2
Karen says: I will help you. I will help you clean the driveway. I will sweep the driveway. I need a broom. I need a broom to sweep the driveway. I need a broom. What does Karen need?	2 Karen needs a broom.	1	3
What is she going to do?	2 1 2 She is going to sweep the driveway.	1	6
Daddy says: I will take a shovel. I will help Bobby shovel the driveway. I will help him. I will help him shovel the driveway. What does Daddy say?	1 4 2 5 I will help him shovel the driveway.	1	13
Daddy and Bobby are shoveling the driveway. They are shoveling the driveway. They are working.			

NARRATIVE	TARGET RESPONSE	SENTENCE POINT	DSS TOTAL
They are working hard. They are working very hard. What are they doing?	3 2 They are working very hard.	1	6
Karen is helping, too. She is working hard. She is sweeping the driveway. She is sweeping it. She is sweeping the driveway. What is she doing?	2 1 She is sweeping the driveway.	1	4
Karen says: Be careful, Daddy. Be careful, Bobby. Don't fall. There is ice on the ground. Be careful! Don't fall on the ice. What does Karen say?	1 4 4 Be careful. Don't fall on the ice.	2	11
Daddy says: Do a good job. Get all the snow off. I want to take the car out of the garage. I want to take it out. I want to take the car out of the garage. What does he want to do?	2 2 2 He wants to take the car out of the garage.	1	7
Bobby says: Oh! Oh! Look, Daddy. Look at Karen. Karen fell down. She fell down. She fell down on the ice. What happened to Karen?	2 2 She fell down on the ice.	1	5
Daddy says: I'm sorry. I'm sorry you fell down. Are you hurt, Karen? Are you? Are you hurt? What does Daddy say?	2 1 1 Are you hurt?	1	5

NARRATIVE	TARGET RESPONSE	SENTENCE POINT	DSS TOTAL
Karen says: No, I am not hurt. I did not hurt myself. I didn't. I did not hurt myself. Did Karen hurt herself?	7 No, Karen did not 6 5 hurt herself.	1	19
Karen says: I am cold. The snow is cold. Let's go into the house. Let's go in and get warm. Let's go into the house and get warm. What does Karen say?	1 2 Let's go into the house 3 2 and get warm.	1	9
Daddy says: Okay, go into the house. You go into the house. You go into the house and get warm. I will finish the job. I will finish cleaning. I will finish cleaning the driveway. What will he do?	2 4 8 He will finish cleaning the driveway.	1	15
Bobby and Karen are in the house. They are in the house. They are getting warm. Mommy says: Let's surprise Daddy. Let's make cocoa. Let's make cocoa for Daddy. Let's make some hot cocoa for Daddy. What does Mommy say?	1 2 3 Let's make some hot cocoa for Daddy.	1	7
Bobby and Karen say: Can we help you? Can we help you make the cocoa? Can we? Can we help you make the cocoa? What do they say?	6 3 4 1 5 Can we help you make the cocoa?	1	20

NARRATIVE	TARGET RESPONSE	SENTENCE POINT	DSS TOTAL
Mommy says: Yes, you can. You can help me. Now they are making cocoa. They are making good hot cocoa. They are making cocoa for Daddy. What are they doing?	3 2 They are making cocoa for Daddy.	1	6
Mommy is calling Daddy. Mommy says: Come into the house. Come into the house. We have a surprise. Come into the house. We have a surprise. What does Mommy say?	1 Come into the house.	1	2
	3 1 We have a surprise.	1	5
Daddy comes into the house. He is in the house. Karen says: Look, Daddy. Here is some cocoa. Here is some hot cocoa for you to drink. Daddy says: Thank you, Karen. Thank you, Bobby and Mommy. I like this cocoa. It was cold outside. Now I am warm again. The cocoa makes me feel warm. Now I am warm again. What does Daddy say?	1 2 Now I am warm again.	1	4
Daddy says: The driveway is all clean. It is all clean. Now I can take the car out.			

LEVEL II: LESSON 2

CONCEPTS

surprise, a new car, waiting

VOCABULARY

bigger, smaller, surprise, different

FLANNEL-BOARD MATERIALS

paper figures: Bobby, Susan, Daddy
paper cutouts: blocks, telephone, window, car

ELICITED STRUCTURES		DSS VALUE
Primary emphasis		
indefinite pronoun	– *something, someone*	3
main verb	– *-s,* copular *am, are,* auxiliary *am, are*	2
secondary verb	– early-developing infinitive	2
Secondary emphasis		
personal pronoun	– *he, she*	2
	– *us, they*	3

DADDY BRINGS HOME A SURPRISE

NARRATIVE	TARGET RESPONSE	SENTENCE POINT	DSS TOTAL
This is Bobby. Who is this?	1 1 This is Bobby.	1	3
This is Susan. Susan is Bobby's sister. She is Bobby's sister. Who is Susan?	1 Susan is Bobby's sister.	1	2
Bobby is building. Bobby is building a tower. He is building with blocks. He is building a tower with blocks. What is he doing?	2 1 He is building a tower with blocks.	1	4
The tower is getting bigger. It is getting bigger. It is getting bigger and bigger. Is the tower getting smaller?	1 No, the tower is getting bigger.	1	2
Oh, oh! What's going to happen? What's going to happen to the tower?	1 The tower is going 2 to fall down.	1	4
Look! The tower is falling down. It is falling. It is falling down. What is happening?	1 The tower is falling down.	1	2

NARRATIVE	TARGET RESPONSE	SENTENCE POINT	DSS TOTAL
Bobby is laughing. He is laughing. What is he doing?	2 1 He is laughing.	1	4
Susan is laughing. She is laughing, too. Bobby and Susan are both laughing. They are both laughing. They are laughing. What are Bobby and Susan doing?	3 Bobby and Susan 2 are laughing.	1	6
Ring! Ring! Ring! It's the phone. The phone is ringing. It is ringing. What is happening?	1 The phone is ringing.	1	2
Bobby says: Someone is calling us. Someone is calling us up. Someone is calling us on the phone. What does Bobby say?	3 1 3 Someone is calling us on the phone.	1	8
Susan says: I'm going to answer. I'm going to answer the phone. I'm going to answer it. I'm going to answer the phone. What does Susan say?	1 2 2 I'm going to answer the phone.	1	6
Bobby says: Oh, no. It's my turn. It's my turn to answer the phone. It's my turn to answer it. It's my turn to answer the phone. What does Bobby say?	1 1 1 3 It's my turn to answer the phone.	1	7
Bobby picks up the phone. Bobby says: Hello. This is Bobby. What does Bobby say?	1 1 Hello, this is Bobby.	1	3
Bobby says: Who is calling? Who is this?			

NARRATIVE	TARGET RESPONSE	SENTENCE POINT	DSS TOTAL
Who is calling? What does Bobby say?	2 1 Who is calling?	1	4
Daddy says: Hello, Bobby. This is Daddy. This is Daddy calling. How are you? Bobby says: I am fine, Daddy. I am fine. What does Bobby say?	1 2 I am fine.	1	4
Bobby says: I am building a tower. It is a big tower. I am building a big tower. What does Bobby say?	1 2 I am building a big tower.	1	4
Daddy says: I am coming home. I will be home soon. I am coming home soon. What does Daddy say?	1 2 I am coming home soon.	1	4
Daddy says: I am going to bring something home. I'm going to bring home something special. I am going to bring something home. What does Daddy say?	1 2 2 I am going to bring 3 something home.	1	9
Daddy says: I'm going to bring a surprise home. I am going to bring home a big surprise. I'm going to bring a surprise home. What is Daddy going to do?	1 2 Daddy is going to bring a surprise home.	1	4
What is it going to be? What is the big surprise? What could it be? Can you guess? Can you guess what it could be?	(Elicit guesses from the children.)		
Daddy says: I am going to bring something special home.			

NARRATIVE	TARGET RESPONSE	SENTENCE POINT	DSS TOTAL
I am going to bring something special for everyone. It's for everyone. I am going to bring something special for everyone. What does Daddy say?	1 2 2 3 I am going to bring something 7 special for everyone.	1	16
Daddy says: You wait and see. I will bring it home. I am going to bring it home. I am going to bring home a big surprise. What is he going to do?	2 1 2 He is going to bring home a big surprise.	1	6
Daddy says: Good-bye, Bobby. Now Bobby and Susan are waiting. They are waiting. They are waiting for Daddy. What is happening?	3 2 Bobby and Susan are waiting for Daddy.	1	6
Bobby and Susan are looking out the window. They are looking. They are looking out the window. What are they doing?	3 2 They are looking out the window.	1	6
Bobby says: I see someone. Someone is coming. I see someone coming. What does he say?	1 1 3 4 I see someone coming.	1	10
Susan says: Is it Daddy? Is it? Is it Daddy? What does Susan say?	1 11 Is it Daddy?	1	4
Bobby says: No, it is not Daddy. Oh! Oh! I see someone else coming. I see someone else. I see someone else coming. What does Bobby say?	1 1 3 4 I see someone else coming.	1	10

NARRATIVE	TARGET RESPONSE	SENTENCE POINT	DSS TOTAL
Susan says: Is it Daddy? Bobby says: It's not Daddy's car, but Daddy is driving it. Daddy is driving a different car. Daddy is driving a new car! He is driving a new car. What is Daddy doing?	1 Daddy is driving a new car.	1	2
Now Daddy is coming in. Daddy is coming into the house. He is coming into the house. What is he doing?	2 1 He is coming into the house.	1	4
Daddy says: Hi, Susan and Bobby! Did you see the surprise? Did you see it? Did you see the surprise? What does Daddy say?	6 1 6 Did you see the surprise?	1	14
What is the big surprise?	(Elicit responses.)		
Daddy has a different car. Daddy has a new car. Daddy is driving a new car. He has a new car. What does Daddy have?	2 Daddy has a new car.	1	3
The big surprise is Daddy's new car. Bobby and Susan are looking at the new car. They are looking at Daddy's new car. They are looking at the new car. What are they doing?	3 2 They are looking at the new car.	1	6
Susan says: It is pretty. Daddy's new car is pretty. The new car is pretty. What does Susan say?	1 The new car is pretty.	1	2
Bobby says: I like it. I like the new car. I like Daddy's new car. What does Bobby say?	1 1 I like Daddy's new car.	1	3

NARRATIVE	TARGET RESPONSE	SENTENCE POINT	DSS TOTAL
Daddy says: Let's do something. Let's do something special. Let's do something special. What does Daddy say?	1 2 3 Let's do something special.	1	7
Daddy says: Let's go for a ride. Let's take a ride. Let's go for a ride. What does Daddysay?	1 2 Let's go for a ride.	1	4
Daddy says: Who's going to go? Who's going to go with me? Who is going to go with me? What does Daddy say?	2 1 2 Who is going to go 1 with me?	1	7
Bobby says: I'm going to go. I'm going to. I'm going to go. What does he say?	1 2 2 I'm going to go.	1	6
Susan says: I'm going to go, too. Susan and Bobby are getting into the car. Daddy is getting into the car. Everyone is getting into the car. Everyone is getting into the car. What's happening?	7 1 Everyone is getting into the car.	1	9
What are they going to do? They are going to ride in Daddy's new car. Susan says: Daddy, this is a good surprise. Your new car is a good surprise.			

LEVEL II: LESSON 3

CONCEPTS

a freight train and its cars,
things a train carries,
a railroad crossing,
waiting for a train to pass

VOCABULARY

railroad, gate, flashing lights, blocking, engineer, freight train, boxcar, flatcar, caboose

FLANNEL-BOARD MATERIALS

paper figures: Daddy, Mommy, Timmy, engineer, flagman
paper cutouts: car, gates for railroad crossing, freight train with engine, flatcar, boxcar, caboose, flag

ELICITED STRUCTURES		DSS VALUE
Primary emphasis		
indefinite pronoun –	*something, someone, somebody, another*	3
personal pronoun –	*they, us*	3
main verb –	auxiliary *am, are,* copular *am, are*	2
Secondary emphasis		
main verb –	obligatory *do* + verb	4
secondary verb –	early-developing infinitive	2
wh-question –	*what, what kind, how many*	2

THE RAILROAD CROSSING

NARRATIVE	TARGET RESPONSE	SENTENCE POINT	DSS TOTAL
This is Mommy. Who is this?	1 1 This is Mommy.	1	3
This is Daddy. Who is this?	1 1 This is Daddy.	1	3
This is Timmy. Who is this?	1 1 This is Timmy.	1	3
Mommy, Daddy, and Timmy are riding in the car. They are riding. They are riding in the car. What are they doing?	3 2 They are riding in the car.	1	6
They are going home. Daddy says: Look over there! Look up ahead! Look over there on the road. I see something. I see something. What does Daddy say?	1 1 3 I see something.	1	6

NARRATIVE	TARGET RESPONSE	SENTENCE POINT	DSS TOTAL
Daddy says: I see bright red lights. The red lights are flashing. They are flashing. The red lights are flashing. What does Daddy say?	2 The red lights are flashing.	1	3
The lights are flashing on. The lights are flashing off. The lights are flashing on and off. Timmy says: Look! Something is blocking the road. Something is blocking it. Something is blocking the road. What does Timmy say?	3 1 Something is blocking the road.	1	5
There is a gate. The gate is coming down. There is a gate across the road. Timmy says: The bells are ringing. They are ringing. The bells are ringing. What are the bells doing?	2 The bells are ringing.	1	3
It is a railroad crossing. Timmy says: A train is going to come. A train will come. A train is going to come. What does Timmy say?	1 2 A train is going to come.	1	4
The lights are flashing. The gate is down. The bells are ringing. Daddy says: I am going to stop the car. I am going to stop. I am going to stop the car. What does Daddy say?	1 2 2 I am going to stop the car.	1	6

NARRATIVE	TARGET RESPONSE	SENTENCE POINT	DSS TOTAL
Daddy says: We are going to wait for the train. We are going to wait. We are going to wait for the train. What does Daddy say?	3 2 2 We are going to wait for the train.	1	8
Here it comes! Daddy says: Timmy, do you see the train? Do you see it? Do you see the train? What does Daddy say?	6 1 4 Do you see the train?	1	12
Timmy says: Yes, I do. I do see it. I do see the train. What does Timmy say?	1 4 I do see the train.	1	6
Timmy says: What kind of train is it? What kind? What kind of train is it? What does Timmy say?	2 111 What kind of train is it?	1	6
Daddy says: It is a freight train. It has lots of cars. The train is coming slowly. The train is coming very slowly. It is coming slowly. What does Daddy say?	1 1 It is coming slowly.	1	3
Timmy says: Look! I see the big engine. The engine is pulling the train. The engine is pulling it. The engine is pulling the train. What is the engine doing?	1 The engine is pulling the train.	1	2
See the wheels move! See the black smoke! Daddy says: I see someone. I see someone on the train.			

NARRATIVE	TARGET RESPONSE	SENTENCE POINT	DSS TOTAL
I see someone. What does Daddy say?	1 1 3 I see someone.	1	6
Daddy says: I see the engineer. An engineer is on the train. I see the engineer. What does Daddy say?	1 1 I see the engineer.	1	3
The engineer is driving the train. He is driving it. The engineer is driving the train. What is the engineer doing?	1 The engineer is driving the train.	1	2
The engineer is waving. The engineer is waving to us. He is waving to us. What is the engineer doing?	1 3 The engineer is waving to us.	1	5
Mommy says: See the boxcars. How many do you see? How many? How many do you see? What does Mommy say?	2 6 1 4 How many do you see?	1	14
Timmy says: I see two boxcars. What's inside the cars? I wonder what is inside. What could be inside? Can you guess?	(Elicit answers from the children.)		
Timmy says: Look! There is a flatcar. It is empty. There is nothing on it. There is nothing on the car. There is nothing on it. What does Timmy say?	1 4 1 There is nothing on it.	1	7
Timmy says: I see another flatcar. There is something on it. Something is on it. What does Timmy say?	3 1 1 Something is on it.	1	6
Timmy says: A tractor is on the flatcar. Look! I see another car.			

NARRATIVE	TARGET RESPONSE	SENTENCE POINT	DSS TOTAL
I see another one. I see another car. What does Timmy say?	1 1 3 I see another car.	1	6
Timmy says: It is the last car. It is on the end of the train. It is a funny car. Daddy says: That car has a funny name. It has a funny name. Timmy says: What is the name of the car? What is it? What is the name of the car? What does Timmy say?	2 1 1 What is the name of the car?	1	5
Do you know what the name is?	(Elicit answers from the children.)		
Daddy says: It is the caboose. It's called a caboose. It is the caboose. What does Daddy say?	1 1 It is the caboose.	1	3
Timmy says: Somebody is inside the caboose. Somebody is inside. Somebody is inside the caboose. What does Timmy say?	3 1 Somebody is inside the caboose.	1	5
Timmy says: A man is waving at us. He is waving. He is waving at us. What is he doing?	2 1 3 He is waving at us.	1	7
Daddy says: See the flag on the end of the caboose. That is the end of the train. The flag is waving. It is waving. The flag is waving. What is the flag doing?	1 The flag is waving.	1	2

NARRATIVE	TARGET RESPONSE	SENTENCE POINT	DSS TOTAL
Now the lights stop flashing.			
The gate goes up.			
Daddy starts the car, and they all drive home.	3 3 1	1	8
What do they do?	They all drive home.		

LEVEL II: LESSON 4

CONCEPTS

running out of food, going shopping

VOCABULARY

none, no one, nobody, nothing, storekeeper, some, counter, refrigerator, freezer

FLANNEL-BOARD MATERIALS

paper figures: Timmy, Mommy, storekeeper
paper cutouts: refrigerator with freezer, store front, store counter, milk carton, carrots, ice-cream carton

ELICITED STRUCTURES		DSS VALUE
Primary emphasis		
indefinite pronoun –	*nothing, nobody, none, no one*	4
Secondary emphasis		
indefinite pronoun –	*some*	3
personal pronoun –	*they*	3
main verb –	*-s, -ed,* copular *are,* auxiliary *are*	2

MOMMY NEEDS TO GO SHOPPING

NARRATIVE	TARGET RESPONSE	SENTENCE POINT	DSS TOTAL
This is Mommy. Who is this?	1 1 This is Mommy.	1	3
This is Timmy. Who is this?	1 1 This is Timmy.	1	3
Mommy is getting ready to make dinner. She is getting ready. She is getting ready to make dinner. What is Mommy doing?	2 1 She is getting ready 3 to make dinner.	1	7
Mommy says: I need some carrots for dinner. Timmy, look in the refrigerator. See if we have any carrots. Timmy is looking in the refrigerator. Timmy says: Mommy, nothing is here. There aren't any carrots here. There is nothing in here. What does Timmy say?	1 4 There is nothing in here.	1	6

NARRATIVE	TARGET RESPONSE	SENTENCE POINT	DSS TOTAL
Mommy is looking in the refrigerator. Mommy says: There are none left. We must have eaten all the carrots. There are none left. What does Mommy say?	2 4 There are none left.	1	7
Mommy says: We will have to go to the store. We will buy some carrots. Mommy says: Timmy, look in the refrigerator. See if we have any milk. Timmy says: Mommy, there is nothing in the refrigerator. There isn't any milk in the refrigerator. There is nothing in the refrigerator. What does Timmy say?	1 4 There is nothing in the refrigerator.	1	6
Mommy is looking in the refrigerator. Mommy says: There is none left. We must have used all the milk. There is none left. What does Mommy say?	1 4 There is none left.	1	6
Mommy says: We will have to go to the store. We will have to buy carrots and milk. What else do we need? What else do we need? What does Mommy say?	2 6 3 4 What else do we need?	1	16
Mommy says: Timmy, look in the freezer. See if we have any ice cream. Timmy is looking in the freezer. Timmy says: Mommy, there is			

NARRATIVE	TARGET RESPONSE	SENTENCE POINT	DSS TOTAL
nothing in the freezer. There isn't any ice cream in the freezer. There is nothing in the freezer. What does Timmy say?	1 4 There is nothing in the freezer.	1	6
Mommy is looking in the freezer. Mommy says: There is none left. We must have eaten all the ice cream. There is none left. What does Mommy say?	1 4 There is none left.	1	6
Mommy says: We will have to go to the store. We will have to buy carrots, milk, and ice cream. Timmy, do you want to go to the store? Do you want to go to the store with me? Do you want to go to the store? What does Mommy say?	6 1 4 2 Do you want to go to the store?	1	14
Timmy says: Yes, Mommy. I want to go. I want to go to the store. I want to go with you. I want to go to the store with you. What does Timmy say?	1 1 2 I want to go to the 1 store with you.	1	6
Mommy says: Okay, let's go. Timmy and Mommy are going to the store. Timmy and Mommy are walking. Timmy and Mommy are walking to the store. They are walking to the store. What are they doing?	3 2 They are walking to the store.	1	6

NARRATIVE	TARGET RESPONSE	SENTENCE POINT	DSS TOTAL
Here is the store. Mommy and Timmy are going inside. Mommy and Timmy are going into the store. They are going into the store. What are they doing?	3 2 They are going into the store.	1	6
Mommy is looking around. She is looking for the storekeeper. She does not see the storekeeper. Mommy says: No one is here. Where is the storekeeper? No one is here. What does Mommy say?	4 1 No one is here.	1	6
Mommy says: Nobody is in the store. I don't see the storekeeper. Nobody is in the store. What does Mommy say?	4 1 Nobody is in the store.	1	6
Timmy says: Oh, oh! I see the storekeeper. He is behind the counter. The storekeeper is behind the counter. He is behind the counter. Where is the storekeeper?	1 The storekeeper is behind the counter.	1	2
Mommy says: Oh, Mr. Storekeeper, I did not see you. I didn't see you before. I did not see you before. What does Mommy say?	1 7 6 1 I did not see you before.	1	16
Mommy says: I need some carrots. I need some milk. I need some ice cream. I need some carrots, some milk, and some			

NARRATIVE	TARGET RESPONSE	SENTENCE POINT	DSS TOTAL
ice cream. What does Mommy need?	2 3 Mommy needs some carrots, 3 3 3 some milk, and some ice cream.	1	15
The storekeeper is giving Mommy the carrots, the milk, and the ice cream. Mommy is paying the storekeeper. Mommy is paying the storekeeper for the food. She is paying the storekeeper for the food. What is Mommy doing?	1 Mommy is paying the storekeeper for the food.	1	2
Now Mommy and Timmy are going home. Mommy says: Now we can make dinner. Now we can have everything we need for dinner.			

LEVEL II: LESSON 5

CONCEPTS

putting out a fire, smoke, burning, big/little

VOCABULARY

smell, smoke, burning, target, empty

FLANNEL-BOARD MATERIALS

paper figures: Mommy, Bobby, two firemen
paper cutouts: two houses, fence, target, bow and arrow, fire truck with hose

ELICITED STRUCTURES		DSS VALUE
Primary emphasis		
personal pronoun	– *he, him, his*	2
main verb	– *-s, -ed,* auxiliary *are,* copular *was*	2
secondary verb	– present participle	4
Secondary emphasis		
main verb	– *can, will* + verb	4

THE FIRE NEXT DOOR

NARRATIVE	TARGET RESPONSE	SENTENCE POINT	DSS TOTAL
This is Bobby. This is Bobby's house. This is his house. Whose house is this?	1 1 This is Bobby's house.	1	3
Bobby is playing in the yard. He is playing alone. He doesn't have anyone to play with. Is he playing alone?	2 1 Yes, he is playing alone.	1	4
Bobby is all alone. He is playing by himself. He is playing all by himself. Is he playing by himself?	2 1 Yes, he is playing by 5 himself.	1	9
Bobby is playing with his bow and arrow. He has a target. The target is on the fence. He is shooting his arrows at the target. Where is he shooting his arrows?	2 1 2 He is shooting his arrows at the target.	1	6

NARRATIVE	TARGET RESPONSE	SENTENCE POINT	DSS TOTAL
Now Bobby is tired. He is tired. He is sitting down to rest. Why is Bobby sitting down?	1 Bobby is sitting down 6 2 1 because he is tired.	1	11
Oh! Oh! Something is happening. Bobby smells something. He smells something burning. Bobby smells something burning. What does he smell?	2 2 3 He smells something 4 burning.	1	12
Bobby sees something, too. He sees smoke. He smells and sees the smoke. What does he see?	2 2 He sees the smoke.	1	5
The smoke is coming from the house next door. It is coming from the house next door. It is coming from the house next door. Where is the smoke coming from?	1 The smoke is coming from the house next door.	1	2
Smoke is coming out of the basement window. The basement is on fire. The fire is in the basement. Where is the fire?	1 The fire is in the basement.	1	2
The basement is on fire. The house next door is burning. Bobby sees the house burning.			

NARRATIVE	TARGET RESPONSE	SENTENCE POINT	DSS TOTAL
He sees the house burning. What does he see?	2 2 4 He sees the house burning.	1	9
Bobby says: I can see the house next door burning. I can see the house burning. I must get help. I can see the house burning. What does Bobby say?	1 4 I can see the house 4 burning.	1	10
Bobby runs home. He runs into his house. Bobby says: Mommy, Mommy, I can see the house next door burning! I can see the house burning. What does Bobby say?	1 4 I can see the house 4 burning.	1	10
Bobby says: Nobody is home. The house is empty. The house next door is empty. Is anybody in the house next door?	4 1 No, nobody is in the house.	1	6
Mommy says: We must call the firemen. The firemen will put out the fire. They will put out the fire. Who will put out the fire?	4 The firemen will put out the fire.	1	5
Here comes the fire engine. The fire engine is red. What color is the fire engine?	1 The fire engine is red.	1	2

NARRATIVE	TARGET RESPONSE	SENTENCE POINT	DSS TOTAL
Bobby sees the fire engine. He sees the fire engine stopping. He sees the fire engine stopping in front of the house next door. What does he see?	2 2 He sees the fire engine 4 stopping in front of the house next door.	1	9
The firemen are getting out. They are pulling a big hose. Bobby sees the firemen pulling out the big hose. He sees them pulling out the big hose. What does he see?	2 2 3 4 He sees them pulling out the big hose.	1	12
The firemen will use the hose to put out the fire. They will use the hose to put out the fire. They are pulling out the big hose. What are they doing?	3 2 They are pulling out the big hose.	1	6
The firemen will use the hose to put out the fire. They will use the hose to put out the fire. Why are they pulling out the hose?	3 2 They are pulling out 3 the hose to put out the fire.	1	9
Water is coming through the hose. The firemen are spraying water into the basement. The water will put out the fire. What will the water do?	4 The water will put out the fire.	1	5

NARRATIVE	TARGET RESPONSE	SENTENCE POINT	DSS TOTAL
Now the fire is out. The firemen put out the fire. It was not a big fire. It was just a little fire. Was it a big fire?	1 2 No, it was a little fire.	1	4
The fire was easy to put out. It was easy to put out because it was little. Why was it easy to put out?	1 2 3 It was easy to put out 6 1 2 because it was little.	1	16
The fireman says: Bobby, you are a good boy. You helped us. You helped us put out the fire. You called us just in time. How did Bobby help?	2 2 He called the firemen just in time.	1	5

LEVEL II: LESSON 6

CONCEPTS

going to a parade

VOCABULARY

band, horn, float, baton, twirling

FLANNEL-BOARD MATERIALS

paper figures: Mommy, Bobby
paper parade figures: man playing a horn, man on horseback, clown carrying balloons, float portraying Snoopy

ELICITED STRUCTURES		DSS VALUE
Primary emphasis		
personal pronoun	– *he, his, him*	2
	– *we, they*	3
main verb	– *-s,* copular *am, are,* auxiliary *am, are*	2
	– *can, will* + verb	4
secondary verb	– present participle	4
Secondary emphasis		
indefinite pronoun	– *some, three*	3
conjunction	– *and*	3

GOING TO A PARADE

NARRATIVE	TARGET RESPONSE	SENTENCE POINT	DSS TOTAL
This is Bobby. Who is this?	1 1 This is Bobby.	1	3
This is Bobby's mommy. Who is this?	1 1 This is Bobby's mommy.	1	3
Today is a special day. Today Mommy and Bobby are going to do something special. They are going to watch a parade. Mommy and Bobby are going to watch a parade. What are they going to do?	3 2 2 They are going to watch a parade.	1	8
Mommy and Bobby are waiting. They are waiting for the parade. They are waiting for the parade to start. What are they doing?	3 2 They are waiting for the 3 parade to start.	1	9

Bobby says:
What will we see, Mommy?

NARRATIVE	TARGET RESPONSE	SENTENCE POINT	DSS TOTAL
What will we see? What will we see in the parade? What does Bobby say?	2 6 3 4 What will we see in the parade?	1	16
What will they see in the parade? Can you guess?	(Elicit responses from the children.)		
Mommy says: We will see men marching in the parade. We will see a band. We will see a band marching. What will they see?	3 4 They will see a band 4 marching.	1	12
Mommy says: We will see a man riding a horse. We will see a man riding. We will see a man riding a horse. What will they see?	3 4 They will see a man 4 riding a horse.	1	12
Mommy says: We will see a funny clown. We will see one. We will see a funny clown. What does Mommy say?	3 4 We will see a funny clown.	1	8
Bobby says: Listen! I hear something! I hear something! The parade is coming. The band is coming. The parade is coming. What does Bobby say?	1 The parade is coming.	1	2
Bobby says: The band is coming. The band is playing music. It is playing music. What is the band doing?	1 The band is playing music.	1	2
Bobby says: Look, I see a man playing a horn.			

NARRATIVE	TARGET RESPONSE	SENTENCE POINT	DSS TOTAL
I see a man playing a horn. What does Bobby say?	1 1 4 I see a man playing a horn.	1	7
Bobby says: I see another man. He is beating a drum. I see a man beating a drum. What does Bobby say?	1 1 4 I see a man beating a drum.	1	7
Bobby says: I see a girl with a baton. She is twirling the baton. I see a girl twirling a baton. What does Bobby say?	1 1 4 I see a girl twirling a baton.	1	7
Bobby says: I like the band, Mommy. I like the music, too. I like the band and the music. What does Bobby say?	1 1 3 I like the band and the music.	1	6
Mommy says: Look, Bobby! Here comes a man and a horse. The man is riding a horse. Here comes a man riding a horse. What does Mommy say?	2 4 Here comes a man riding a horse.	1	7
Mommy says: The man is waving to all the people. He is waving to everybody. What is he doing?	2 1 7 He is waving to everybody.	1	11
Bobby says: The man is waving to me, Mommy. I can see him waving at me. What does Bobby say?	1 4 2 4 I can see him waving 1 at me.	1	13

NARRATIVE	TARGET RESPONSE	SENTENCE POINT	DSS TOTAL
Mommy says: Look, Bobby! Here come some men. They are carrying flags. The men are carrying flags. What are they doing?	3 2 They are carrying flags.	1	6
Mommy says: I see three men. I see three flags. There are three men and three flags. How many men are there?	2 3 There are three men.	1	6
How many flags are there?	2 3 There are three flags.	1	6
Bobby says: The flags are red and green. They are red and green. What color are the flags?	2 3 The flags are red and green.	1	6
Bobby says: Look, Mommy! Look at what's coming next. What is it? Mommy says: It is a float. A car is pulling a float. A float is coming. What is coming?	1 A float is coming.	1	2
Bobby says: Snoopy is on the float. The float looks like Snoopy. It looks like Snoopy. What does the float look like?	2 8 The float looks like Snoopy.	1	11
Mommy says: Snoopy is turning his head. He is looking at everybody. He is turning his head and looking at everybody. What is he doing?	2 1 2 He is turning his head 3 1 7 and looking at everybody.	1	17

NARRATIVE	TARGET RESPONSE	SENTENCE POINT	DSS TOTAL
Bobby says: Snoopy is wagging his tail. He is wagging his tail. What is he doing?	2 1 2 He is wagging his tail.	1	6
Bobby is happy. He is jumping up and down. Bobby says: Snoopy is wagging his tail. I can see Snoopy wagging his tail. What does Bobby say?	1 4 I can see Snoopy 4 2 wagging his tail.	1	12
Mommy says: Look, Bobby! Here comes a funny clown. The clown has big ears and red hair. He has a big red nose. Here comes the clown. What does Mommy say?	2 Here comes the clown.	1	3
The clown is carrying some balloons. He is carrying some balloons. What is he doing?	2 1 3 He is carrying some balloons.	1	7
Oh! Oh! The clown is coming. The clown is coming toward Bobby. The clown is coming up to Bobby. Is Bobby afraid? Do you think Bobby is afraid? Would you be afraid of the clown?	(Elicit responses from the children.)		
The clown says: Hello, little boy. Do you like the parade? Are you having fun? What does the clown say?	4 1 2 Are you having fun?	1	8
Bobby says: Oh, yes! I like the parade.			

NARRATIVE	TARGET RESPONSE	SENTENCE POINT	DSS TOTAL
I am having fun. What does Bobby say?	1 2 I am having fun.	1	4
Now the clown is giving something to Bobby. The clown is giving a balloon to Bobby. What is the clown doing?	2 1 He is giving a balloon to Bobby.	1	4
Bobby says: I had a good time, Mommy. It was a good parade!			

LEVEL II: LESSON 7

CONCEPTS

a loose tooth, losing a tooth, finding, exchanging a tooth for money, time concepts

VOCABULARY

loose, wiggly, wiggling, isn't, soon, bedtime, dinnertime, morning

FLANNEL-BOARD MATERIALS

paper figures: Timmy, Daddy
paper cutouts: mirror, table, plate, two chairs, bed with pillow, penny, tooth

ELICITED STRUCTURES		DSS VALUE
Primary emphasis		
personal pronoun	– *he, him, his*	2
negative	– *isn't*	5
Secondary emphasis		
indefinite pronoun	– *six, seven, something*	3
main verb	– irregular past, auxiliary *are*	2
	– *can, will, do* + verb	4
secondary verb	– early-developing infinitive	2

TIMMY LOSES A TOOTH

NARRATIVE	TARGET RESPONSE	SENTENCE POINT	DSS TOTAL
This is Timmy. Timmy is a boy. Timmy is the boy in our story. Who is the boy in our story?	1 Timmy is the boy 3 in our story.	1	5
Timmy is six years old. He is six years old. He is six. How old is Timmy?	1 3 Timmy is six (years old).	1	5
Is he seven?	2 1 5 3 No, he isn't seven.	1	12
This is Daddy. This is Timmy's daddy. Who is this?	1 1 This is Daddy.	1	3
Timmy says: Look! Look, Daddy. Look in my mouth. What does Timmy say?	1 1 Look in my mouth.	1	3
Daddy is looking in Timmy's mouth.			

NARRATIVE	TARGET RESPONSE	SENTENCE POINT	DSS TOTAL
He is looking in Timmy's mouth. Where is Daddy looking?	2 1 He is looking in Timmy's mouth.	1	4
Timmy says: Look at my tooth. My tooth is loose. My tooth is wiggly. It is wiggly. My tooth is wiggly. What does Timmy say?	1 1 My tooth is wiggly.	1	3
Daddy says: Where? Where is the tooth? Where is it? Where is the loose tooth? What does Daddy say?	2 1 1 Where is the (loose) tooth?	1	5
Timmy says: Here. My tooth is on the bottom. It is on the bottom. My loose tooth is on the bottom. Where is the loose tooth?	1 The (loose) tooth is on the bottom.	1	2
Daddy is looking on the bottom. He is looking on the bottom. He is looking for the loose tooth. He is looking on the bottom. What is Daddy doing?	1 Daddy is looking on the bottom.	1	2
Daddy says: Which tooth? Which tooth is wiggly? Is it this tooth? Daddy is touching Timmy's tooth. Timmy says: No. It isn't that tooth. It isn't that one. It isn't that tooth. What does Timmy say?	1 1 5 1 It isn't that tooth.	1	9
Daddy says: Is it this tooth? Is it this one?			

NARRATIVE	TARGET RESPONSE	SENTENCE POINT	DSS TOTAL
Timmy says: Yes. That is the tooth. That is the loose tooth. That is the tooth. What does Timmy say?	1 1 That is the tooth.	1	3
Daddy says: I see the tooth. I see it. I see the loose tooth. What does Daddy say?	1 1 I see the loose tooth.	1	3
Daddy is wiggling the tooth. He is wiggling the tooth. He is wiggling the loose tooth. What is Daddy doing?	1 Daddy is wiggling the (loose) tooth.	1	2
He is wiggling Timmy's tooth. Is he wiggling the tooth?	2 1 Yes, he is wiggling the tooth.	1	4
Timmy says: When is the tooth going to come out? When is it gonna come out? When is my tooth going to come out? What does Timmy say?	5 4 1 1 When is my tooth going 2 to come out?	1	14
Daddy says: Soon. Not now. It will come out soon. When will Timmy's tooth come out?	1 4 It will come out soon.	1	6
Daddy says: This tooth is very loose. This tooth is gonna come out soon. It will come out soon. Will it come out soon?	1 4 Yes, it will come out soon.	1	6
Daddy says: It is dinnertime. It is time to eat dinner. It is time to eat. It is dinnertime. What time is it?	1 1 It is dinnertime.	1	3

NARRATIVE	TARGET RESPONSE	SENTENCE POINT	DSS TOTAL
Timmy is eating meat. Daddy is eating meat, too. Daddy says: Oh, oh! I see a hole. I see a hole in Timmy's mouth. I see a hole. What does Daddy say?	1 1 I see a hole.	1	3
Daddy says: The tooth isn't there. The tooth is gone. It isn't there. Your tooth isn't there. What does Daddy say?	1 15 Your tooth isn't there.	1	8
Timmy says: Where is the tooth? Where is it? Where is my tooth? What does Timmy say?	5 11 1 Where is my tooth?	1	9
Daddy says: There is a hole. The tooth isn't there. The tooth fell out. It isn't there. What does Daddy say?	1 15 It isn't there.	1	8
Timmy says: I want to see. I want to see the hole. I want to see where the tooth fell out. I want to see the hole. What does Timmy say?	1 1 2 I want to see the hole.	1	5
Timmy is going to look in the mirror. He is going to look in the mirror. Timmy is going to look in the mirror. What is Timmy going to do?	1 2 Timmy is going to look (in the mirror).	1	4
Timmy says: I see the hole. It is on the bottom. The hole is on the bottom. Where is the hole?	1 The hole is on the bottom.	1	2
Timmy says: My tooth fell out. My loose tooth fell out.			

NARRATIVE	TARGET RESPONSE	SENTENCE POINT	DSS TOTAL
It isn't there. My tooth isn't there. What does Timmy say?	1 1 5 My tooth isn't there.	1	8
Timmy and Daddy are going back to the kitchen. They are going back to look for the tooth. They are going to look for the tooth. Timmy is looking. Timmy is looking for his tooth. He is looking for his tooth. What is Timmy doing?	1 Timmy is looking for 2 his tooth.	1	4
Is he looking for his tooth?	2 1 Yes, he is looking for 2 his tooth.	1	6
Daddy is looking, too. Timmy and Daddy are looking. Timmy and Daddy are both looking. They are both looking for the tooth. What are they doing?	3 7 2 They are both looking for the tooth.	1	13
Daddy is looking on the floor. Daddy says: The tooth isn't on the floor. It isn't on the floor. What does Daddy say?	1 5 The tooth isn't on the floor.	1	7
Timmy says: I found my tooth. I found it. What does Timmy say?	1 2 1 I found my tooth.	1	5
Timmy says: Here is my tooth. Here it is. What does Timmy say?	1 1 Here it is.	1	3
Daddy says: Where? Where is it? Where is your tooth? What does Daddy say?	2 1 1 1 Where is your tooth?	1	6

NARRATIVE	TARGET RESPONSE	SENTENCE POINT	DSS TOTAL
Timmy says: My tooth is on my plate. It is on my plate. Where is Timmy's tooth?	1 1 2 It is on his plate.	1	5
Now it is bedtime. It is time to go to bed. It is bedtime. What time is it?	1 1 It is bedtime.	1	3
Timmy is in bed. He is in bed. Where is Timmy?	1 Timmy is in bed.	1	2
Timmy is not asleep. Timmy isn't asleep. He isn't asleep. Is he asleep?	2 1 5 No, he isn't asleep.	1	9
Timmy is putting his tooth under the pillow. Timmy is putting his tooth under his pillow. He is putting his tooth under his pillow. What is Timmy putting under his pillow?	1 2 Timmy is putting his 2 tooth under his pillow.	1	6
Where is Timmy putting his tooth?	1 2 Timmy is putting his tooth 2 under his pillow.	1	6
Now Timmy is asleep. He is asleep. He is sleeping. Is Timmy asleep?	1 Yes, Timmy is asleep.	1	2
Now it is morning. It is morning, and Timmy is awake. Timmy isn't asleep. He is awake. Is Timmy asleep?	1 5 No, Timmy isn't asleep.	1	7
Timmy is awake. Timmy is looking. Timmy is looking for his tooth. He is looking for his tooth. What is he doing?	2 1 2 He is looking for his tooth.	1	6
Timmy is looking for his tooth.			

NARRATIVE	TARGET RESPONSE	SENTENCE POINT	DSS TOTAL
He is looking under his pillow. Timmy is looking for his tooth under his pillow. He is looking for his tooth under his pillow. What is he doing?	2 1 2 He is looking for his 2 tooth under his pillow.	1	8
Where is he looking?	2 1 2 He is looking under his pillow.	1	6
Timmy can't find the tooth. Timmy can't find it. He can't find the tooth. Can he find the tooth?	2 4 4 No, he can't find the tooth.	1	11
The tooth is not under his pillow. The tooth isn't under his pillow. It isn't there. Is the tooth under his pillow?	1 5 No, the tooth isn't under 2 his pillow.	1	9
Timmy says: Look. I see something. I see something. What does Timmy say?	1 1 3 I see something.	1	6
Timmy says: Something is under my pillow. It isn't my tooth. My tooth isn't there. What does he say?	1 1 5 My tooth isn't there.	1	8
Timmy says: My tooth isn't there. I see something else. It is a penny. A penny is under my pillow. I see a penny. What is under Timmy's pillow?	1 A penny is under Timmy's pillow.	1	2
Timmy says: Daddy, look. I found something.			

NARRATIVE	TARGET RESPONSE	SENTENCE POINT	DSS TOTAL
I found a penny. I found a penny under my pillow. I found a penny. What does Timmy say?	1 2 I found a penny.	1	4
Timmy is happy. Timmy is happy because he found a penny. He is happy because he found a penny. Why is Timmy happy?	1 6 Timmy is happy because 2 2 he found a penny.	1	12
Is he happy?	2 1 Yes, he is happy.	1	4

LEVEL II: LESSON 8

CONCEPTS

surprise, birthday, wagon, putting things together

VOCABULARY

wagon, wheels, handle, tools, hammer, screwdriver

FLANNEL-BOARD MATERIALS

paper figures: Daddy, Timmy
paper cutouts: bed, table, package, wagon with separate handle and wheels

ELICITED STRUCTURES		DSS VALUE
Primary emphasis		
personal pronoun –	*he, him, his*	2
secondary verb –	early-developing infinitive	2
negative –	*isn't, won't*	3

A BIRTHDAY SURPRISE

NARRATIVE	TARGET RESPONSE	SENTENCE POINT	DSS TOTAL
This is Timmy. He is the boy in our story. Who is this?	1 1 This is Timmy.	1	3
Timmy is sleeping. He isn't awake. He is sleeping. Is Timmy awake?	1 5 No, Timmy isn't awake.	1	7
He is sleeping. What is he doing?	2 1 He is sleeping.	1	4
It is morning. It is time to get up. It isn't time for sleeping. It is time to get up. Is it time for sleeping?	1 1 5 No, it isn't time for 8 sleeping.	1	16
This is Timmy's daddy. This is his daddy. Who is this?	1 1 This is Timmy's daddy.	1	3
Daddy is going to wake Timmy up. He is going to wake up Timmy. He is going to wake him up. What is he going to do?	2 1 2 2 He is going to wake him up.	1	8

NARRATIVE	TARGET RESPONSE	SENTENCE POINT	DSS TOTAL
Daddy says: Wake up, Timmy. Won't you get up? Won't you? Won't you get up? What does Daddy say?	5 6 1 4 Won't you get up?	1	17
Daddy says: Today is a special day. Today is special. Today is your birthday. Today is special. Today's is Timmy's birthday. Today is his birthday. What is today?	1 2 Today is his birthday.	1	4
Mommy and Daddy have a surprise for Timmy. They have a birthday present for Timmy. Daddy says: We have a surprise for you. We have one. We have a surprise for you. What does Daddy say?	3 1 We have a surprise 1 for you.	1	6
Timmy is happy. He is very happy. It is his birthday. He is happy because it is his birthday. Why is Timmy happy?	2 1 6 He is happy because 1 1 2 it is his birthday.	1	14
Timmy is getting dressed. He is hurrying. Timmy says: I want to go downstairs. I want to find my birthday present. I want to go downstairs and find my birthday present. What does Timmy say?	1 1 2 I want to go downstairs 3 2 1 and find my birthday present.	1	11

NARRATIVE	TARGET RESPONSE	SENTENCE POINT	DSS TOTAL
Timmy is running down the stairs. Where is his birthday present? Oh! There it is! It is on the table. The birthday present is on the table. Where is it?	1 1 It is on the table.	1	3
Timmy says: What is my present? What could it be? Is it a bicycle? Daddy says: No, it isn't a bicycle. It isn't a bike. It isn't a bicycle. What does Daddy say?	1 1 5 It isn't a bicycle.	1	8
What could it be? Can you guess?	(Elicit responses from the children.)		
Timmy says: I want to open my present. I want to see my surprise. I want to open my present. What does Timmy say?	1 1 2 1 I want to open my present.	1	6
Timmy is going to open his present. He is going to see what's inside the package. He is going to see what's inside. What is he going to do?	2 1 2 6 1 He is going to see what's inside.	1	13
Look! It is a wagon. It is a red wagon. But where are the wheels? Where is the handle? Daddy says: The wheels are in the box. The handle is in the box. They are all in the box. Where are the wheels?	2 The wheels are in the box.	1	3
Where is the handle?	1 The handle is in the box.	1	2

NARRATIVE	TARGET RESPONSE	SENTENCE POINT	DSS TOTAL
Daddy is going to put the wheels on the wagon. Daddy is going to put the handle on the wagon. He is going to put the wagon together. What is he going to do?	2 1 2 He is going to put the wagon together.	1	6
Daddy is getting his tools. He is getting his hammer. He is getting his screwdriver. He is getting his tools. What is he getting?	2 1 2 He is getting his tools.	1	6
Daddy is going to put the wagon together. He is going to put it together with his tools. He is going to put the wagon together with his tools. What is he going to do?	2 1 2 He is going to put the wagon together with 2 his tools.	1	8
Daddy is putting the wheels on the wagon. Now he is putting the handle on the wagon. He is putting the wheels and the handle on the wagon. What is he doing?	2 1 He is putting the wheels 3 and the handle on the the wagon.	1	7
Now the wagon is all put together. Daddy is giving Timmy a ride. He is pulling the wagon. He is giving Timmy a ride. What is he doing?	2 1 He is giving Timmy a ride.	1	4
Daddy says: Isn't this fun on your birthday? Isn't it? Isn't this fun on your birthday? What does Daddy say?	1 5 1 1 1 Isn't this fun on your birthday?	1	10

LEVEL II: LESSON 9

CONCEPTS

getting lost, going to a grocery store, obeying

VOCABULARY

food, grocery store, lost, cart, waiting, here, there

FLANNEL-BOARD MATERIALS

paper figures: Timmy, Mommy
paper cutouts: two coats, two boots, car, store front, grocery cart, clown

ELICITED STRUCTURES		DSS VALUE
Primary emphasis		
personal pronoun	– *he, his, she*	2
main verb	– copular *am, are,* auxiliary *am, are,* irregular past, *-s, -ed*	2
	– *can, will,* + verb, obligatory *do* + verb	4
negative	– *isn't, won't*	5
Secondary emphasis		
indefinite pronoun	– *some*	3
personal pronoun	– *we, they*	3
negative	– *can't, don't*	4
main verb	– passive	7
secondary verb	– early-developing infinitive	2
conjunction	– *and*	3

TIMMY GETS LOST

NARRATIVE	TARGET RESPONSE	SENTENCE POINT	DSS TOTAL
This is Timmy. Who is this?	1 1 This is Timmy.	1	3
This is Timmy's mommy. She is Timmy's mommy. She is his mommy. This is Timmy's mommy. Who is this?	1 1 This is Timmy's mommy.	1	3
Mommy says: We are going somewhere. Put on your coat. Put on your boots. Put on your coat and boots. Timmy is putting on his coat. He is putting on his boots. He is putting on his coat and boots. What is he doing?	2 1 2 He is putting on his 3 2 coat and his boots.	1	11

NARRATIVE	TARGET RESPONSE	SENTENCE POINT	DSS TOTAL
Mommy says: We are going to get into the car. We are going to go to the store. I want to buy some food. I want to go to the store. I want to buy some food. What does Mommy say?	1 1 2 3 I want to buy some food.	1	8
Mommy says: Timmy, get into the car. We are going to go to the store. We are going to the grocery store. We are going to go to the grocery store. What does Mommy say?	3 2 2 We are going to go to the grocery store.	1	8
Timmy and Mommy are driving to the store. They are driving in the car. They are driving to the store in the car. They are driving to the store. What are they doing?	3 2 They are driving to the store.	1	6
Now Timmy and Mommy are at the store. Timmy is going into the store. Mommy is going into the store. Timmy and Mommy are going into the store. They are going into the store. Where are they going?	3 2 They are going into the store.	1	6
Mommy says: Be careful, Timmy. Stay with me in the store. Don't get lost. Don't get lost. What does Mommy say?	4 7 Don't get lost.	1	12

NARRATIVE	TARGET RESPONSE	SENTENCE POINT	DSS TOTAL
Timmy says: I won't, Mommy. I won't get lost. I won't get lost. What does Timmy say?	1 5 7 I won't get lost.	1	14
Now Mommy is pushing a cart. Mommy is pushing a big cart. She is pushing a big cart. What is she doing?	2 1 She is pushing a big cart.	1	4
Mommy is putting bread into the cart. Mommy is putting meat into the cart. Mommy is putting bread and meat into the cart. She is putting bread and meat into the cart. What is she doing?	2 1 3 She is putting bread and meat into the cart.	1	7
Mommy says: Remember, Timmy, don't go away. Don't go away from me. Don't get lost. Don't get lost. What does Mommy say?	4 7 Don't get lost.	1	12
Timmy says: I won't go away. I won't get lost. I won't go away. What does Timmy say?	1 5 4 I won't go away.	1	11
Now Mommy is putting milk into the cart. Mommy is putting ice cream into the cart. Mommy is putting milk and ice cream into the cart. She is putting milk and ice cream into the cart. What is Mommy doing?	2 1 3 She is putting milk and ice cream into the cart.	1	7
Mommy says: There are some apples. I see some apples. I see some apples over there.			

NARRATIVE	TARGET RESPONSE	SENTENCE POINT	DSS TOTAL
There are some apples over there. What does Mommy say?	2 3 There are some apples over there.	1	6
Mommy says: I'm going to get some apples. I want to get some apples. I'm going to get some apples. What does Mommy say?	1 2 2 3 I'm going to get some apples.	1	9
Mommy says: I'm going to get some apples. Timmy, you wait here. Don't go away. Wait by the cart. Don't go away. What does Mommy say?	4 4 Don't go away.	1	9
Timmy says: I won't go away. I won't get lost. I won't go away. What does Timmy say?	1 5 4 I won't go away.	1	11
Timmy is waiting by the cart. Timmy is waiting and waiting. Timmy is waiting for a long time. He is waiting for a long time. What is he doing?	2 1 He is waiting for a long time.	1	4
Timmy can't see Mommy. Timmy is tired of waiting. Timmy sees a big picture over there. Timmy sees a big picture of a clown. Timmy sees a picture of a funny clown. He sees a picture of a funny clown. What does he see?	2 2 He sees a picture of a funny clown.	1	5
Timmy says: I'm going to look at the picture. Timmy is going to look at the picture.			

NARRATIVE	TARGET RESPONSE	SENTENCE POINT	DSS TOTAL
Timmy is going to look at the clown. Timmy is running. Timmy is running fast. Timmy is running over to the clown. He is running over to the clown. Timmy is going to see the clown. Where is Timmy going?	1 2 Timmy is going to see the clown.	1	4
Timmy is looking at the clown. The clown has a big nose. The clown has a big red nose. He has a big red nose. What does the clown have?	2 The clown has a big red nose.	1	3
The clown is funny. The clown is big. The clown is big and funny. What does Timmy think of the clown?	2 Timmy thinks the clown 1 3 is big and funny.	1	7
Mommy is over here. Mommy is looking at the apples. Mommy is over here looking at the apples. She is over here looking at the apples. Where is Mommy?	1 Mommy is over here 4 looking at the apples.	1	6
Mommy is putting some apples into a bag. Mommy is coming back to the cart. Mommy is putting the apples into the cart. She is putting the apples into the cart. What is she doing?	2 1 She is putting the apples into the cart.	1	4
Mommy says: Oh, where is Timmy? Timmy isn't here. He isn't near the cart. Timmy isn't here. What does Mommy say?	1 5 Timmy isn't here.	1	7

NARRATIVE	TARGET RESPONSE	SENTENCE POINT	DSS TOTAL
Timmy is over there. He is over there. Where is Timmy?	1 Timmy is over there.	1	2
Timmy says: Oh, oh! Where is Mommy? Mommy isn't here. She isn't here. Mommy isn't here. What does Timmy say?	1 5 Mommy isn't here.	1	7
Timmy says: Mommy isn't here. I can't find Mommy. I am lost. I am lost. What does Timmy say?	1 2 I am lost.	1	4
Timmy is starting to cry. He is starting to cry. Timmy is starting to cry. What is Timmy doing?	1 5 Timmy is starting to cry.	1	7
Timmy says: I can't find my mommy. I can't find her. I am lost. I can't find my mommy. What does Timmy say?	1 4 4 1 I can't find my mommy.	1	11
Timmy says: Where is Mommy? Mommy is looking for Timmy. She is looking for Timmy. Mommy is looking for Timmy. What is Mommy doing?	1 Mommy is looking for Timmy.	1	2
Timmy is crying. Timmy calls: Mommy, Mommy. Where are you? Where are you? What does Timmy say?	2 2 1 1 Where are you?	1	7
Oh! Oh! Timmy sees Mommy. Timmy is running. Timmy is running to Mommy. He is running to Mommy. What is he doing?	2 1 He is running to Mommy.	1	4

NARRATIVE	TARGET RESPONSE	SENTENCE POINT	DSS TOTAL
Timmy is crying.			
Timmy says:			
Mommy, I went away.			
I got lost.			
I wanted to see the clown.			
I went to see the clown.			
I got lost.			
I didn't stay by the cart.			
I got lost.	1 7	1	9
What does Timmy say?	I got lost.		
Timmy says:			
I went away from you.			
I won't go away again.			
I won't go away.			
I won't go away again.	1 5 4	1	11
What does Timmy say?	I won't go away again.		

LEVEL II: LESSON 10

CONCEPTS	ELICITED STRUCTURES	DSS VALUE
playing outside in the snow, how snow feels, wintertime activities	**Primary emphasis**	
	personal pronoun – *he, she, her, his*	2
	– *we, they, their*	3
VOCABULARY	main verb – *-s,* copular *are,* auxiliary *are*	2
soft, wet, cold, snow-bank, bubbles, snow-balls, sled, hurt	secondary verb – early-developing infinitive	2
FLANNEL-BOARD MATERIALS	– later infinitival complement	5
paper figures: Timmy, Susan	conjunction – *and*	3
paper cutouts: window, bubble-blowing pipe, paint brush, two coats, two hats, two pairs of boots, snowballs, sled, hill		
additional materials: cotton to represent snow at bottom of hill		

PLAYING IN THE SNOW

NARRATIVE	TARGET RESPONSE	SENTENCE POINT	DSS TOTAL
This is Timmy. Who is this?	1 1 This is Timmy.	1	3
This is Susan. Who is this?	1 1 This is Susan.	1	3
Susan is Timmy's friend. She is Timmy's friend. She is his friend. Who is she?	2 1 She is Timmy's friend.	1	4
Timmy is playing in the house. Timmy is blowing bubbles. He is blowing bubbles. Timmy is blowing bubbles. What is Timmy doing?	1 Timmy is blowing bubbles.	1	2
See the bubbles go up, up, up. The bubbles are going to break. They are going to break. What are the bubbles going to do?	2 The bubbles are going 2 to break.	1	5

NARRATIVE	TARGET RESPONSE	SENTENCE POINT	DSS TOTAL
Susan is playing in the house. She is playing in Timmy's house. She is painting. Susan is painting a picture. She is painting a picture. What is she doing?	2 1 She is painting a picture.	1	4
Susan says: Oh, look outside. It is snowing. It is snowing outside. What does Susan say?	1 1 It is snowing outside.	1	3
Timmy says: I see lots of white snow. Lots of snow is coming down. I see lots of white snow coming down. What does Timmy say?	1 1 3 I see lots of white snow 4 coming down.	1	10
Susan says: I want to go out and play. I want to play in the snow. I want to play in the snow. What does Susan say?	1 1 2 I want to play in the snow.	1	5
Susan says: The snow is cold. The snow is soft. It is soft and cold. The snow is soft and cold. What does Susan say?	1 3 The snow is soft and cold.	1	5
Susan says: I want to ride on my sled. I want to ride on it. I want to ride on my sled. What does Susan say?	1 1 2 1 I want to ride on my sled.	1	6
Timmy says: I want to play in the snow, too. I want to make snowballs. I want to make some.			

NARRATIVE	TARGET RESPONSE	SENTENCE POINT	DSS TOTAL
I want to make some snowballs. What does Timmy say?	1 1 2 3 I want to make some snowballs.	1	8
Timmy is putting on his hat. He is putting on his coat. He is putting on his hat and coat. What is he doing?	2 1 2 He is putting on his 3 hat and coat.	1	9
Susan is putting on her hat. She is putting on her coat. She is putting on her hat and coat. What is she doing?	2 1 2 She is putting on her 3 hat and coat.	1	9
Timmy is putting on his boots. Susan is putting on her boots. They are both putting on their boots. They are both putting on their boots. What are they doing?	3 7 2 They are both putting on 3 their boots.	1	16
Now Susan and Timmy are outside. Susan and Timmy are playing in the snow. They are playing in the snow. Where are Susan and Timmy?	3 2 Susan and Timmy are outside.	1	6
What are they doing?	3 2 They are playing in the snow.	1	6
Timmy is making a snowball. He is taking some snow in his hands. He is rolling the snow around in his hands. He is making a snowball. What is he doing?	2 1 He is making a snowball.	1	4
Timmy is throwing the snowball at Susan.			

NARRATIVE	TARGET RESPONSE	SENTENCE POINT	DSS TOTAL
Susan is trying to duck. She is trying to duck. What is she doing?	2 1 5 She is trying to duck.	1	9
Susan is ducking because she does not want the snowball to hit her. Oh! The snowball is hitting Susan. Timmy says: Oh, oh! The snowball hit you, Susan. Are you hurt? Are you? Are you hurt? What does Timmy say?	2 1 1 Are you hurt?	1	5
Susan says: No, I'm not hurt. The snowball is soft. I am not hurt. Is Susan hurt?	1 7 No, Susan is not hurt.	1	9
Susan says: I have to ride on my sled. I have to ride on my red sled. I have to ride on my sled. What does Susan say?	1 1 5 1 I have to ride on my sled.	1	9
Susan says: I'm going to ride down the hill. I'm going to ride down the hill on my sled. I'm going to ride down the hill on my sled. What is she going to do?	2 1 2 She is going to ride down the hill.	1	6
Susan and Timmy are climbing up the hill. Now they are on the top of the hill. Susan and Timmy are on the top. They are on the top of the hill. Where are they?	3 2 They are on the top of the hill.	1	6
Susan is getting on her sled. She is getting on it. She is getting on her sled. What is she doing?	2 1 2 She is getting on her sled.	1	6

NARRATIVE	TARGET RESPONSE	SENTENCE POINT	DSS TOTAL
Timmy is pushing the sled. Timmy is pushing it. He is pushing the sled. What is he doing?	2 1 He is pushing the sled.	1	4
Susan is going down the hill on her sled. Down, down, down the hill. She is going down the hill on her sled. What is she doing?	2 1 She is going down the 2 hill on her sled.	1	6
Oh, oh! The sled is going into a pile of snow. It is going into a big pile of snow. Susan is going into a snowbank. Susan is trying to stop the sled. Susan says: Timmy, I can't stop the sled. Susan is trying to stop the sled. She is trying to stop the sled. What is she doing?	2 1 5 She is trying to stop the sled.	1	9
Timmy is running down the hill. He is running after Susan. He is running down the hill after Susan. What is Timmy doing?	1 Timmy is running down the hill after Susan.	1	2
Timmy says: Where is Susan? I can't see Susan. I can't. I can't see Susan. What does Timmy say?	1 4 4 I can't see Susan.	1	10
Susan says: Here I am. Here I am. I am in the snowbank. I am covered with snow. I am in the snowbank. Where is Susan?	1 Susan is in the snowbank.	1	2

NARRATIVE	TARGET RESPONSE	SENTENCE POINT	DSS TOTAL
Timmy says: Are you hurt? Are you? Susan, are you hurt? What does Timmy say?	2 1 1 Are you hurt?	1	5
Susan says: No, I am not hurt. The snow feels soft. It feels cold. It feels wet. The snow feels soft and cold and wet. How does the snow feel?	2 3 The snow feels soft and 3 cold and wet.	1	9
Is Susan hurt?	1 5 No, Susan isn't hurt.	1	7
Why isn't she hurt?	2 1 5 6 She isn't hurt because 1 the snow is soft.	1	16
Susan says: I like to play in the snow. I like it. I like to play in the snow. What does Susan say?	1 1 5 I like to play in the snow.	1	8
Timmy says: I like to play in the snow, too. We both like to play in the snow. We both like it. We like to play in the snow. What does Timmy say?	3 1 5 We like to play in the snow.	1	10
Susan says: Oh, oh! I am getting cold. Timmy says: We ought to go in, now. We ought to. We ought to go in. What does Timmy say?	3 1 5 We ought to go in.	1	10

LEVEL II: LESSON 11

CONCEPTS

baking a cake, being careful, being together, mixing

VOCABULARY

mix, together, oven, surprise

FLANNEL-BOARD MATERIALS

paper figures: Mommy, Bobby, Aunt Sally
paper cutouts: bed, bowl, spoon, box of cake mix, two eggs, measuring cup, refrigerator, oven, cake

ELICITED STRUCTURES		DSS VALUE
Primary emphasis		
personal pronoun	– *he, she, him, his, her*	2
	– *they, we, them, their*	3
main verb	– *-s, ed,* copular *am, are,* auxiliary *am, are*	2
	– *can, will* + verb, obligatory *do* + verb	4
secondary verb	– later infinitival complement, infinitive with wh-word	5
Secondary emphasis		
interrogative	– reversal of modal, obligatory *do*	6

MAKING A CAKE

NARRATIVE	TARGET RESPONSE	SENTENCE POINT	DSS TOTAL
It is eight o'clock. It is eight o'clock in the morning. What time is it?	1 1 3 It is eight o'clock in the morning.	1	6
This is Bobby. Bobby is sleeping. He is sleeping in bed. What is he doing?	2 1 He is sleeping in bed.	1	4
This is Mommy. This is Bobby's mommy. This is his mommy. Who is this?	1 1 2 This is his mommy.	1	5
Mommy wants Bobby to get up. She wants Bobby to get up. She wants him to get up. What does she want?	2 2 2 5 She wants him to get up.	1	12
Mommy says: Wake up, Bobby. It is eight o'clock in the morning. It is time to get up. What does Mommy say?	1 1 3 It is time to get up.	1	6

NARRATIVE	TARGET RESPONSE	SENTENCE POINT	DSS TOTAL
Mommy says: I have a surprise for you. I have a surprise. I have a surprise for you. What does Mommy say?	1 1 1 I have a surprise for you.	1	4
Bobby says: What is the surprise? Mommy says: This is a special day. Someone is coming to see us. Aunt Sally is coming. Aunt Sally is coming to see us. Who is coming to see them?	1 Aunt Sally is coming 3 3 to see them.	1	8
Bobby says: Oh, goody. I like Aunt Sally. I'm glad she is coming to see us. I am happy. Why is Bobby happy?	1 6 Bobby is happy because 1 Aunt Sally is coming.	1	9
Bobby is getting up. He is going downstairs. He is going down to the kitchen. Where is Bobby going?	2 1 He is going to the kitchen.	1	4
Mommy is in the kitchen. Bobby is going into the kitchen, too. Now Bobby and Mommy are in the kitchen together. Is Mommy in the kitchen alone?	3 2 No, Mommy and Bobby are in the kitchen together.	1	6
Bobby says: When is Aunt Sally coming? Mommy says: She is coming after lunch. She is coming this afternoon. When is she coming?	2 1 1 She is coming this afternoon.	1	5

NARRATIVE	TARGET RESPONSE	SENTENCE POINT	DSS TOTAL
Bobby says: I can't wait! I can hardly wait. But what can I do now, Mommy? What can I do this morning? Will you play with me? Will you? Will you play with me? What does Bobby say?	6 1 4 1 Will you play with me?	1	13
Mommy says: I am too busy to play. I have to bake a cake. I have to bake a cake for Aunt Sally. Can Mommy play with Bobby?	2 2 5 No, she has to bake a cake.	1	10
Bobby says: Can I help? Mommy says: Yes, you can. Bobby says: Can I help you bake the cake? Mommy says: Yes, you can. You can help me. You can help me bake the cake. Can Bobby help?	2 4 Yes, he can help.	1	7
Bobby says: What do we do? What do we do first? What does Bobby say?	2 6 3 4 What do we do first?	1	16
Mommy says: First, we need a bowl. We need to get a bowl for the cake. We need to get a bowl. What do they need to get first?	3 1 5 They need to get a bowl.	1	10
Mommy says: Next, we need a big spoon. We need to get a big spoon to mix the cake. We need to get a big spoon. What do they need to get next?	3 1 5 They need to get a big spoon.	1	10

NARRATIVE	TARGET RESPONSE	SENTENCE POINT	DSS TOTAL
Bobby is getting the bowl and the spoon. He is getting them for Mommy. He is helping Mommy. What is he doing?	2 1 He is helping Mommy.	1	4
Mommy says: We need the cake mix. We need two eggs and some water. What do they need?	3 1 3 They need a cake mix, two 3 eggs, and water.	1	11
Mommy says: I will put the cake mix into the bowl. Bobby, do you know what to do next? Do you? Do you know what to do next? What does Mommy say?	6 1 4 6 Do you know what 5 to do next?	1	23
Bobby says: Yes, I will pour the water into the bowl. I will pour the water. What is he doing?	2 1 He is pouring the water into the bowl.	1	4
Mommy says: I will mix the cake mix and water. I will mix them together. What does Mommy say?	1 4 3 I will mix them together.	1	9
Mommy says: Give me the eggs, Bobby. Give me the eggs. What is Bobby doing?	1 Bobby is giving Mommy the eggs.	1	2
Mommy says: Be careful, Bobby. Be careful with the eggs. Don't drop the eggs. What does Mommy say?	4 4 Don't drop the eggs.	1	9
Oh, oh! Mommy says: What happened?			

NARRATIVE	TARGET RESPONSE	SENTENCE POINT	DSS TOTAL
Bobby says: I dropped the eggs. The eggs fell on the floor. The eggs are broken. What happened?	2 Bobby dropped the eggs.	1	3
Bobby says: I'm sorry, Mommy. I'm sorry. What does Bobby say?	1 2 I'm sorry.	1	4
Mommy says: I will wipe up the eggs. You can get me some more eggs. Now Bobby is very careful. He is getting two more eggs. He is giving them to Mommy. Did the eggs break?	7 6 No, the eggs did not break.	1	14
Mommy is putting the eggs into the bowl. She is mixing the cake and eggs together. She is pouring the cake into the pan. What is she doing?	2 1 She is pouring the cake into the pan.	1	4
Bobby is opening the oven. Mommy is putting the cake into the oven. Bobby is closing the door. Where is the cake?	1 The cake is inside the oven.	1	2
Bobby and Mommy are waiting. They are waiting for the cake to bake. They are waiting for the cake. What are they doing?	3 2 They are waiting for the cake.	1	6
Now Mommy looks into the oven. Mommy says: Look at the cake. Look at it bake. Look at it bake. What does Mommy say?	1 1 5 Look at it bake.	1	8

NARRATIVE	TARGET RESPONSE	SENTENCE POINT	DSS TOTAL
Mommy says: Now the cake is ready. We can take it out of the oven. Is the cake ready?	1 Yes, the cake is ready.	1	2
Here comes Aunt Sally. Aunt Sally is here. Who is here?	1 Aunt Sally is here.	1	2
Aunt Sally says: Something smells good. What does Aunt Sally smell?	(Elicit responses from the children.)		
Mommy says: It is a cake. We made a cake for you. Aunt Sally says: Oh, thank you! I love cake. Thank you for making a cake for me. What does Aunt Sally say?	1 1 8 Thank you for making a 1 cake for me.	1	12

LEVEL II: LESSON 12

CONCEPTS

finding a home, where animals live, being sad, being homeless

VOCABULARY

sad, nobody, where, nest, cage, zoo, tree, water, house, swim

FLANNEL-BOARD MATERIALS

paper cutouts: horse, bird, bear, duck, dog, squirrel, cat, barn, a group of horses

ELICITED STRUCTURES		DSS VALUE
Primary emphasis		
indefinite pronoun	– *nobody, no one*	4
personal pronoun	– *he*	2
main verb	– *-s,* copular *am, are,* auxiliary *am, are*	2
	– *can* + verb, *do* + verb	4
secondary verb	– noncomplementing infinitive	3
negative	– *can't, don't*	4
interrogative	– reversal of modal, obligatory *do, does, did*	6
Secondary emphasis		
secondary verb	– early-developing infinitive	2
wh-question	– *where, what . . . do*	2
conjunction	– *and*	3

THE HORSE FINDS A HOME

NARRATIVE	TARGET RESPONSE	SENTENCE POINT	DSS TOTAL
This is a horse. The horse is brown. This is a brown horse. What is this?	1 1 This is a brown horse.	1	3
The horse is sad. He is very sad. He is not happy. Is he happy?	2 1 7 No, he is not happy.	1	11
The horse has no place to live. He has no place to live. He has nobody to live with. The horse is sad because he has nobody to live with. He is sad because he has nobody to live with. Why is the horse sad?	2 1 6 2 He is sad because he 2 4 3 has nobody to live with.	1	21

NARRATIVE	TARGET RESPONSE	SENTENCE POINT	DSS TOTAL
The horse doesn't have a home. He doesn't have a home. Does the horse have a home?	2 7 6 No, he doesn't have a home.	1	16
The horse says: I'm going to look for a home. I'm going to look for someplace to live. I'm going to look for a home. What is the horse going to do?	1 The horse is going 2 to look for a home.	1	4
The horse sees something. Something is coming. It is a bird. A bird is coming. What is coming?	1 A bird is coming.	1	2
The horse says: I'm going to talk to the bird. I'm going to talk to him. I'm going to talk to the bird. What does the horse say?	1 2 2 I'm going to talk to the bird.	1	6
The horse says: Hello, bird. I don't have a home. I have nobody to live with. I have nobody to live with. What does the horse say?	1 1 4 3 I have nobody to live with.	1	10
The horse says: Can I live with you? Can I? Can I live with you? The bird says: Oh, no. I live in a nest. The nest is in a tree. A horse can't live in a nest. A horse can't climb a tree.			

NARRATIVE	TARGET RESPONSE	SENTENCE POINT	DSS TOTAL
A horse can't live in a nest. What does the bird say?	4 4 A horse can't live in a nest.	1	9
The horse says: Oh, dear. You are right. I can't live in a nest. I can't climb a tree. I can't live in a nest. What does the horse say?	1 4 4 I can't live in a nest.	1	10
The horse says: I see something. It is a bear. A bear is coming. What is coming?	1 A bear is coming.	1	2
The horse says: I'm going to talk to the bear. Hello, bear. I don't have a home. I have no one to live with. I have no one to live with. What does he say?	1 1 4 3 I have no one to live with.	1	10
The horse says: Can I live with you? The bear says: Oh, no. I live in a cage. I live at the zoo. I live in a cage at the zoo. Where does the bear live?	2 The bear lives in a cage at the zoo.	1	3
The bear says: I live in a cage. I do tricks. The horse says: I don't want to live in a cage. I don't want to do tricks. I don't want to live in a cage and do tricks. What does the horse say?	1 4 4 2 I don't want to live in 3 2 a cage and do tricks.	1	17
The horse says: I see something. I see a duck.			

NARRATIVE	TARGET RESPONSE	SENTENCE POINT	DSS TOTAL
A duck is coming. What is coming?	1 A duck is coming.	1	2
The horse says: Hello, duck. I don't have a home. Can I live with you? The duck says: Horse, can you swim? Can you? Can you swim? What does the duck say?	6 1 4 Can you swim?	1	12
The horse says: No, I can't swim. I can't swim. I can't. What does the horse say?	1 4 4 I can't swim.	1	10
The duck says: Then you can't live with me. You can't live with me. because I live in water. You can't live with me. Can the horse live with the duck?	2 4 4 No, he can't live with the duck.	1	11
The horse sees something. The horse sees a dog. He sees a dog. What does the horse see?	2 The horse sees a dog.	1	3
The horse says: Where do you live? Do you have a home? Where do you live? What does the horse say?	2 6 1 4 Where do you live?	1	14
The dog says: I live in a house. I live with a little boy. I live in a house. The horse says: Can I live in a house, too? Can I live with you? Can I? Can I live with you? What does the horse say?	61 4 1 Can I live with you?	1	13
The dog says: Oh, no. I am little. You are big.			

NARRATIVE	TARGET RESPONSE	SENTENCE POINT	DSS TOTAL
I am little, and you are big. What does the dog say?	1 2 3 1 I am little, and you 2 are big.	1	10
The dog says: You can't live in a house. You are too big. A horse can't live in a house. What does the dog say?	4 4 A horse can't live in a house.	1	9
The horse says: Oh, dear. What can I do? I don't have a home. What can I do? What does the horse say?	2 6 1 4 What can I do?	1	14
The horse says: I see something. It is a squirrel. I see a squirrel. What does the horse see?	2 The horse sees a squirrel.	1	3
The horse says: Hello, squirrel. How are you? I am very sad. I don't have a home. I have no place to live. The squirrel says: I live in a tree. I live on the ground. I live in a tree and on the ground. What does the squirrel say?	1 1 3 I live in a tree and on the ground.	1	6
The squirrel says: I can run up and down the tree. I can run up and down. Can you run up and down a tree? Can you run up and down? Can you run up and down a tree? What does the squirrel say?	6 1 4 3 Can you run up and down a tree?	1	15
The horse says: No, I can't do that. I can run, but I can't			

NARRATIVE	TARGET RESPONSE	SENTENCE POINT	DSS TOTAL
run up and down a tree. I can't live with you. I can't live in a tree. Can the horse live in a tree?	4 4 No, the horse can't live in a tree.	1	9
The horse is very sad. He is very sad. The horse says: I can't find a home. I can't find a place to live. Nobody wants to live with me. Nobody wants me. Nobody wants to live with me. What does the horse say?	4 2 2 Nobody wants to live 1 with me.	1	10
The horse says: I can't live in a nest. I can't live in a cage at the zoo. Can a horse live in a nest?	4 4 No, a horse can't live in a nest.	1	9
Can a horse live in a cage at the zoo?	4 4 No, a horse can't live in a cage at the zoo.	1	9
The horse says: I can't live in the water. I can't live in a tree. Where can I live? Where? Where can I live? What does the horse say?	2 6 1 4 Where can I live?	1	14
Do you know? Do you know where a horse can live?	(Elicit guesses from the children.)		
The horse says: I'm going to try one more time. I'm going to try once more. The horse sees a cat. He sees a cat. The horse says: Oh, cat! I am sad. I have no one.			

NARRATIVE	TARGET RESPONSE	SENTENCE POINT	DSS TOTAL
I have no one to live with. I have no one to live with. What does the horse say?	1 1 4 3 I have no one to live with.	1	10
The horse says: Can I live with you? The cat says: You can't live with me, but I know where you can live. I know. I know where you can live. What does the cat say?	1 1 8 1 4 I know where you can live.	1	16
The cat says: Come with me. The cat is going to a big red building. It is on a farm. It is where horses live. What is it?	(Elicit guesses from the children.)		
It is a barn. What is it?	1 1 It is a barn.	1	3
There are many horses in the barn. The horse says: Can I live here? Can I live here with you? Can I? Can I live with you? What does the horse say?	6 1 4 1 Can I live with you?	1	13
The other horses say: Yes, you can. You can live with us. You can live with us. What do the other horses say?	1 4 3 You can live with us.	1	9
The horse says: Now I have a home. Now I have somebody to live with. I have somebody to live with. What does the horse say?	1 1 3 I have somebody 3 to live with.	1	9

LEVEL II: LESSON 13

CONCEPTS	ELICITED STRUCTURES		DSS VALUE
warm, cold, shapes, building a birdhouse	**Primary emphasis**		
	personal pronoun	– *he, his, she, her*	2
VOCABULARY		– *we, they, their*	3
warm, cold, roof, sides, door, wood, nails, hammer, circle, square, triangle	main verb	– copular and auxiliary *are*	2
		– *can, will* + verb	4
FLANNEL-BOARD MATERIALS	interrogative	– reversal of modal, obligatory *do*	6
paper figures: Bobby, Karen paper cutouts: window, bird, wood, hammer, nails, birdhouse parts consisting of a square, a triangle, and a circle	wh-question	– *how, when*	5

THE BIRD FINDS A HOME

NARRATIVE	TARGET RESPONSE	SENTENCE POINT	DSS TOTAL
This is Karen. Who is this?	1 1 This is Karen.	1	3
This is Bobby. Bobby is Karen's brother. He is her brother. Who is he?	2 1 2 He is her brother.	1	6
This is Karen's and Bobby's house. This is where they live. This is their house. What is this?	1 1 3 This is their house.	1	6
Karen and Bobby are inside their house. They are playing. They are playing inside the house. What are they doing?	3 2 They are playing.	1	6
Where are they playing?	3 2 They are playing inside the house.	1	6

NARRATIVE	TARGET RESPONSE	SENTENCE POINT	DSS TOTAL
Karen says: I like to play inside. It is warm inside our house. It is warm inside, but it is cold outside. Is it cold inside their house?	1 1 1 3 It is not cold inside their house.	1	7
Bobby says: I like to play inside, too. It is warm inside our house. It is warm inside, but it is cold outside. What does Bobby say?	1 1 5 1 1 It is warm inside, but it is cold outside.	1	10
Karen says: Look, Bobby. Look out the window. I can see a bird. I can see a bird outside. What can she see?	2 4 She can see a bird.	1	7
Karen says: The bird is in the tree. He is outside. He is outside in a tree. Where is the bird?	1 The bird is in the tree.	1	2
Karen says: How cold is it outside? Is it very cold? How cold is it outside? What does Karen say?	5 111 How cold is it outside?	1	9
Bobby says: It is very cold outside. It is very cold. Karen says: The bird is outside. The bird must be cold. Where does the bird live? Does he have a house? Does he have a place to keep warm? Where does the bird live? What does Karen say?	2 6 6 Where does the bird live?	1	15
Bobby says: Let's make a house. Let's make a birdhouse.			

NARRATIVE	TARGET RESPONSE	SENTENCE POINT	DSS TOTAL
Let's make a house for the bird. Let's make a birdhouse. What does Bobby say?	1 2 Let's make a birdhouse.	1	4
Bobby says: Let's make a birdhouse so the bird can keep warm. Then the bird can go into his house when he is cold. He can go inside to get warm. Why are they going to build the birdhouse?	3 2 2 They are going to build a 5 birdhouse so the bird 4 can keep warm.	1	17
Karen says: How do you make a birdhouse? How do you make one? How do you make a birdhouse? What does Karen say?	5 6 1 4 How do you make a birdhouse?	1	17
Bobby says: I will show you. I will show you how to make a birdhouse. Karen says: What will we need? What will we need to make the birdhouse? Bobby says: We will need wood. We will need lots of it. We will need lots of wood. What will they need?	3 4 They will need wood.	1	8
Bobby says: First we will make the sides of the birdhouse. Karen says: How will we make the sides? How will we make them?			

NARRATIVE	TARGET RESPONSE	SENTENCE POINT	DSS TOTAL
How will we make the sides of the birdhouse? What does Karen say?	5 6 3 4 How will we make the sides of the birdhouse?	1	19
Bobby says: We will use some nails. We will use nails to hold the house together. We will use nails. What will they use?	3 4 They will use nails.	1	8
Bobby says: We will need a hammer. We will use a hammer to pound the nails. We will use a hammer. What will they use?	3 4 They will use a hammer.	1	8
Karen is getting the hammer and nails. Bobby is getting some wood. Karen and Bobby are going to build a birdhouse. They will build one. They will build a birdhouse. What will they do?	3 4 They will build a birdhouse.	1	8
Bobby says: Let's build the sides of the house. There are four sides. Let's build the four sides of the house. How many sides are there?	2 3 There are four sides.	1	6
Bobby says: Each side is the same shape. Each side is a square. Each side is shaped like a square. What shape is each side?	7 1 Each side is a square.	1	9
Karen is holding the nail. Bobby is pounding the nail. They are building the sides. They are building the sides of the house. What are they doing?	3 2 They are building the sides of the house.	1	6

NARRATIVE	TARGET RESPONSE	SENTENCE POINT	DSS TOTAL
Bobby says: Now we will make a roof. Karen says: How will we make the roof? How will we make it? How will we make the roof? What does Karen say?	5 6 3 4 How will we make the roof?	1	19
Bobby says: We will make the roof out of wood, too. We will use the hammer and nails. The roof is a different shape than the sides. The roof is a triangle. The roof is not a square. The roof is a triangle. What shape is the roof?	1 The roof is a triangle.	1	2
Karen is holding the nail. Bobby is pounding the nail. They are building the roof. They are building one. They are building the roof. What are they doing?	3 2 They are building the roof.	1	6
Bobby says: Let's put the roof on the sides. We are almost finished. Karen says: How will the bird get inside? How can he? How can he get inside his house? What does Karen say?	5 6 2 4 How can he get inside 2 his house?	1	20
What does the house need?	(Elicit guesses from the children.)		
Bobby says: We will cut a circle in the side of the birdhouse.			

NARRATIVE	TARGET RESPONSE	SENTENCE POINT	DSS TOTAL
The door is a different shape than the roof. The door is a circle. What shape is the door?	1 The door is a circle.	1	2
Bobby is cutting a circle in the side. He is cutting a door in the side. He is making a door. What is he doing?	2 1 He is making a door.	1	4
Karen says: When will the birdhouse be finished? When? When will it be finished? What does Karen say?	5 61 7 When will it be finished?	1	20
Bobby says: Pretty soon. Oh, look! Now they are all done. Bobby says: Now we are all done. The birdhouse is finished. Is it finished?	1 7 Yes, it is finished.	1	9
Karen says: Let's put the birdhouse outside. Let's put the birdhouse in the tree. Now the bird has a home. The bird has a home so he can keep warm.			

LEVEL II: LESSON 14

CONCEPTS	ELICITED STRUCTURES		DSS VALUE
going to a circus, activities at the circus	**Primary emphasis**		
	indefinite pronoun –	*one, two, some*	3
VOCABULARY	personal pronoun –	*he, him, his*	2
elephants, bears, lions, clowns, circus, popcorn man, lion trainer, cage	main verb –	*-s, -ed,* copular *am, are,* auxiliary *am, are,* irregular past	2
FLANNEL-BOARD MATERIALS	–	*can* + verb, obligatory *do* + verb	4
paper figures: Bobby, Daddy, popcorn man, lion trainer	interrogative –	reversal of modal, obligatory *do*	6
paper cutouts: two lions, two bears, two elephants, two clowns, bag of popcorn, stick, cage, one horse with rider	**Secondary emphasis**		
	conjunction –	*and*	3

BOBBY GOES TO THE CIRCUS

NARRATIVE	TARGET RESPONSE	SENTENCE POINT	DSS TOTAL
This is Bobby. Who is this?	1 1 This is Bobby.	1	3
This is Daddy. Who is this?	1 1 This is Daddy.	1	3
Bobby and Daddy are going somewhere. They are going somewhere. They are going somewhere special. They are going to the circus. Bobby and Daddy are going to go to the circus. What are they going to do?	3 2 2 They are going to go to the circus.	1	8
It's going to be lots of fun. Have you ever been to a circus?	(Elicit spontaneous responses.)		

NARRATIVE	TARGET RESPONSE	SENTENCE POINT	DSS TOTAL
Now Bobby and Daddy are at the circus. They are at the circus. Bobby says: Oh, look, Daddy. The circus is starting. Do you see the elephants? Do you see them? Do you see the elephants? What does Bobby say?	6 1 4 Do you see the elephants?	1	12
Daddy says: Yes, I do. I see them. Look at who is riding on the elephants. Two clowns are riding. They are riding on the elephants. Two clowns are riding on the elephants. What does Daddy say?	3 2 Two clowns are riding on the elephants.	1	6
Daddy says: The clowns are funny, aren't they? Aren't they funny? Aren't the clowns funny? What does Daddy say?	2 7 1 Aren't the clowns funny?	1	11
Bobby says: Yes, the clowns are funny. They have funny red noses. They are wearing funny hats. They are wearing funny clothes. They are wearing funny hats and funny clothes. What are the clowns wearing?	2 The clowns are wearing funny 3 hats and funny clothes.	1	6
Bobby says: Oh, look, Daddy. Do you see the bear? Do you see it? Do you see the bear? What does Bobby say?	6 1 4 Do you see the bear?	1	12

NARRATIVE	TARGET RESPONSE	SENTENCE POINT	DSS TOTAL
Daddy says: Yes, I see the bear. He is wearing a jacket. He is wearing a tie. He is wearing a hat. The bear is wearing a jacket, a tie, and a hat. What is the bear wearing?	1 The bear is wearing a jacket, 3 a tie, and a hat.	1	5
Daddy says: Look at what is coming now. A horse is coming. The horse is running. The horse is jumping. He is running and jumping. What is the horse doing?	2 1 3 1 He is running and jumping.	1	8
Daddy says: There is a man. A man is riding the horse. There is a man riding the horse. What does Daddy say?	1 4 There is a man riding the horse.	1	6
Daddy says: The man is jumping. The man is jumping through a big hoop. He is jumping through a big hoop. What is he doing?	2 1 He is jumping through a big hoop.	1	4
Daddy says: Now the man is riding away. Bobby says: Look, Daddy, a man is coming toward us. He is carrying something. The man says: Popcorn, popcorn! Who wants popcorn? Bobby says: The man is selling popcorn. He is selling popcorn. Can I have some popcorn? Can I have some?			

NARRATIVE	TARGET RESPONSE	SENTENCE POINT	DSS TOTAL
Daddy, can I have some popcorn? What does Bobby say?	6 1 4 3 Can I have some popcorn?	1	15
Daddy says: Yes, you can. You can have some popcorn. You can have some. What does Daddy say?	1 4 3 Yes, you can have some.	1	9
Here is the popcorn man. Bobby says: Can I have a bag of popcorn? Can I have one, please? Can I have one bag of popcorn? What does Bobby say?	6 1 4 3 Can I have one bag of popcorn?	1	15
The popcorn man says: Yes, you can. You can have one bag. You can have one bag of popcorn. What does the popcorn man say?	1 4 3 You can have one bag of popcorn.	1	9
The popcorn man says: Popcorn costs a dime. It costs a dime. Popcorn costs a dime. How much is the popcorn?	1 1 It is a dime.	1	3
Daddy gives the popcorn man a dime. Daddy gives him a dime. He gives the popcorn man a dime. What does Daddy do?	2 Daddy gives the popcorn man a dime.	1	3
Bobby says: Thank you. Now Bobby is eating the popcorn. Bobby says: Oh, look, Daddy. Two elephants are coming. One elephant is standing. He is standing up.			

NARRATIVE	TARGET RESPONSE	SENTENCE POINT	DSS TOTAL
The elephant is standing on his back legs. He is standing on his back legs. What is he doing?	2 1 2 He is standing on his back legs.	1	6
Daddy says: Look at the elephant's trunk. Look at his trunk. The elephant is picking up a stick with his trunk. He is picking up a stick with his trunk. What is he doing?	2 1 He is picking up a stick 2 with his trunk.	1	6
Bobby says: Someone else is coming. He is silly. He has funny clothes. He is wearing funny big shoes. Who is coming? Can you guess?	(Elicit spontaneous answers.) 1 A clown is coming.	1	2
Daddy says: It is a clown. He is funny. The clown is waving. The clown is waving to everybody. He is waving to everybody. What is he doing?	2 1 7 He is waving to everybody.	1	11
Bobby says: What's coming? What is coming next? What is coming next? What does Bobby say?	2 1 What is coming next?	1	4
Daddy says: Listen. I hear something. I hear a roar. Something is roaring. It sounds scary. It's scary. It sounds scary. How does it sound?	1 2 It sounds scary.	1	4
What is roaring? Can you guess?	(Elicit spontaneous answers.)		

NARRATIVE	TARGET RESPONSE	SENTENCE POINT	DSS TOTAL
Daddy says: I see lions. The lions are coming. The lions are in a cage. The lions can't get out. They can't get out. They can't get out of the cage. Can the lions get out?	3 4 4 No, they can't get out.	1	12
Bobby says: Look, Daddy. A man is going into the cage! He is going inside the cage. Who is that man? Who is the man? Who is he? What does Bobby say?	2 11 2 Who is he?	1	7
Daddy says: He is the lion trainer. That man is the lion trainer. He is the lion trainer. Who is he?	21 He is the lion trainer.	1	4
Daddy says: The man is talking to the lions. He is talking to the lions. The man is saying, "Sit up." The man is saying, "Sit up, lions." He is saying, "Sit up, lions." What is he saying?	2 1 1 He is saying, "Sit up, lions."	1	5
Daddy says: The lions are listening to the man. They are listening to the man. The lions are sitting. The lions are sitting up. They are sitting up. What are the lions doing?	2 The lions are sitting up.	1	3
Bobby says: The lion trainer is leaving.			

NARRATIVE	TARGET RESPONSE	SENTENCE POINT	DSS TOTAL
Now the circus is over. Daddy says: Do you want to go home? Are you ready? Do you want to go home? What does Daddy say?	6 1 4 2 Do you want to go home?	1	14
Bobby says: Yes, I am ready to go home. Thank you, Daddy. I had a good time. What does Bobby say?	1 1 Thank you, Daddy. 1 2 I had a good time.	2	7

LEVEL II: LESSON 15

CONCEPTS

going shopping, numbers, food types

VOCABULARY

fruit, vegetable, meat, drink, dessert

FLANNEL-BOARD MATERIALS

paper figures: Mommy, Timmy
paper cutouts: store front, grocery cart, small articles of food, including apples, hot dogs, carrots, a bottle of pop, and an ice-cream carton

ELICITED STRUCTURES		DSS VALUE
Primary emphasis		
indefinite pronoun	– *some, two, three*	3
personal pronoun	– *we, they*	3
main verb	– *-s,* copular *am, are,* auxiliary *am, are*	2
	– *can* + verb, obligatory *do* + verb	4
secondary verb	– early-developing infinitive	2
interrogative	– reversal of modal, obligatory *do*	6
Secondary emphasis		
conjunction	– *and*	3

GOING TO THE GROCERY STORE

NARRATIVE	TARGET RESPONSE	SENTENCE POINT	DSS TOTAL
This is Mommy. This is Timmy. Mommy says: I am going to go to the grocery store. I am going to buy something for dinner. I am going to buy some food for dinner.			
Why is Mommy going to the grocery store?	1 Mommy is going to the 3 grocery store to buy 3 some food for dinner.	1	8
Timmy says: Can I go to the grocery store, too, Mommy? Can I? Can I go, too?			
What does Timmy say?	6 1 4 Can I go, too?	1	12

NARRATIVE	TARGET RESPONSE	SENTENCE POINT	DSS TOTAL
Mommy says: Yes, you can go to the grocery store. You can go. You can go with me. What does Mommy say?	1 4 1 You can go with me.	1	7
Mommy says: Let's hurry. Daddy will be home pretty soon. We'd better hurry. Why are they going to hurry?	3 2 2 They are going to hurry 6 4 because Daddy will be home pretty soon.	1	18
Mommy and Timmy are walking to the grocery store. They are walking. They are walking to the grocery store. What are they doing?	3 2 They are walking to the grocery store.	1	6
Now Mommy and Timmy are at the grocery store. Timmy says: Do we need a shopping cart? Do we, Mommy? Do we need a shopping cart? What does Timmy say?	6 3 4 Do we need a shopping cart?	1	14
Mommy says: Yes, we do need a shopping cart. Timmy says: Can I push the cart, Mommy? Can I? Can I push it? What does Timmy say?	6 1 4 1 Can I push it?	1	13
Mommy says: Yes, you can. You can push the cart. You can push it. What does Mommy say?	1 4 1 You can push it.	1	7

NARRATIVE	TARGET RESPONSE	SENTENCE POINT	DSS TOTAL
Mommy says: Here is the fruit. What kind of fruit should we buy? What kind of fruit can they buy? Can you guess?	(Elicit responses from the children.)		
Timmy says: Can we buy some apples? Can we? Can we buy some apples? What does Timmy say?	6 3 4 3 Can we buy some apples?	1	17
Mommy says: Yes, we can buy some apples. Let's buy five. Let's buy five apples. How many apples are they going to buy?	3 2 2 They are going to buy 3 five apples.	1	11
Mommy says: The meat is over here. What kind of meat should we buy, Timmy? What kind? What kind of meat should we buy? What does Mommy say?	2 What kind of meat 6 3 6 should we buy?	1	18
What kind of meat can they buy? Can you guess?	(Elicit responses from the children.)		
Mommy says: Do you want some hot dogs? Daddy likes hot dogs. Do you want some? Do you want some hot dogs? What does Mommy say?	6 1 4 3 Do you want some hot dogs?	1	15
Timmy says: Yes, I want some hot dogs. Mommy says: Okay, let's get two packages of hot dogs.			

NARRATIVE	TARGET RESPONSE	SENTENCE POINT	DSS TOTAL
Let's get two. Let's get two packages of hot dogs. What does Mommy say?	1 2 3 Let's get two packages of hot dogs.	1	7
How many packages of hot dogs are they going to buy?	3 2 2 3 They are going to buy two packages of hot dogs.	1	11
Mommy says: Put the hot dogs in the cart, Timmy. Let's find the vegetables. Timmy is pushing the cart. He is pushing it. He is pushing the cart. What is he doing?	2 1 He is pushing the cart.	1	4
Timmy says: Here are the vegetables. Here they are. Here are the vegetables. What does Timmy say?	2 Here are the vegetables.	1	3
What kind of vegetables can they buy? Can you guess?	(Elicit responses from the children.)		
Mommy says: I like carrots. Do you want to buy some carrots? Do you, Timmy? Do you want to buy some carrots? What does Mommy say?	6 1 4 2 3 Do you want to buy some carrots?	1	17
Timmy says: Yes, let's buy some carrots. Let's buy three. Let's buy three carrots. How many carrots are they going to buy?	3 2 2 3 They are going to buy three carrots.	1	11
Now Mommy and Timmy are looking for things you can drink.			

NARRATIVE	TARGET RESPONSE	SENTENCE POINT	DSS TOTAL
What can they buy to drink? Can you guess?	(Elicit responses from the children.)		
Timmy says: Can we buy some pop, Mommy? Can we? Can we buy some pop? What does Timmy say?	6 3 4 3 Can we buy some pop?	1	17
Mommy says: Okay, but let's buy only two bottles of pop. Let's buy only two. Let's buy only two bottles of pop. How many bottles of pop are they going to buy?	3 2 2 3 They are going to buy two bottles of pop.	1	11
Now Mommy says: We need some dessert. Let's buy some dessert. What can they buy for dessert? Can you guess?	(Elicit responses from the children.)		
Timmy says: I like ice cream. Can we buy ice cream? Can we? Can we buy ice cream? What does Timmy say?	6 3 4 Can we buy ice cream?	1	14
Mommy says: Yes, let's buy some ice cream. Let's buy chocolate. Let's buy some chocolate ice cream. What does Mommy say?	1 2 3 Let's buy some chocolate ice cream.	1	7
Mommy says: Now we are finished. We have everything we need. We bought apples. We bought hot dogs. We bought carrots. We bought pop. We bought ice cream.			

NARRATIVE	TARGET RESPONSE	SENTENCE POINT	DSS TOTAL
It's going to be a good dinner. What did they buy?	They (3) bought (2) apples and (3) hot dogs and (3) carrots and (3) pop and (3) ice cream.	1	18

LEVEL II: LESSON 16

CONCEPTS

making a kite, windy weather, independence

VOCABULARY

windy, kite, glue, sticks

FLANNEL-BOARD MATERIALS

paper figures: Daddy, Susan, Timmy

additional materials: paper cut in diamond shape for kite, toothpick sticks, glue, string

ELICITED STRUCTURES		DSS VALUE
Primary emphasis		
personal pronoun	– *we, our, us, they, them, their*	3
	– *myself, themselves*	5
main verb	– *can, will* + verb, obligatory *do* + verb	4
secondary verb	– early-developing infinitive	2
	– later-developing infinitive, infinitive with wh-word	5
conjunction	– *because*	6
Secondary emphasis		
indefinite pronoun	– *all*	3
personal pronoun	– *what*	6
main verb	– *-s, -ed,* copular *am, are,* auxiliary *am, are,* irregular past tense	2
negative	– *can't, don't*	4
interrogative	– reversal of modal, obligatory *do*	6

MAKING A KITE

NARRATIVE	TARGET RESPONSE	SENTENCE POINT	DSS TOTAL
This is Timmy. Who is this?	1 1 This is Timmy.	1	3
This is Susan. Who is this?	1 1 This is Susan.	1	3
This is Daddy. Who is this?	1 1 This is Daddy.	1	3
Timmy says: The sun is shining. It is warm today. It is warm because the sun is shining. It is warm today because the sun is shining. What does Timmy say?	1 1 6 It is warm today because 1 the sun is shining.	1	10

NARRATIVE	TARGET RESPONSE	SENTENCE POINT	DSS TOTAL
Susan says: Yes, it is warm today. It is a good day to go riding. I want to ride my bike. I want to ride my bike because it is a nice day. I want to ride my bike because it is a nice day. What does Susan say?	1 1 2 1 I want to ride my bike 6 1 1 because it is a nice day.	1	14
Timmy says: The wind is blowing. The wind is blowing very hard. The wind is very strong. The wind is very strong today. What does Timmy say?	1 The wind is very strong today.	1	2
Timmy says: We can't go riding. The wind is too strong. We can't go bike riding because the wind is too strong. We can't go riding because the wind is too strong. Why can't they go riding?	3 4 4 8 6 They can't go riding because 1 the wind is too strong.	1	27
Susan says: Yes, the wind is too strong. The wind is too strong to go riding. But what can we do? I don't know what to do. What should we do? I don't know what to do. What does Susan say?	1 4 4 6 5 I don't know what to do.	1	21
Timmy says: Let's ask Daddy. Let's ask Daddy what to do. He'll know. Let's ask Daddy what to do. What does Timmy say?	1 2 6 Let's ask Daddy what 5 to do.	1	15

NARRATIVE	TARGET RESPONSE	SENTENCE POINT	DSS TOTAL
Timmy and Susan are looking for Daddy. They are looking for Daddy. What are they doing?	3 2 They are looking for Daddy.	1	6
Timmy says: Daddy, we can't ride our bikes. It is too windy.. We can't ride because it is too windy. We can't ride our bikes because it is too windy. What does Timmy say?	3 4 4 3 We can't ride our 6 1 1 bikes because it is too windy.	1	23
Susan says: Daddy, what can we do? Can you tell us? Can you tell us what we can do? Can you tell us what to do? What does Susan say?	6 1 4 3 6 Can you tell us what 5 to do?	1	26
Daddy says: Let's make a kite. The wind is strong. The strong wind will fly the kite. The kite will fly because the wind is strong. The kite will fly because the wind is strong. What does Daddy say?	4 6 The kite will fly because 1 the wind is strong.	1	12
Timmy says: I like to fly kites. I want to make a kite. I want to make one all by myself. I want to make a kite all by myself. What does Timmy say?	1 1 2 I want to make a kite 3 5 all by myself.	1	13

NARRATIVE	TARGET RESPONSE	SENTENCE POINT	DSS TOTAL
Susan says: I like to fly kites. I want to make a kite. I want to make one all by myself. I want to make a kite all by myself. What does Susan say?	1 1 2 I want to make a kite 3 5 all by myself.	1	13
Daddy says: I will help you. We need string and paper for kites. We need string, paper, and sticks. We need string, paper, and sticks for the kite. What do they need?	3 1 They need string, paper, 3 and sticks for the kite.	1	8
Timmy says: I will help. I will get the string and paper and sticks. I will do it myself. I will get them myself. What does Timmy say?	1 4 3 5 I will get them myself.	1	14
Susan says: We need glue for the kite. We need glue to make the kite. I'd better get the glue. I'd better get it myself. I'd better do it myself. What does Susan say?	1 2 5 1 5 I'd better do it myself.	1	15
Here comes Timmy. Here comes Susan. Timmy is bringing the string, paper, and sticks. Susan is bringing the glue. What is Timmy bringing?	1 Timmy is bringing the 3 string, paper, and sticks.	1	5

NARRATIVE	TARGET RESPONSE	SENTENCE POINT	DSS TOTAL
What is Susan bringing?	1 Susan is bringing the glue.	1	2
Timmy says: I will cut the paper. I will cut the paper, but I need help. I can't do it myself. Susan, will you help me? Will you help me because I can't do it myself? What does Timmy say?	6 1 4 1 6 Will you help me because 1 4 4 1 5 I can't do it myself?	1	34
Susan says: Yes, I can help you. I can help you cut. I can help you cut the paper. What does Susan say?	1 4 1 5 I can help you cut the paper.	1	12
Daddy says: The sticks are ready. Is the paper ready? Is it cut? Is the paper cut? What does Daddy say?	4 7 Is the paper cut?	1	12
Susan says: Yes, the paper is cut. Let's make the kite. Daddy, can you help us make the kite? Can you? Can you help us make the kite? What does Susan say?	6 1 4 3 5 Can you help us make the kite?	1	20
Daddy is making the kite. Now he is all done. The kite is ready to fly. They made the kite all by themselves. They made it. They made it all by themselves. What did they do?	3 2 3 They made the kite all 5 by themselves.	1	14
Susan and Timmy and Daddy are going outside.			

NARRATIVE	TARGET RESPONSE	SENTENCE POINT	DSS TOTAL
They are going outside.			
They are going to fly the kite.			
They are going outside to fly the kite.		1	9
What are they doing?	3 2 They are going outside 3 to fly the kite.		

LEVEL II: LESSON 17

CONCEPTS

being hungry, emptiness, finding a bone

VOCABULARY

empty, hungry, finding, bone, doghouse

FLANNEL-BOARD MATERIALS

paper cutouts: two dogs, doghouse, dog's food dish, playground slide, swing, store front, garbage cans, ice-cream truck, tree, bone

ELICITED STRUCTURES		DSS VALUE
Primary emphasis		
indefinite pronoun	– *another, all*	3
	– *some, something*	3
	– *any*	7
main verb	– *can, will* + verb, obligatory *do* + verb	4
secondary verb	– early-developing infinitive	2
negative	– *isn't, won't*	5
Secondary emphasis		
personal pronoun	– *he, his*	2
main verb	– copular *am, are,* auxiliary *am*	2
negative	– *can't, don't*	4
interrogative	– reversal of modal, obligatory *do*	6

TAFFY FINDS A BONE

NARRATIVE	TARGET RESPONSE	SENTENCE POINT	DSS TOTAL
This is Taffy. Taffy is a dog. Taffy is the dog in our story. Who is this?	1 1 This is Taffy.	1	3
This is Taffy's house. It is a doghouse. Taffy lives in this house. What is this?	1 1 It is a doghouse.	1	3
The doghouse has Taffy's name on it. See? The letters spell T A F F Y. Taffy is sitting in front of his doghouse. He is getting very hungry. He wants to eat something. What do dogs eat?	(Elicit guesses from the children.)		

NARRATIVE	TARGET RESPONSE	SENTENCE POINT	DSS TOTAL
Taffy says: I'm hungry. I'm going to look for something to eat. I want to eat. I'm going to look for something to eat. What does Taffy say?	1 2 2 I'm going to look for 3 3 something to eat.	1	12
Taffy gets up. He runs to his food dish. But there is nothing in the dish. The dish is empty. Taffy says: My dish is empty. Where can I go to look for food? Where can I go? Where can I go to look for food? What does Taffy say?	2 6 1 4 3 Where can I go to look for food?	1	17
Taffy says: I am hungry, but there isn't any food here. There isn't any food left. I am hungry, but there isn't any food here. What does Taffy say?	1 2 5 I am hungry, but there 1 5 7 isn't any food here.	1	22
Taffy says: My dish is empty. I'm going to go to the playground. Maybe some children will be there. Maybe they'll have candy or bread or even meat for me. I hope they have some food for me. I'm going to hurry to to the playground. Taffy is running to the playground. He is hurrying. He wants to see the children. He is running to the playground. What is Taffy doing?	1 Taffy is running to the playground.	1	2

NARRATIVE	TARGET RESPONSE	SENTENCE POINT	DSS TOTAL
Now Taffy is at the playground. He is very hungry. Taffy says: I don't see any children. I don't see any. I don't see any children. What does Taffy say?	1 4 4 7 I don't see any children.	1	17
Taffy says: Nobody is on the swing. The swing is empty. Nobody is on the slide. The slide is empty. Oh! Oh! The children must be in school. They are not here. All the children are in school. Where are all the children?	3 2 All the children are in school.	1	6
Taffy is sad. Taffy is very sad. Is Taffy happy?	1 5 No, Taffy isn't happy.	1	7
Taffy says: I'm going to look in another place. I'm going to find some food. I'm going to find some. I'm going to find some food. What is Taffy going to do?	1 2 3 Taffy is going to find some food.	1	7
Taffy says: I'm going to look near the grocery store. Taffy runs to the front of the grocery store, but there isn't any food there. No one has dropped any food. There isn't any food near the grocery store. Is there any food near the grocery store?	1 5 7 No, there isn't any food near the grocery store.	1	14
Taffy says: I'm going to look near the garbage cans.			

NARRATIVE	TARGET RESPONSE	SENTENCE POINT	DSS TOTAL
I'm going to look for food. I'm going to look near the garbage cans. What does Taffy say?	1 2 2 I'm going to look near the garbage cans.	1	6
Taffy says: Maybe I can find an old bone or a piece of meat. Taffy runs to the garbage cans, but there isn't any food there. There isn't any food. The garbage cans are empty. Is there any food near the garbage cans?	1 5 7 No, there isn't any food near the garbage cans.	1	14
Then Taffy hears something. Ding-a-ling. A bell is ringing. The ice-cream truck is coming. The Good Humor man is coming. The ice-cream truck is coming. What is happening?	The ice-cream truck 1 is coming.	1	2
Taffy says: I love ice cream. But then Taffy remembers. Taffy says: I have no money. I don't have any money. I can't buy ice cream. I don't have any money, so I can't buy ice cream. What does Taffy say?	1 4 4 7 5 I don't have any money, so 1 4 4 I can't buy ice cream.	1	31
So Taffy walks home. He walks past all the houses. He comes to his yard. He sees his doghouse. He sees his empty dish. He is so hungry.			

NARRATIVE	TARGET RESPONSE	SENTENCE POINT	DSS TOTAL
Taffy says: What can I do now? What? What can I do? What can I do now? What does Taffy say?	2 6 1 4 What can I do now?	1	14
Taffy says: I have looked everywhere. There isn't any food. There isn't any. There isn't any food. What does Taffy say?	1 5 7 There isn't any food.	1	14
What is Taffy going to do?	(Elicit guesses from the children.)		
Taffy says: Look! Another dog! Another dog is coming. What does Taffy say?	3 1 Another dog is coming.	1	5
Taffy says: Oh, it's my friend Mimi. Hello, Mimi. Can you help me? Can you? Can you help me? What does Taffy say?	6 1 4 1 Can you help me?	1	13
Taffy says: I want to find something to eat. I have looked everywhere. I looked at the playground and the grocery store. I looked near the garbage cans and the ice-cream truck. But I can't find anything to eat. Mimi says: I know! I know what to do. Go over to the big tree. A big bone is over there. Yesterday I dug a hole. Then I put a big bone into the hole. The bone is under the ground.			

NARRATIVE	TARGET RESPONSE	SENTENCE POINT	DSS TOTAL
You can have the bone. You can have it. What does Mimi say?	1 4 1 You can have it.	1	7
Taffy says: Thank you, Mimi. I'm going to go to the big tree. I'm going to dig up the bone. I'm going to eat the bone. What is Taffy going to do?	1 2 Taffy is going to eat the bone.	1	4
Taffy is running to the big tree. He is running to the big tree. What is he doing?	2 1 He is running to the big tree.	1	4
Taffy is digging in the ground. He is digging a hole. He is digging a deep hole. He is digging deeper and deeper. What is Taffy doing?	1 3 Taffy is digging deeper and deeper.	1	5
He is looking for the bone. Taffy says: I see something! It is white. I see something white. What does Taffy say?	1 1 3 I see something white.	1	6
Taffy says: I feel something. It is hard. I feel something hard. What does Taffy say?	1 1 3 I feel something hard.	1	6
Taffy says: I found something hard and white. What do you think it is?	(Elicit guesses from the children.)		
Taffy says: It is a bone. It is a big bone. Taffy puts the bone in his mouth.			

NARRATIVE	TARGET RESPONSE	SENTENCE POINT	DSS TOTAL
He is running. He is running to his doghouse. What is he doing?	2 1 2 He is running to his doghouse.	1	6
Taffy says: Thank you, Mimi. You helped me find some food. I won't be hungry. Now I won't be hungry. What does Taffy say?	1 5 4 I won't be hungry.	1	11
Taffy says: Let's eat the bone together, Mimi. You are a real friend.			

LEVEL II: LESSON 18

CONCEPTS

cold weather, building things, painting, top, bottom

VOCABULARY

back yard, cold, garage, wood, roof, smell

FLANNEL-BOARD MATERIALS

paper figures: Bobby, Susan, Daddy
paper cutouts: dog, wood, hammer, nails, doghouse, can of paint, three paintbrushes

ELICITED STRUCTURES		DSS VALUE
Primary emphasis		
indefinite pronoun	– *any, anything, everything, everyone*	7
personal pronoun	– *he, she, him, her, his*	2
	– *we, they, their, our, them*	3
main verb	– *-s, -ed,* copular *am, are,* auxiliary *am, are*	2
	– *could, would, might* + verb	6
secondary verb	– early-developing infinitive	2
conjunction	– *and*	3
Secondary emphasis		
main verb	– *can, will* + verb, obligatory *do* + verb	4

BUILDING SPOT A HOUSE

NARRATIVE	TARGET RESPONSE	SENTENCE POINT	DSS TOTAL
This is Bobby. Who is this?	1 1 This is Bobby.	1	3
This is Susan. Who is this?	1 1 This is Susan.	1	3
This is Daddy. He is Bobby's daddy. He is Susan's daddy. He is Bobby's and Susan's daddy. He is their daddy. Who is he?	2 1 3 He is their daddy.	1	7
This is Spot. He is a dog. He is Bobby's and Susan's dog. He is their dog. Who is he?	2 1 3 He is their dog.	1	7
Spot lives with Bobby and Susan. He lives in their yard.			

NARRATIVE	TARGET RESPONSE	SENTENCE POINT	DSS TOTAL
He lives in their back yard. Where does Spot live?	2 3 Spot lives in their back yard.	1	6
Susan says: It is getting cold outside. Spot might get cold outside. He might get sick outside. Spot might get cold and sick outside. What does Susan say?	6 3 Spot might get cold and sick outside.	1	10
Daddy says: We could build a house for Spot. We could build it in the back yard. We could build a house for Spot in the back yard. What could they do?	3 6 They could build a house for Spot in the back yard.	1	10
Daddy says: What could we use to build Spot's house? What could we use to build? What could we use? What does Daddy say?	2 6 3 6 3 What could we use to build?	1	21
Bobby and Susan say: We could use a hammer to build Spot's house. We could use wood to build his house. We could use nails to build. We could use a hammer, wood, and nails to build. What do Bobby and Susan say?	3 6 We could use a hammer, 3 3 wood, and nails to build.	1	16
Daddy says: Look in the garage, Bobby. We might have a hammer. We might have wood. We might have nails.			

NARRATIVE	TARGET RESPONSE	SENTENCE POINT	DSS TOTAL
We might have a hammer, wood, and nails in the garage. What does Daddy say?	3 6 We might have a hammer, 3 wood, and nails in the garage.	1	13
Bobby says: I see the nails. I see the hammer. I see the wood. I see everything. What does he see?	2 2 7 He sees everything.	1	12
Daddy says: Now we are going to build a house. We are going to build a house for Spot. What are they going to do?	3 2 2 They are going to build a house for Spot.	1	8
Susan says: I want to pound a nail. I want to pound a nail into the wood. What does she want to do?	2 2 2 She wants to pound a nail into the wood.	1	7
Bobby says: I am going to pound a nail. I'm going to pound a nail into the wood. What is he going to do?	2 1 2 He is going to pound a nail into the wood.	1	6
Daddy says: Let's put the wood together. Let's put all the wood together. Let's put everything together. What does Daddy say?	1 2 7 Let's put everything together.	1	11
Susan is putting her wood on the ground. She is putting her wood on the ground. What is she doing?	2 1 2 She is putting her wood on the ground.	1	6
Bobby is putting his wood on top.			

NARRATIVE	TARGET RESPONSE	SENTENCE POINT	DSS TOTAL
He is putting his wood on top of Susan's. Where is he putting his wood?	2 1 2 He is putting his wood on top of Susan's.	1	6
Daddy is looking at Spot's house. Daddy says: Spot's house needs a roof. It needs a roof. Spot's house needs a roof. What does Spot's house need?	2 Spot's house needs a roof.	1	3
Daddy is putting the roof on. He is putting the roof on Spot's house. What is he doing?	2 1 He is putting the roof on Spot's house.	1	4
Susan says: Spot's house is not pretty. It is not very pretty. Spot's house is not very pretty. What does Susan say?	1 7 Spot's house is not very pretty.	1	9
Daddy says: We could paint the house. We could paint it. We could paint the house a pretty color. What does Daddy say?	3 6 We could paint the house a pretty color.	1	10
Susan and Bobby say: We want to paint Spot's house. We want to paint his house a pretty color. Are Susan and Bobby going to paint Spot's house?	3 Yes, Bobby and Susan 2 2 are going to paint Spot's house.	1	8
Daddy says: What color do you want to paint it?			

NARRATIVE	TARGET RESPONSE	SENTENCE POINT	DSS TOTAL
Susan says: We could paint it green. Bobby says: We could paint it blue. Daddy says: We could paint it yellow. What color could they paint Spot's house?	3 6 1 They could paint it green 5 5 or yellow or blue.	1	21
Daddy says: Look in the garage. Do we have any paint? Do we? Do we have any paint? What does Daddy say?	6 3 4 7 Do we have any paint?	1	21
Bobby says: I don't see any paint. I don't see any. What does Bobby say?	1 4 4 7 I don't see any.	1	17
Susan says: I see some. I see some green paint. I see some green paint. What does Susan say?	1 1 3 I see some green paint.	1	6
Daddy says: Then we will paint Spot's house green. We will paint it green. What color will they paint Spot's house?	3 4 They will paint Spot's house green.	1	8
Daddy is giving Susan a paintbrush. He is giving Bobby a paintbrush. He is giving both of them paintbrushes. What is Daddy doing?	1 3 Daddy is giving Bobby and Susan paintbrushes.	1	5
Now Susan is painting the top of the house. She is painting the top. She is painting the top of Spot's house. What is she doing?	2 1 She is painting the top of Spot's house.	1	4

NARRATIVE	TARGET RESPONSE	SENTENCE POINT	DSS TOTAL
Bobby is painting the bottom. He is painting the bottom of the house. He is painting the bottom of Spot's house. What is he doing?	2 1 He is painting the bottom of Spot's house.	1	4
Daddy is painting, too. They are painting. They are all painting. What are they doing?	3 3 2 They are all painting.	1	9
Bobby says: Look, Daddy! Spot is near the paint. Spot is smelling the paint. What is Spot doing?	1 Spot is smelling the paint.	1	2
Daddy says: Be careful, Spot; you might spill the green paint. You might spill the green paint on yourself. You might spill the paint on yourself. What does Daddy say?	1 6 You might spill the 5 paint on yourself.	1	13
Susan says: Look, Daddy, look! Spot is spilling the paint. He is spilling the green paint. Spot is spilling the green paint. What is he doing?	2 1 He is spilling the green paint.	1	4
Daddy says: Oh, look! Spot has green paint on his tail. Now everything is green. Spot is green. Spot's house is green. The ground is green. Everything is green. What does Daddy say?	7 1 Everything is green.	1	9

NARRATIVE	TARGET RESPONSE	SENTENCE POINT	DSS TOTAL
Bobby says: Spot looks funny. Spot has a green tail. He has a green tail. He has a funny green tail. What does Spot have?	2 Spot has a funny green tail.	1	3
Daddy says: I am going to wash Spot's tail. I'm going to wash Spot's green tail. What is Daddy going to do?	1 2 Daddy is going to wash Spot's tail.	1	4
Now Spot is happy. Bobby says: I had fun. I am happy. Everyone is happy. What does Bobby say?	7 1 Everyone is happy.	1	9

LEVEL II: LESSON 19

CONCEPTS	ELICITED STRUCTURES		DSS VALUE
big/little, warm/cold, building a snowman	**Primary emphasis**		
	personal pronoun	– *he, she, his, her*	2
VOCABULARY		– *we, our, they, their*	3
snowman, snowball, warm, cold, inside, outside	secondary verb	– early-developing infinitive	2
FLANNEL-BOARD MATERIALS	negative	– N + *is not, doesn't*	7
	conjunction	– *and*	3
paper figures: Timmy, Susan, Mommy	**Secondary emphasis**		
paper cutouts: two coats, big snowball, little snowball, middle-sized snowball, small pieces of black paper for eyes, nose, and mouth, hat	indefinite pronoun	– *some, one, another*	3
	main verb	– -*s*, copular *am, are,* auxiliary *am, are*	2
		– obligatory *does* + verb	6

BUILDING A SNOWMAN

NARRATIVE	TARGET RESPONSE	SENTENCE POINT	DSS TOTAL
This is Susan. She is the girl in our story. Who is this?	1 1 This is Susan.	1	3
This is Timmy. Who is this?	1 1 This is Timmy.	1	3
This is Mommy. This is Timmy's and Susan's mommy. This is their mommy. Who is this?	1 1 3 This is their mommy.	1	6
Timmy says: Susan, I want to play. I want to go outside. I want to play outside. What does Timmy say?	1 1 2 I want to play outside.	1	5
Susan says: Okay, Timmy. Let's ask Mommy. Let's ask her. Let's ask Mommy. What does Susan say?	1 2 Let's ask Mommy.	1	4

NARRATIVE	TARGET RESPONSE	SENTENCE POINT	DSS TOTAL
Timmy says: Mommy, Susan and I want to play. We want to go outside. We want to play outside. What does Timmy say?	3 1 2 We want to play outside.	1	7
Mommy says: You can go outside, but it is cold. It is cold outside. It is not warm outside. Is it warm outside?	1 1 1 No, it is not warm outside.	1	4
Mommy says: Wear your warm clothes. Wear your warm clothes outside. Susan says: Look, Mommy. I am putting on my coat. I am putting on my hat. I am putting on my coat and hat. What is she putting on?	2 1 2 She is putting on her 3 coat and hat.	1	9
Timmy says: I am putting on my mittens. I am putting on my boots. I am putting on my mittens and my boots. What is he putting on?	2 1 2 He is putting on his 3 2 mittens and his boots.	1	11
Susan says: Timmy and I are putting on our warm clothes. We are getting dressed. We are putting on our warm clothes. What does Susan say?	3 2 3 We are putting on our warm clothes.	1	9
Why are they putting on their warm clothes?	3 2 3 They are putting on their 6 warm clothes because 1 1 it is cold outside.	1	17

NARRATIVE	TARGET RESPONSE	SENTENCE POINT	DSS TOTAL
Mommy says: Now you are ready. You can play outside. Timmy says: Look, Susan. Look at the snow. I want to play in the snow. I want to play in the snow. What does Timmy say?	1 1 2 I want to play in the snow.	1	5
Susan says: Let's make something, Timmy. Let's make something with the snow. What can Susan and Timmy make? Can you guess?	(Elicit guesses from the children.)		
Timmy says: Oh, I know. We can make a snowman. Look, Susan. I am making a snowball. What is he making?	2 1 He is making a snowball.	1	4
The snowball is getting bigger and bigger. It is getting bigger. Now it is very big. It is not little. Is the snowball little?	1 7 No, the snowball is not little.	1	9
Timmy says: This is a big snowball. It can be the bottom of the snowman. Susan says: Let's make another snowball. Let's make another one. What does Susan say?	1 2 3 3 Let's make another one.	1	10
Susan says: Look, Timmy. This snowball can be the middle of the snowman. Timmy says: Now I am making a little snowball.			

NARRATIVE	TARGET RESPONSE	SENTENCE POINT	DSS TOTAL
The snowball is not very big. The snowball is little. Is the snowball big?	1 . 7 No, the snowball is not big.	1	9
Timmy says: I am putting this snowball on top. I am putting this one on top. I am putting it on top. What does Timmy say?	1 2 1 I am putting it on top.	1	5
Susan says: The little snowball can be the snowman's head. It can be the snowman's head. What can it be?	1 4 It can be the snowman's head.	1	6
Timmy says: The big snowball is on the bottom. It is on the bottom. The little snowball is on the top. It is on the top. Where is the big snowball?	1 The big snowball is on the bottom.	1	2
Susan says: Look, Timmy. The snowman doesn't have eyes. He doesn't have a nose. He doesn't have a mouth. Does the snowman have eyes?	No, the snowman 7 6 doesn't have eyes.	1	14
Does he have a mouth?	2 7 6 No, he doesn't have a mouth.	1	16
Does he have a nose?	2 7 6 No, he doesn't have a nose.	1	16
Susan says: What can we do, Timmy? What can we do? Can you guess?	(Elicit guesses from the children.)		

NARRATIVE	TARGET RESPONSE	SENTENCE POINT	DSS TOTAL
Timmy says: I know. I'm going to get buttons. I'm going to get some. I'm going to get some buttons. What is he going to get?	2 1 2 3 He is going to get some buttons.	1	9
Timmy says: We can make the eyes with buttons. We can make the nose with buttons. We can make the mouth with buttons. What can they make with buttons?	3 4 They can make the eyes 3 3 and nose and mouth.	1	14
Timmy says: Now look, Susan. Now look at our snowman. He has eyes. He has a nose. He has a mouth. What does the snowman have?	2 The snowman has eyes 3 3 and a nose and a mouth.	1	9
Susan says: I am going to get a hat. I am going to get a hat for the snowman. I am going to get an old hat. What is she going to get?	2 1 2 She is going to get an old hat.	1	6
Now Susan is putting the hat on the snowman. Susan says: I am cold, Timmy. It is cold outside. I am not warm. Is she warm?	2 1 7 No, she is not warm.	1	11
What should Susan do?	(Elicit responses from the children.)		
Susan says: I want to go in, Timmy.			

NARRATIVE	TARGET RESPONSE	SENTENCE POINT	DSS TOTAL
I want to go in. What does Susan say?	1 1 2 I want to go in.	1	5
Timmy says: Okay, Susan. Let's go in. Let's go in and get warm. Let's go in. What does Timmy say?	1 2 Let's go in.	1	4

LEVEL II: LESSON 20

CONCEPTS	ELICITED STRUCTURES	DSS VALUE
running away, walking a dog, dogs and cats, being alone	**Primary emphasis**	
	personal pronoun – *he, him*	2
	main verb – *-s, -ed,* auxiliary *are,* irregular past	2
	– *can* + verb	4
	negative – any uncontracted negative	7
	conjunction – *because*	6

VOCABULARY
alone, outside, sidewalk, lost

FLANNEL-BOARD MATERIALS
paper figures: Timmy, Mommy
paper cutouts: dog, cat, kitchen door, sidewalk, leash, house front

PRINCE CHASES THE CAT

NARRATIVE	TARGET RESPONSE	SENTENCE POINT	DSS TOTAL
This is Timmy. Who is this?	1 1 This is Timmy.	1	3
This is Prince. Prince is Timmy's dog. He is his dog. Who is this?	1 1 This is Prince.	1	3
Whose dog is Prince?	2 1 He is Timmy's dog.	1	4
Timmy is playing inside. He is playing with Prince. Timmy and Prince are playing inside. They are playing together. Is Timmy playing alone?	7 No, Timmy is not 1 playing alone.	1	9
Who is he playing with?	2 1 He is playing with Prince.	1	4
Now Prince is going to the door. Prince is scratching at the door. Why is Prince scratching at the door? Can you guess?	(Elicit guesses from the children.)		

NARRATIVE	TARGET RESPONSE	SENTENCE POINT	DSS TOTAL
Prince wants to go outside. Prince is scratching at the door because he wants to go outside. He is scratching at the door because he wants to go outside. Why is he scratching at the door?	2 1 He is scratching at the door 6 2 2 2 because he wants to go outside.	1	16
Mommy is in the kitchen. Timmy is running into the kitchen. Timmy is running to see Mommy. Timmy is running into the kitchen to see Mommy. Why is Timmy running into the kitchen?	1 Timmy is running into the 3 kitchen to see Mommy.	1	5
Timmy says: Mommy, Mommy, Prince is scratching at the door. He is scratching at the door because he wants to go outside. Can I take him outside? Can I? Can I take him outside? What does Timmy say?	6 1 4 2 Can I take him outside?	1	14
Mommy says: Yes, you can. Yes, you can take Prince outside. Yes, you can take him out. What does Mommy say?	1 4 2 Yes, you can take him out.	1	8
Now Timmy is putting the leash on Prince. He is putting on Prince's leash. What is Timmy doing?	2 1 He is putting the leash on Prince.	1	4
Timmy and Prince are going outside.			

NARRATIVE	TARGET RESPONSE	SENTENCE POINT	DSS TOTAL
Timmy and Prince are walking on the sidewalk. They are walking on the sidewalk together. What are they doing?	3 2 They are walking on the sidewalk.	1	6
Is Timmy alone?	21 7 No, he is not alone.	1	11
Prince and Timmy are walking together. They are walking together. Timmy is not alone. Oh, oh. Prince sees a cat. He is running toward the cat. He is chasing the cat. He is chasing the cat. What is he doing?	2 1 He is chasing the cat.	1	4
Prince is pulling Timmy. Prince is pulling Timmy toward the cat. Prince is pulling hard. Timmy drops the leash. He cannot hold the leash. Timmy cannot hold the leash. Can Timmy hold the leash?	7 4 No, Timmy cannot hold the leash.	1	12
Prince pulled too hard. Why did Timmy drop the leash?	2 Timmy dropped the leash 6 2 because Prince pulled too hard.	1	11
Prince is running away. He is chasing the cat. He is chasing the cat. What is he doing?	2 1 He is chasing the cat.	1	4
Where did Prince go? Timmy is looking for Prince. Timmy cannot find Prince. Can Timmy find Prince?	7 4 No, Timmy cannot find Prince.	1	12
First he looked in the yard.			

NARRATIVE	TARGET RESPONSE	SENTENCE POINT	DSS TOTAL
Then he looked behind the tree. He looked in the yard and behind the tree. Where did Timmy look?	2 2 He looked in the yard 3 and behind the tree.	1	8
Timmy says: Prince is not here. He is gone. Prince is not here. What did Timmy say?	1 7 Prince is not here.	1	9
Timmy cannot find Prince. Timmy is going home. He is going home because he cannot find Prince. Why is Timmy going home?	2 1 6 He is going home because 2 7 4 he cannot find Prince.	1	23
Now Timmy is home. Timmy is crying. He is crying because he cannot find Prince. He is crying because he cannot find Prince. Why is he crying?	2 1 6 He is crying because 2 7 4 he cannot find Prince.	1	23
Oh, oh! Timmy sees something. He sees something on his porch. It's Prince!! Prince is standing on the porch. Prince came home. Where is Prince?	1 Prince is on the porch.	1	2
Now Timmy is happy. He is happy because Prince came home. Timmy is happy because Prince came home. Why is he happy?	21 6 He is happy because 2 Prince came home.	1	12

LEVEL II: LESSON 21

CONCEPTS

steering a wagon,
being careful,
breaking/fixing

VOCABULARY

handle, steer,
fix, doorbell

FLANNEL-BOARD MATERIALS

paper figures: Mommy, Timmy, mailman
paper cutouts: door, package, wagon, hill

ELICITED STRUCTURES	DSS VALUE
Primary emphasis	
personal pronoun – *he, she, his, her*	2
main verb – *-s,* copular *am, are,* auxiliary *am, are*	2
secondary verb – early-developing infinitive	2
wh-question – *why, how come*	7
Secondary emphasis	
personal pronoun – *they, their*	3
main verb – *can* + verb, obligatory *do* + verb	4
conjunction – *and*	3

TIMMY GETS A WAGON

NARRATIVE	TARGET RESPONSE	SENTENCE POINT	DSS TOTAL
This is Timmy. He is the boy in our story. Timmy is in our story. Who is this?	1 1 This is Timmy.	1	3
This is Mommy. This is Timmy's mommy. This is his mommy. Who is this?	1 1 This is Timmy's mommy.	1	3
Timmy is in the house. Timmy and Mommy are in the house. They are in the house. Where are they?	3 2 They are in the house.	1	6
Timmy hears something. He hears something ringing. He hears the doorbell ringing. What does he hear?	2 2 He hears the doorbell 4 ringing.	1	9
Mommy says: Why is the doorbell ringing?			

NARRATIVE	TARGET RESPONSE	SENTENCE POINT	DSS TOTAL
Why? Why is it ringing? What does Mommy say?	7 4 1 1 Why is it ringing?	1	14
Timmy says: The mailman might be ringing the doorbell. He might be ringing the doorbell. The mailman might be ringing it. Who might be ringing the doorbell?	The mailman might be 8 ringing the doorbell.	1	9
Timmy looks out the window. He sees the mailman. The mailman is ringing the doorbell. He is ringing the doorbell. What is he doing?	2 1 He is ringing the doorbell.	1	4
The mailman has a package. He has a big package. He has a big package for Timmy. What does he have?	2 2 He has a big package.	1	5
Timmy says: Mommy, Mommy, come here. Come here and see the package. Come here and see the big package. What does Timmy say?	1 3 1 Come here and see the big package.	1	6
Mommy says: The package is for you. It is for you, Timmy. The big package is for you. What does Mommy say?	1 1 The package is for you.	1	3
Mommy says: Open the package, Timmy. Open it. Open the big package. What does Mommy say?	1 Open the big package.	1	2

NARRATIVE	TARGET RESPONSE	SENTENCE POINT	DSS TOTAL
Mommy says: Let's see what's inside. Let's see. Let's see what's inside the package. What does Mommy say?	1 2 6 1 Let's see what's inside the package.	1	11
Timmy says: Look, Mommy. It's a wagon. It's a red wagon. It's a shiny red wagon. What is it?	1 1 It's a shiny red wagon.	1	3
Timmy says: I want to take my wagon outside. I want to. I want to take it outside. What does he want to do?	2 2 2 2 He wants to take his wagon outside.	1	9
Mommy says: Why do you want to take the wagon outside? Why? Why do you want to take it outside? What does Mommy say?	7 6 1 4 2 Why do you want to take 1 it outside?	1	22
Timmy says: I want to take my new wagon outside to play. I want to take my wagon out to play. I want to take it out to play. What does he want to do?	2 2 2 2 He wants to take his 3 wagon out to play.	1	12
Mommy and Timmy are going to take the new wagon outside. They are going to take the shiny new wagon outside. They are going to take it outside. What are they going to do?	3 2 2 They are going to take the wagon outside.	1	8

NARRATIVE	TARGET RESPONSE	SENTENCE POINT	DSS TOTAL
Timmy says: Look, Mommy, look! There is a hill. There is a big hill. What does Timmy say?	1 There is a big hill.	1	2
Timmy and Mommy are walking up the hill. They are going up the hill. They are walking up the hill. What are they doing?	3 2 They are walking up the hill.	1	6
Timmy is holding the wagon. Mommy says: You steer. You hold the handle and steer. You hold the wagon handle and steer. What does Mommy say?	1 1 You hold the wagon 3 1 handle and steer.	1	7
The wagon is rolling down the hill. It is going down the hill. It is rolling down the big hill. What is happening?	1 The wagon is rolling down the big hill.	1	2
The wagon is going fast. It is going very fast. What is happening?	1 The wagon is going very fast.	1	2
Mommy yells: Watch out, Timmy. Hang on to the wagon. Watch out, and hang on to the wagon. What does Mommy say?	1 3 1 Watch out, and hang on to the wagon.	1	6
Mommy says: Oh, Timmy. Your wagon tipped. Your wagon tipped, and you fell. Why did the wagon tip, Timmy? Why did it? Why did your wagon tip? What does Mommy say?	7 6 1 6 Why did your wagon tip?	1	21

NARRATIVE	TARGET RESPONSE	SENTENCE POINT	DSS TOTAL
Timmy says: My wagon tipped because it is broken. It is broken. My new wagon is broken. What does Timmy say?	1 1 My new wagon is broken.	1	3
Mommy says: Your wagon is broken! How come your wagon is broken? How come? How come it is broken? What does Mommy say?	7 1 1 How come it is broken?	1	10
Timmy says: Oh, Mommy! The wheels fell off. They fell off. The wheels fell off my new wagon. What happened?	2 The wheels fell off Timmy's wagon.	1	3
Mommy says: You look sad, Timmy. Why? Why are you sad? Why are you sad, Timmy? What does Mommy say?	7 2 1 1 Why are you sad?	1	12
Timmy says: I am sad because my wagon is broken. I can't put the wheels on my wagon. I can't put the wheels on my new wagon. I can't fix my wagon. Can Timmy fix the wagon?	4 4 No, Timmy can't fix the wagon.	1	9
Why is Timmy sad?	1 6 Timmy is sad because 2 4 4 he can't fix the wagon.	1	18
Mommy says: Don't worry, Timmy. Daddy will put the wheels on your wagon. Daddy will fix your new wagon.			

NARRATIVE	TARGET RESPONSE	SENTENCE POINT	DSS TOTAL
He will fix your wagon. What is Daddy going to do?	1 2 Daddy is going to fix Timmy's wagon.	1	4
Now Timmy is happy. He is very happy. Daddy is going to put the wheels on his wagon. Daddy is going to fix his wagon. Why is Timmy happy?	1 6 Timmy is happy because 1 2 2 Daddy is going to fix his wagon.	1	13

LEVEL II: LESSON 22

CONCEPTS	ELICITED STRUCTURES		DSS VALUE
going to the park, losing a ball, finding a dog, feeding a dog	**Primary emphasis**		
	personal pronoun	– *he, his, him*	2
		– *we, they, our, their*	3
VOCABULARY	main verb	– -*s,* copular *am, are,* auxiliary *am, are*	2
how about, miss, catch, bone	wh-question	– *why, what if, how come, how about* + gerund	7
FLANNEL-BOARD MATERIALS			
paper figures: Daddy, Susan, Timmy	**Secondary emphasis**		
paper cutouts: dog, ball, bone, hill	secondary verb	– early-developing infinitives	2
		– gerund	8

ADVENTURE AT THE PARK

NARRATIVE	TARGET RESPONSE	SENTENCE POINT	DSS TOTAL
This is Timmy. Who is this?	1 1 This is Timmy.	1	3
This is Susan. Who is this?	1 1 This is Susan.	1	3
This is Daddy. This is Timmy's and Susan's daddy. This is their daddy. Who is this?	1 1 3 This is their daddy.	1	6
Daddy says: I'm going to go to the park. I am going to go to the park, but I don't want to go alone. I want you to go, too. How about coming with me? How about it? How about coming with me? What does Daddy say?	7 8 How about coming 1 with me?	1	17

NARRATIVE	TARGET RESPONSE	SENTENCE POINT	DSS TOTAL
Timmy and Susan say: We will go to the park. We will go to the park with you. Timmy and Susan are going to the park with Daddy. They are going to go with Daddy. They are going to go to the park with Daddy. What are they going to do?	3 2 2 They are going to go to the park with Daddy.	1	8
Daddy is going to the park. Susan and Timmy are going to the park. They are going to the park. Where are they going?	3 2 They are going to the park.	1	6
Now they are at the park. Susan wants to play ball. Susan says: How about playing ball? How about it? How about playing ball? What does Susan say?	7 8 How about playing ball?	1	16
Susan is throwing the ball. She is throwing the ball to Timmy. Susan says: Catch the ball, Timmy. Catch the ball. What does Susan say?	1 Catch the ball.	1	2
Timmy says: Oh, Susan! I am going to miss the ball. I can't catch the ball. I can't catch it. I can't catch the ball. What does Timmy say?	1 4 4 I can't catch the ball.	1	10
The ball is rolling away. It is rolling away. It is rolling down a hill. What is happening?	1 The ball is rolling away.	1	2

NARRATIVE	TARGET RESPONSE	SENTENCE POINT	DSS TOTAL
Susan says: Run, Timmy. Run after the ball. Get the ball. What does Susan say?	1 Get the ball.	1	2
Timmy is running after the ball. He is running to get the ball. He wants to get the ball. Why is he running?	2 1 3 He is running to get the ball.	1	7
Timmy says: Oh, Susan! I see a dog. The dog is going to get the ball. Susan says: What will happen if the dog gets the ball? What if the dog gets it? What if the dog gets the ball? What does Susan say?	7 2 What if the dog gets the ball?	1	10
Timmy says: If the dog gets the ball, he might run away. He might run away. The dog might run away if he gets the ball. What does Timmy say?	6 The dog might run away 5 2 2 if he gets the ball.	1	16
Oh, oh! The dog got the ball. The dog is running with the ball. The dog is running away with the ball. What is the dog doing?	1 The dog is running away with the ball.	1	2
Susan says: Daddy! Daddy! The dog is running away with our ball. He has our ball. The dog is running with our ball. What does Susan say?	1 The dog is running with 3 our ball.	1	5

NARRATIVE	TARGET RESPONSE	SENTENCE POINT	DSS TOTAL
Daddy says: I'll get the ball. I will get it. I will get the ball from the dog. What will Daddy do?	4 Daddy will get the ball from the dog.	1	5
Daddy says: Come here, doggie. Come here. Bring me the ball. Daddy calls the dog because he wants the ball. Daddy wants the ball. Why is Daddy calling the dog?	1 Daddy is calling the dog 6 2 2 because he wants the ball.	1	12
The dog is looking at Daddy. Now he is running. He is running to Daddy. What is he doing?	2 1 He is running to Daddy.	1	4
The dog is bringing the ball. He is bringing the ball to Daddy. What is happening?	1 The dog is bringing the ball to Daddy.	1	2
Daddy says: Good dog. You are a good dog. What does Daddy say?	1 2 You are a good dog.	1	4
Susan says: Oh! Oh! The doggie is growling. Why is the doggie growling? Why? Why is the doggie growling? What does Susan say?	7 4 Why is the doggie 1 growling?	1	13
Daddy says: Maybe the doggie is hungry. Susan says: The doggie looks hungry.			

NARRATIVE	TARGET RESPONSE	SENTENCE POINT	DSS TOTAL
How about getting the doggie some food? How about it? How about getting the doggie some food? What does Susan say?	7 8 How about getting the 3 doggie some food?	1	19
Daddy says: Okay! Daddy is going to feed the dog. Daddy is going to feed the dog because the dog is hungry. How come Daddy is going to feed the dog?	1 2 Daddy is going to feed 6 the dog because the 1 dog is hungry.	1	11
Timmy says: Can we take the doggie home? Daddy says: Yes, we can take the doggie home. Let's take the doggie home. Is the doggie going to go home?	1 Yes, the doggie is going 2 to go home.	1	4
Daddy is walking home. Timmy and Susan are walking home. The doggie is walking home. They are all walking home. What are they doing?	3 3 2 They are all walking home.	1	9
Now they are home. Daddy is going to give the doggie a bone. He is going to give the doggie a bone. What is he going to do?	2 1 2 He is going to give the doggie a bone.	1	6
Susan says: Why is Daddy giving the dog a bone?			

NARRATIVE	TARGET RESPONSE	SENTENCE POINT	DSS TOTAL
Why? Why is Daddy giving the dog a bone?			
What does Susan say?	7 4 1 Why is Daddy giving the dog a bone?	1	13
Can you guess why?	(Elicit responses from the children.)		

LEVEL II: LESSON 23

CONCEPTS	ELICITED STRUCTURES		DSS VALUE
breaking, fixing, repairing	**Primary emphasis**		
	personal pronoun –	*we, they, us, our, their, them*	3
VOCABULARY	main verb –	*can, will* + verb, obligatory *do* + verb	4
TV repairman, cartoons, fix	–	*have* + verb + *-en*	7
FLANNEL-BOARD MATERIALS	secondary verb –	early-developing infinitives	2
paper figures: Mommy, Daddy, Timmy, Susan, TV repairman	negative –	*have* + *not*, N + *is not*	7
paper cutouts: TV set, telephone, truck, window	**Secondary emphasis**		
	personal pronoun –	*he, she, him, her*	2
	main verb –	*-s*, copular *am, are*, auxiliary *am, are*	2
	secondary verb –	later infinitival complement, infinitive with wh-word	5

GETTING THE TV FIXED

NARRATIVE	TARGET RESPONSE	SENTENCE POINT	DSS TOTAL
This is Timmy. Who is this?	1 1 This is Timmy.	1	3
This is Susan. Who is this?	1 1 This is Susan.	1	3
Timmy and Susan are eating breakfast. They are eating. They are eating breakfast. What are they doing?	3 2 They are eating breakfast.	1	6
It is Saturday. Today is Saturday. Timmy and Susan do not have to go to school on Saturday. Timmy says: I don't have to go to school on Saturday.			

NARRATIVE	TARGET RESPONSE	SENTENCE POINT	DSS TOTAL
I don't have to go on Saturday. I don't have to go. What does Timmy say?	1 4 4 5 I don't have to go.	1	15
Timmy and Susan are hurrying. They want to finish their breakfast. They want to watch television. They want to watch TV. What do they want to do?	3 1 2 They want to watch TV.	1	7
Mommy says: When you finish breakfast, you can watch TV. You can watch TV when you finish. When you finish, you can watch TV. What does Mommy say?	8 1 1 1 When you finish, you 4 can watch TV.	1	16
Mommy says: Susan and Timmy, you have not finished eating breakfast. You have not finished eating. You have not finished. What does Mommy say?	1 7 7 You have not finished.	1	16
Now Susan and Timmy have finished. They have finished. Now they want to watch television. Now they want to watch TV. What do they want?	3 1 2 They want to watch TV.	1	7
Susan says: Let's turn on the TV. Let's watch the cartoons. Let's turn on the TV and watch the cartoons. What does Susan say?	1 2 3 Let's turn on the TV and 2 watch the cartoons.	1	9

NARRATIVE	TARGET RESPONSE	SENTENCE POINT	DSS TOTAL
Timmy says: I will turn on the TV. I will. I will turn it on. What does Timmy say?	1 4 1 I will turn it on.	1	7
Timmy is turning the dial. He is turning the TV on. He is turning on the TV. What is Timmy doing?	2 1 He is turning on the TV.	1	4
What has happened? What is wrong? There isn't any picture. There isn't any sound. The TV set is not working. The TV set is broken. Timmy says: The TV set is broken. What does Timmy say?	1 The TV set is broken.	1	2
Susan says: Daddy! Daddy! The TV set is broken. The TV won't work. The TV won't work. What is wrong with the TV?	5 4 The TV won't work.	1	10
Timmy says: Daddy, can you fix the TV? Can you? Can you fix it? What does Timmy say?	6 1 4 1 Can you fix it?	1	13
Daddy says: I will try. I will try to fix the TV. I will try to fix it. I will try to make the TV work. What does Daddy say?	1 4 5 I will try to make the 5 TV work.	1	16
The TV won't work; it is broken. Daddy cannot fix it. He cannot fix it. Can Daddy fix the TV?	7 4 No, Daddy cannot fix the TV.	1	12
Timmy says: Daddy, you have not made the TV work.			

NARRATIVE	TARGET RESPONSE	SENTENCE POINT	DSS TOTAL
You have not fixed the TV. You have not fixed it. What does Timmy say?	1 7 7 1 You have not fixed it.	1	17
Who will make the TV work? Who will fix the TV? Who knows how to fix the TV? Can you guess?	(Elicit responses from the children.)		
Daddy says: The TV repairman knows how to fix the TV. He knows how to fix it. The TV repairman knows. Who knows how to fix the TV?	2 The TV repairman knows 8 5 how to fix the TV.	1	16
Daddy says: I will call the TV repairman. I will call him. I will call the TV repairman. What will Daddy do?	4 Daddy will call the TV repairman.	1	5
Mommy says: Call the TV man at home. The TV repairman has not gone to work yet. He has not gone to work. The TV repairman has not gone to work yet. What does Mommy say?	7 The TV repairman has not 7 gone to work yet.	1	15
Daddy is calling the TV repairman. He is calling. He is calling the TV repairman. What is Daddy doing?	1 Daddy is calling the TV repairman.	1	2

NARRATIVE	TARGET RESPONSE	SENTENCE POINT	DSS TOTAL
Daddy says: Hello, this is Mr. Jones. Our TV is broken. Our TV needs to be fixed. Can you come to our house? Can you fix our TV? Can you come to our house and fix our TV? What does Daddy say?	6 1 4 3 Can you come to our 3 4 3 house and fix our TV?	1	25
The TV repairman says: I can come to your house. I can fix your TV. I can come to your house and fix your TV. Will the TV repairman fix the TV?	Yes, the TV repairman 4 will fix the TV.	1	5
The TV repairman says: I will be at your house soon. I will be there. I will be there soon. What does he say?	1 4 I will be there soon.	1	6
Susan and Timmy are looking for the TV repairman. They are looking for the repairman. They are looking out the window. They are looking for the TV repairman. What are they doing?	3 2 They are looking for the TV repairman.	1	6
Timmy and Susan have not seen the TV repairman's truck. They have not seen his truck. Have they seen the TV repairman's truck?	3 7 7 No, they have not seen the TV repairman's truck.	1	18
Timmy says: I have not seen the TV man's truck.			

NARRATIVE	TARGET RESPONSE	SENTENCE POINT	DSS TOTAL
I have not seen his truck. I have not seen it. What does Timmy say?	1 7 7 1 I have not seen it.	1	17
Here comes a truck! Here comes the TV repairman. Hooray! Here he comes. Who is coming?	The TV repairman 1 is coming.	1	2
The TV repairman is looking at the TV. He wants to see what's wrong. He wants to see what's broken. What does he want to do?	2 2 2 6 1 He wants to see what's broken.	1	14
Now the TV repairman is fixing the TV. He is fixing it. He is fixing the TV. What is he doing?	2 1 He is fixing the TV.	1	4
The TV is fixed. Here comes the picture. Here comes the sound. It is not broken any more. Is the TV broken?	1 7 No, the TV is not broken.	1	9
Timmy says: Now, we can watch TV. We have not missed the cartoons on TV. We have not missed the cartoons. We have not missed them. What does Timmy say?	3 7 7 3 We have not missed them.	1	21
Timmy and Susan are happy. Now they can see the cartoons.			

LEVEL II: LESSON 24

CONCEPTS	ELICITED STRUCTURES		DSS VALUE
going to the park, activities at the park	**Primary emphasis**		
	personal pronoun	– *he, his, she*	2
VOCABULARY		– *we, us, they, them, their, those, these*	3
wagon, swing, sandbox, trucks	main verb	– irregular past, *-s,* copular *are,* auxiliary *am, are*	2
FLANNEL-BOARD MATERIALS		– *can, will* + verb	4
paper figures: Daddy, Bobby, Karen	secondary verb	– early-developing infinitives	2
paper cutouts: wagon, four swings, sandbox, four trucks	conjunction	– *if, so*	5
	Secondary emphasis		
	indefinite pronoun	– *some, more*	3

FUN AT THE PARK

NARRATIVE	TARGET RESPONSE	SENTENCE POINT	DSS TOTAL
This is Bobby. Who is this?	1 1 This is Bobby.	1	3
This is Karen. Who is this?	1 1 This is Karen.	1	3
Karen is Bobby's sister. Karen is his sister. She is Bobby's sister. Who is she?	2 1 She is Bobby's sister.	1	4
This is Daddy. Who is this?	1 1 This is Daddy.	1	3
This is Bobby's and Karen's daddy. This is their daddy. He is their daddy. Who is he?	2 1 3 He is their daddy.	1	7
Bobby says: I want to go to the park. I want to go. I want to go to the park. What does Bobby say?	1 1 2 I want to go to the park.	1	5
Karen says: I want to go, too.			

NARRATIVE	TARGET RESPONSE	SENTENCE POINT	DSS TOTAL
I want to go to the park. I want to go, too. What does Karen say?	1 1 2 I want to go, too.	1	5
Daddy says: We will go to the park if the sun is shining. If the sun is shining, we will go. We will go to the park if the sun is shining. What does Daddy say?	3 4 We will go to the park 5 1 if the sun is shining.	1	14
Look! The sun is shining. It is a nice day. Daddy says: We will go to the park. The sun is shining, so we will go. The sun is shining, so we will go to the park. What does Daddy say?	1 5 3 The sun is shining, so we 4 will go to the park.	1	14
Daddy and Bobby and Karen are going to the park. They are all going. They are going to the park. Where are they going?	3 2 They are going to the park.	1	6
This is Karen's wagon. This is her wagon. Whose wagon is this?	1 1 It is Karen's.	1	3
Daddy will pull the wagon. Daddy will pull the wagon if Karen is in it. He will pull the wagon if Karen is in it. What will Daddy do?	4 Daddy will pull the wagon 5 1 1 if Karen is in it.	1	12
Karen is in the wagon. She is in the wagon. Is Karen in the wagon?	1 Yes, Karen is in the wagon.	1	2

NARRATIVE	TARGET RESPONSE	SENTENCE POINT	DSS TOTAL
Karen says: I got into the wagon, so now Daddy can pull it. I got in, so Daddy can pull it. I got into the wagon, so Daddy can pull it. What does Karen say?	1 2 5 I got into the wagon, so 4 1 Daddy can pull it.	1	14
Bobby is riding his bicycle. He is riding. He is riding his bicycle. What is he doing?	2 1 2 He is riding his bicycle.	1	6
Now Bobby, Karen, and Daddy are at the park. They are at the park. They are at the park. Where are they?	3 2 They are at the park.	1	6
What are they gonna do? Can you guess?	(Elicit guesses from the children.)		
Bobby wants to go on those swings. He wants to go on those swings. He wants to go on them. He wants to go on those swings. What does he want?	2 2 2 He wants to go on 3 those swings.	1	10
Karen wants to go on those swings, too. She wants to go on those swings. What does she want?	2 2 2 She wants to go on 3 those swings.	1	10
They both want to go on those swings. Bobby says: We can swing if Daddy pushes us. If Daddy pushes us, we can swing.			

NARRATIVE	TARGET RESPONSE	SENTENCE POINT	DSS TOTAL
We can swing if Daddy pushes us. What does Bobby say?	3 4 5 We can swing if Daddy 2 3 pushes us.	1	18
Karen says: Push me. Push me, Daddy. What does Karen say?	1 1 Push me, Daddy.	1	3
Daddy is pushing Karen. Karen is swinging. Daddy says: I am pushing you. I am pushing you so you can swing. I am pushing you so you can swing. What does Daddy say?	1 2 1 5 1 I am pushing you so you 4 can swing.	1	15
Bobby says: Give me a big push, Daddy. I want to go up high. Give me a big push so I will go up high. Give me a big push so I will go up high. What does Bobby say?	1 1 5 1 Give me a big push so I 4 will go up high.	1	13
Now Bobby and Karen are getting off the swings. They are getting off. They are getting off the swings. What are they doing?	3 2 They are getting off the swings.	1	6
Now Bobby says: I want to play in the sandbox. I want to play over there. I want to play in the sandbox. What does Bobby say?	1 1 2 I want to play in the sandbox.	1	5
Karen says: I want to play in the sandbox, too.			

NARRATIVE	TARGET RESPONSE	SENTENCE POINT	DSS TOTAL
I want to play in the sandbox. What does Karen say?	1 1 2 I want to play in the sandbox.	1	5
Bobby and Karen are playing in the sandbox. They are both playing in the sandbox. They are playing in the sandbox. What are they doing?	3 2 They are playing in the sandbox.	1	6
Bobby is playing with these trucks. Bobby is playing with these. He is playing with these trucks. What is he doing?	2 1 He is playing with 3 these trucks.	1	7
Karen wants to play with those trucks. She wants to play with those. She wants those trucks, too. What does Karen want?	2 3 Karen wants those trucks.	1	6
But Bobby will get mad. Bobby will get mad if Karen takes those trucks. He will get mad if she takes them. He will get mad if she takes those trucks. Why will he get mad?	2 4 5 2 He will get mad if she 2 3 takes those trucks.	1	19
Oh! Oh! Daddy has some more trucks. He has some more. He has some more trucks. What does Daddy have?	2 3 3 Daddy has some more trucks.	1	9
Daddy says: These trucks are for you, Karen. These trucks are for you. What does Daddy say?	3 2 1 These trucks are for you.	1	7

NARRATIVE	TARGET RESPONSE	SENTENCE POINT	DSS TOTAL
Daddy gives the trucks to Karen. Daddy gives them to Karen. He gives them to Karen. What does he do?	2 2 3 He gives them to Karen.	1	8
Now Bobby and Karen both have trucks. They both have trucks. They are happy. Daddy says: You both have trucks, so you are happy. You have trucks, so you are happy. You both have some trucks, so you are happy. What does Daddy say?	1 7 1 3 You both have some trucks, 5 1 2 so you are happy.	1	21
Bobby is getting tired. Karen is getting tired. They are getting tired. It is time to go home. Bobby wants to come back tomorrow. Karen wants to come back tomorrow. They both want to come back. They want to come back tomorrow. What do they want?	3 1 2 They want to come back tomorrow.	1	7
Daddy says: You can come back if you are good. If you are good, you can come back. You can come back if you are good. What does Daddy say?	1 4 5 You can come back if 1 2 you are good.	1	14
Do you think they will be good?	(Elicit spontaneous responses.)		

LEVEL II: LESSON 25

CONCEPTS

going to the airport, ordering lunch, meeting someone at a plane, finding baggage, why people visit

VOCABULARY

airport, airplane, restaurant, suitcases

FLANNEL-BOARD MATERIALS

paper figures: Mommy, Daddy, Karen, Uncle Bill
paper cutouts: car, two airplanes, table, four suitcases

ELICITED STRUCTURES		DSS VALUE
Primary emphasis		
personal pronoun	– *he, she*	2
	– *we, us, they, them, these, those*	3
main verb	– *-s,* irregular past, copular *am, are,* auxiliary *am, are*	2
	– *can* + verb	4
secondary verb	– early-developing infinitives	2
conjunction	– *so, if*	5
Secondary emphasis		
indefinite pronoun	– *six, all*	3

PICKING UP UNCLE BILL AT THE AIRPORT

NARRATIVE	TARGET RESPONSE	SENTENCE POINT	DSS TOTAL
This is Karen. Who is this?	1 1 This is Karen.	1	3
Karen is six. She is six. She is six years old. How old is she?	2 1 3 She is six years old.	1	7
This is Mommy. This is Karen's mommy. This is her mommy. Who is this?	1 1 This is Karen's mommy.	1	3
This is Daddy. This is Karen's daddy. This is her daddy. Who is this?	1 1 This is Karen's daddy.	1	3
Daddy says: Guess who is coming. Guess who is coming so he can see us. Karen says: Oh! Oh! I know! Uncle Bill is coming.			

NARRATIVE	TARGET RESPONSE	SENTENCE POINT	DSS TOTAL
He is coming so he can see us. Uncle Bill is coming so he can see us. Why is Uncle Bill coming?	1 5 Uncle Bill is coming so 2 4 3 he can see us.	1	16
Uncle Bill is coming on an airplane. He is coming on an airplane so he can see them. Were you ever on an airplane?	(Elicit responses from the children.)		
Daddy says: I'm going to meet Uncle Bill at the airport. I'm going to the airport so I can meet him. I'm going to the airport so I can meet Uncle Bill. Why is Daddy going to the airport?	1 Daddy is going to the 5 2 4 airport so he can meet Uncle Bill.	1	13
Daddy says: Who wants to go? Who wants to go to the airport? Who wants to go to the airport to meet Uncle Bill? What does Daddy say?	2 2 2 Who wants to go to the 3 airport to meet Uncle Bill?	1	10
Mommy says: I want to go to the airport. I want to go to the airport so I can meet Uncle Bill. I want to go to the airport so I can meet him. I want to go to the airport so I can meet Uncle Bill. What does Mommy say?	1 1 2 I want to go to the airport 5 1 4 so I can meet Uncle Bill.	1	15
Karen says: I want to go, too. I want to go so I can meet Uncle Bill.			

NARRATIVE	TARGET RESPONSE	SENTENCE POINT	DSS TOTAL
I can meet Uncle Bill if I go to the airport. I want to go so I can meet Uncle Bill. What does Karen say?	1 1 2 5 1 4 I want to go so I can meet Uncle Bill.	1	15
Mommy, Daddy, and Karen are driving to the airport. They are driving to the airport so they can meet Uncle Bill. They are driving so they can meet Uncle Bill. Why are they driving?	3 2 5 3 They are driving so they 4 can meet Uncle Bill.	1	18
Karen says: Oh, look at the sky. You can see airplanes if you look at the sky. If you look at the sky, you can see airplanes. You can see airplanes if you look at the sky. What does Karen say?	1 4 5 You can see airplanes if 1 1 you look at the sky.	1	13
Daddy says: We are near the airport, so you can see lots of airplanes. There are lots of airplanes in the sky. Look at all those airplanes. Look at them. Look at all those airplanes. What does Daddy say?	1 3 3 Look at all those airplanes.	1	8
Now Mommy, Daddy, and Karen are at the airport. They are at the airport so they can meet Uncle Bill. Who is at the airport?	3 Mommy, Daddy, and Karen 2 are at the airport.	1	6
Karen says: Let's watch the planes land.			

NARRATIVE	TARGET RESPONSE	SENTENCE POINT	DSS TOTAL
Let's watch the planes come down. Let's watch them come down. Let's watch the planes come down. What does Karen say?	1 2 Let's watch the planes 5 come down.	1	9
Mommy says: Look at the people coming off the plane. Look at all those people. Look at all those people coming off the plane. What does Mommy say?	1 3 3 Look at all those people 4 coming off the plane.	1	12
Karen says: Oh! Here comes Uncle Bill. Uncle Bill is getting off the plane so he can visit us. He is coming so he can visit us. He is getting off the plane so he can visit us. Why is Uncle Bill getting off the plane?	1 Uncle Bill is getting off 5 2 4 3 the plane so he can visit them.	1	16
Uncle Bill looks around so he can see Mommy, Daddy, and Karen. Uncle Bill looks around so he can see them. He looks around so he can see all of them. Why does he look around?	2 2 5 2 He looks around so he 4 3 can see them.	1	19
Uncle Bill says: Hello, Karen. Hello everybody. How are you? Daddy says: Are you hungry? If you are hungry, let's eat.			

NARRATIVE	TARGET RESPONSE	SENTENCE POINT	DSS TOTAL
Let's eat if you are hungry. Let's eat at the restaurant if you are hungry. What does Daddy say?	1 2 Let's eat at the restaurant 5 1 2 if you are hungry.	1	12
Uncle Bill says: Good. I am hungry. Now they are at the restaurant. They are sitting at a table. Karen says: I want a hamburger so I can eat it. I want a hamburger. I want a hamburger so I can eat it. What does Karen say?	1 1 5 I want a hamburger so 1 4 1 I can eat it.	1	14
Mommy says: I want a hot dog so I can eat it. Daddy says: I want a hot dog so I can eat it. Uncle Bill says: I want a hot dog so I can eat it. They all want hot dogs so they can eat them. Why do they want hot dogs?	3 3 1 5 They all want hot dogs so 3 4 3 they can eat them.	1	23
Everybody is eating lunch. They are hungry, so they are eating lunch. They are all eating lunch. They are hungry, so they are eating lunch. Why are they eating lunch?	3 2 5 3 They are hungry, so they 2 are eating lunch.	1	16
Karen says: I like the airport. I like eating here. I like eating at the airport. What does Karen say?	1 1 8 I like eating at the airport.	1	11

NARRATIVE	TARGET RESPONSE	SENTENCE POINT	DSS TOTAL
Now they are finished. They are finished eating lunch. Uncle Bill says: Let's go downstairs. Let's get my suitcases. Let's go downstairs so I can get my suitcases. What does Uncle Bill say?	1 2 5 1 Let's go downstairs so I 4 1 can get my suitcases.	1	15
They are looking for Uncle Bill's suitcases. Karen says: Are these your suitcases, Uncle Bill? Are these yours? Are these your suitcases? What does Karen say?	2 1 3 1 Are these your suitcases?	1	8
Uncle Bill says: No, my suitcases are black. Mommy says: Look. Those suitcases are black. See if those suitcases are yours, Uncle Bill. See if those suitcases are yours. What does Mommy say?	1 5 3 See if those suitcases 2 1 are yours.	1	13
Uncle Bill says: Yes, these suitcases are mine. These are mine. These suitcases are mine. What does Uncle Bill say?	3 2 1 These suitcases are mine.	1	7
Uncle Bill says: We can go home. You found my suitcases, so we can go home. You found my suitcases, so we can go home now. What does Uncle Bill say?	1 2 1 You found my suitcases, 5 3 4 so we can go home now.	1	17
Daddy says: Let me carry your suitcases. Now we can go home.			

LEVEL II: LESSON 26

CONCEPTS

baiting a hook,
camping,
fishing,
hurrying

VOCABULARY

bait, campfire

FLANNEL-BOARD MATERIALS

paper figures: Mommy, Daddy, Timmy, Bobby
paper cutouts: tent, table, four fishing poles with strings and hooks, worms, pond, boot

ELICITED STRUCTURES		DSS VALUE
Primary emphasis		
personal pronoun	– *he, she, his, her, him*	2
	– *we, us, our, them, their, they*	3
main verb	– *-s, -ed,* copular *am, are,* auxiliary *am, are*	2
	– *can, will* + verb, obligatory *do* + verb	4
	– *could, should* + verb, obligatory *does, did* + verb	6
secondary verb	– gerund	8
negative	– uncontracted negative, *couldn't, doesn't*	7
conjunction	– *because*	6
Secondary emphasis		
secondary verb	– later-developing infinitive	5
interrogative	– reversal of modal and obligatory *do*	6

FISHING ON A CAMPING TRIP

NARRATIVE	TARGET RESPONSE	SENTENCE POINT	DSS TOTAL
This is Mommy. Who is this?	1 1 This is Mommy.	1	3
This is Daddy. Who is this?	1 1 This is Daddy.	1	3
Mommy and Daddy are on a camping trip. Mommy and Daddy are fixing breakfast on their camping trip. They are fixing breakfast. They are hungry. What are they doing?	3 2 They are fixing breakfast.	1	6

NARRATIVE	TARGET RESPONSE	SENTENCE POINT	DSS TOTAL
Where are Timmy and Bobby? I do not see them. Where are they? Do you see them?	1 7 4 3 I do not see them.	1	16
Here are Timmy and Bobby! They were playing in the woods. They smelled the bacon, so they came back. They are hungry. They came back because they smelled the bacon. Why did they come back?	3 2 6 They came back because 3 2 they smelled the bacon.	1	17
Timmy and Bobby say: We're hungry. Mommy and Daddy say: We're hungry. Mommy says: Breakfast is not ready yet. We will have to wait because breakfast is not ready. We will have to wait because breakfast is not ready. What does Mommy say?	3 4 5 We will have to wait 6 1 because breakfast is 7 not ready.	1	27
Now breakfast is ready. Mommy says: Breakfast is ready. Come and eat. Come and eat, because breakfast is ready. What does Mommy say?	1 3 1 6 Come and eat, because 1 breakfast is ready.	1	13
Everyone is sitting around the campfire. Timmy says: I wish we could stay longer. This is fun.			

NARRATIVE	TARGET RESPONSE	SENTENCE POINT	DSS TOTAL
I wish we could stay longer. What does Timmy say?	1 1 3 6 I wish we could stay longer.	1	12
Bobby says: Couldn't we stay, Daddy? Couldn't we? Couldn't we stay? What does Bobby say?	7 6 3 6 Couldn't we stay?	1	23
Daddy says: I would like to, but I have to go back to work. We will come again. We will come again sometime. What does Daddy say?	3 4 We will come again sometime.	1	8
Bobby is eating fast. Mommy says: Why are you hurrying? Why are you eating so fast? Why are you hurrying? What does Mommy say?	7 4 1 2 Why are you hurrying?	1	15
Bobby says: I am eating fast because I want to go fishing again. I had so much fun yesterday. I am hurrying because I want to go fishing again. What does Bobby say?	1 2 6 1 I am hurrying because I 1 2 8 want to go fishing.	1	22
Now Timmy is eating fast, too. Timmy says: Can we go fishing again, Daddy? Can we go fishing again? Can we go again? What does Timmy say?	6 3 4 8 Can we go fishing again?	1	22
Oh, oh! Daddy is getting upset. The boys are eating too fast.			

NARRATIVE	TARGET RESPONSE	SENTENCE POINT	DSS TOTAL
He doesn't like the boys to eat so fast. Why is Daddy getting upset?	1 Daddy is getting upset 6 because the boys 2 are eating too fast.	1	10
Daddy says: We can go fishing if you slow down. We can go fishing if you eat slower. What does Daddy say?	3 4 8 5 1 We can go fishing if you 1 eat slower.	1	23
Timmy and Bobby are eating slower. They want to go fishing again. They are eating slower. Why are they eating slower?	3 2 They are eating slower 6 3 1 because they want 2 8 to go fishing.	1	26
Everyone is finished now. They are all finished. Everyone is ready to go fishing. What is everyone ready to do?	7 1 3 Everyone is ready to go 8 fishing.	1	20
Mommy says: Oh, wait!! I want to put the food away. Will you wait if I hurry? Will you? Will you wait if I hurry? What does Mommy say?	6 1 4 5 1 1 Will you wait if I hurry?	1	19
Daddy says: Take your time. We can wait. We can wait for you. What does Daddy say?	3 4 1 We can wait for you.	1	9
Timmy and Bobby have their fishing poles. Daddy has his pole and Mommy's pole.			

NARRATIVE	TARGET RESPONSE	SENTENCE POINT	DSS TOTAL
Mommy is ready now. Mommy says: I am ready, so we can go. We can go because I am ready. We can go now because I am ready. What does Mommy say?	3 4 6 We can go now because 1 2 I am ready.	1	17
Now everyone is at the lake. Daddy is putting the worm on his hook. He is baiting his hook. Daddy is putting the worm on his hook. He is baiting his hook. What is Daddy doing?	2 1 2 He is baiting his hook.	1	6
Mommy says: Oh, I don't like to do that. I could not do that. I could not do it. What does Mommy say?	1 7 6 1 I could not do that.	1	16
Mommy says: Could you help me, Timmy? Could you help me put the worm on my hook? Could you help me bait my hook? What does Mommy say?	6 1 6 1 5 Could you help me bait 1 my hook?	1	21
Why does Mommy want help?	2 6 Mommy wants help because 2 7 6 5 she doesn't like to bait 2 her hook.	1	31
Timmy and Bobby are laughing. Mommy says: Why are you laughing? Why are you laughing at me? What does Mommy say?	7 4 1 2 1 Why are you laughing at me?	1	16

NARRATIVE	TARGET RESPONSE	SENTENCE POINT	DSS TOTAL
Daddy says: I know why they are laughing. I know why. They are laughing because you're afraid of a little worm. They are laughing because you are afraid. What does Daddy say?	3 2 6 They are laughing because 1 2 you are afraid.	1	15
Timmy is putting a worm on Mommy's hook. He is baiting her hook so she can fish. He is baiting her hook. What is he doing?	2 1 2 He is baiting her hook.	1	6
Timmy and Bobby put worms on their hooks. They bait their hooks. Now everyone is ready to fish. Who is ready to fish?	7 1 3 Everyone is ready to fish.	1	12
They are all fishing. Everyone is fishing at the edge of the lake. Oh! Oh! Mommy's pole is moving. It is bending down. What do you think is happening?	(Elicit responses from the children.)		
Mommy says: I think I have a fish. I think I caught a fish on my hook. I think I caught a fish. What does Mommy say?	1 1 1 2 I think I caught a fish.	1	6
Mommy is pulling up on her pole. She is excited. Mommy says: We can have this fish with dinner. It will be good. We can have this fish with dinner. What does Mommy say?	3 4 1 We can have this fish with dinner.	1	9

NARRATIVE	TARGET RESPONSE	SENTENCE POINT	DSS TOTAL
Oh! Oh! Timmy and Bobby and Daddy are laughing. They are all laughing. What are they doing?	3 3 2 They are all laughing.	1	9
Now Mommy is laughing, too. Everyone is laughing. Everying is laughing because Mommy didn't catch a fish. Why are they laughing?	3 2 They are laughing 6 7 because Mommy didn't 6 catch a fish.	1	25
What do you think Mommy caught?	(Elicit responses from the children.)		
Mommy pulls a boot out of the water.			

LEVEL II: LESSON 27

CONCEPTS	ELICITED STRUCTURES		DSS VALUE
making choices, amusement-park activities, being on vacation.	**Primary emphasis**		
	personal pronoun –	*we, they*	3
	main verb –	*-s,* copular *are,* auxiliary *am, are*	2
	–	*could, should* + verb	6
	conjunction –	*or*	5
	interrogative –	reversal of modal	6
	Secondary emphasis		
	main verb –	*will* + verb, emphatic *do* + verb	4
	secondary verb –	early-developing infinitive	2

VOCABULARY

vacation, decide, which one, Kiddyland, Ferris wheel, roller coaster, merry-go-round

FLANNEL-BOARD MATERIALS

paper figures: Mommy Daddy, Timmy
paper cutouts: Ferris wheel, roller coaster, merry-go-round, hot-dog stand

GOING TO KIDDYLAND

NARRATIVE	TARGET RESPONSE	SENTENCE POINT	DSS TOTAL
This is Timmy. Timmy is a boy. He is the boy in our story. Timmy is the boy in our story. Who is this?	1 1 This is Timmy.	1	3
This is Mommy. This is Daddy. They are Timmy's mommy and daddy. They are his mommy and daddy. Who are they?	3 2 They are Timmy's 3 mommy and daddy.	1	9
It is summertime. Daddy is on vacation. He is on vacation. He is not going to work today. He has the day off.			

NARRATIVE	TARGET RESPONSE	SENTENCE POINT	DSS TOTAL
Daddy is on vacation. Why isn't Daddy going to work today?	5 1 Daddy isn't going to work 6 2 1 today because he is on vacation.	1	16
Daddy says: I have today off. I am not going to work today. I am on vacation. Let's do something special. Let's do something special on my day off. Let's do something special today. What does Daddy say?	1 2 3 Let's do something special today.	1	7
Mommy says: What should we do? Can you think of something special? What should we do? What does Mommy say?	2 6 3 6 What should we do?	1	18
Daddy says: We could go to the zoo or to Kiddyland. We could go to the zoo. It would be fun to see the animals. It would be fun to see the lions and tigers and monkeys. Or, we could go to Kiddyland. It would be fun to go on the rides. It would be fun to go on the Ferris wheel and the roller coaster. We could go to the zoo or to Kiddyland. What does Daddy say?	3 6 We could go to the zoo 5 or to Kiddyland.	1	15
Mommy says: Oh, Daddy, those are good ideas.			

NARRATIVE	TARGET RESPONSE	SENTENCE POINT	DSS TOTAL
We could go to the zoo or to Kiddyland. Which one should we do? Should we go to the zoo or to Kiddyland? You decide, Timmy. Should we go to the zoo or to Kiddyland? What does Mommy say?	6 3 6 Should we go to the 5 zoo or to Kiddyland?	1	21
Timmy says: Oh! Let's go to Kiddyland. I like to go on rides. I like to go on the roller coaster. I like to go to Kiddyland. What does Timmy say?	1 1 5 I like to go to Kiddyland.	1	8
Daddy says: Okay, Timmy. We will go to Kiddyland. We will go on lots of rides. It will be fun. We will have fun at Kiddyland. What does Daddy say?	3 4 We will have fun at Kiddyland.	1	8
Now Mommy, Daddy, and Timmy are at Kiddyland. They are at Kiddyland. Mommy says: Oh! Look at all the rides. What shall we do first? There are so many things to do. What shall we do first? What does Mommy say?	2 6 3 7 What shall we do first?	1	19
Daddy says: We could go on the Ferris wheel.			

NARRATIVE	TARGET RESPONSE	SENTENCE POINT	DSS TOTAL
Or we could go on the roller coaster. Which should we do first? Should we go on the Ferris wheel or the roller coaster? You decide, Timmy. Should we go on the Ferris wheel or the roller coaster? What does Daddy say?	6 3 6 Should we go on the 5 Ferris wheel or the roller coaster?	1	21
Timmy says: Oh, let's go on the roller coaster. I like the roller coaster. I like to go fast. I like to go up and down. Let's go on the roller coaster first. What does Timmy say?	1 2 Let's go on the roller coaster first.	1	4
Daddy says: Okay. We will go on the roller coaster first. Now Mommy, Daddy, and Timmy are on the roller coaster. The roller coaster is going fast. It is going up and down. Mommy, Daddy, and Timmy are having fun. They are having fun. Do Mommy, Daddy, and Timmy like the roller coaster? Do they?	3 4 Yes, they do like the roller coaster.	1	8
Now the roller-coaster ride is finished. Mommy says: What should we do next? We could go on the Ferris wheel. The Ferris wheel is right here.			

NARRATIVE	TARGET RESPONSE	SENTENCE POINT	DSS TOTAL
It is right here. Or, we could go on the merry-go-round. The merry-go-round is over there. It is over there. Which one should we do? Should we go on the Ferris wheel or the merry-go-round? You decide, Timmy. Should we go on the Ferris wheel or the merry-go-round? What does Mommy say?	6 3 6 Should we go on the 5 Ferris wheel or the merry-go-round?	1	21
Timmy says: I can't decide. I like them both. I like the Ferris wheel, and I like the merry-go-round, too. I can't decide. You help me, Daddy. Should we go on the Ferris wheel or the merry-go-round? Which one should we do? Should we go on the Ferris wheel or the merry-go-round? What does Timmy say?	6 3 6 Should we go on the 5 Ferris wheel or the merry-go-round?	1	21
Daddy says: Let's go on the Ferris wheel. I like the Ferris wheel because it goes up high. I like to go up high. I like the Ferris wheel because it goes up high. Why does Daddy like the Ferris wheel?	2 Daddy likes the Ferris 6 1 2 wheel because it goes up high.	1	12

NARRATIVE	TARGET RESPONSE	SENTENCE POINT	DSS TOTAL
Mommy and Timmy say: Okay. We will go on the Ferris wheel. Now Mommy, Daddy, and Timmy are on the Ferris wheel. They are going up. They are going up high on the Ferris wheel. Mommy, Daddy, and Timmy are having fun. They are having fun. Do Mommy, Daddy, and Timmy like the Ferris wheel? Do they?	3 4 Yes, they do like the Ferris wheel.	1	8
Now the Ferris-wheel ride is finished. Daddy says: I am hungry. Mommy says: So am I. Timmy says: I am hungry, too. Daddy says: What shall we eat? Should we have hot dogs or hamburgers? I like hot dogs. But I like hamburgers, too. Which should we have, hot dogs or hamburgers? You decide, Mommy. Should we have hot dogs or hamburgers? What does Daddy say?	6 3 6 Should we have hot dogs 5 or hamburgers?	1	21
Mommy says: Let's have hot dogs. I like hot dogs. Let's eat hot dogs. What are they going to eat?	3 2 2 They are going to eat hot dogs.	1	8
Daddy says: Okay. We will have hot dogs.			

NARRATIVE	TARGET RESPONSE	SENTENCE POINT	DSS TOTAL
Daddy is buying the hot dogs. Daddy, Mommy, and Timmy are eating. They are eating hot dogs. Timmy says: This is fun. I like going to Kiddyland. I am having a good time. Thank you, Daddy. Thank you, Mommy. I am having a good time. What does Timmy say?	1 2 I am having a good time.	1	4

LEVEL II: LESSON 28

CONCEPTS	ELICITED STRUCTURES		DSS VALUE
making breakfast	**Primary emphasis**		
	personal pronoun –	*he, she, him, her*	2
VOCABULARY			
toast, orange juice, Tang, breadbox, pitcher	interrogative –	reversal of auxiliary *have*, reversal of any two auxiliaries	8
FLANNEL-BOARD MATERIALS	**Secondary emphasis**		
paper figures: Karen, Timmy	personal pronoun –	*we, they*	3
paper cutouts: slice of bread, toaster, pitcher	main verb –	*will, can* + verb	4
	–	*have* + verb + *-en*, *have got*	7

MAKING BREAKFAST FOR MOMMY

NARRATIVE	TARGET RESPONSE	SENTENCE POINT	DSS TOTAL
This is Timmy. Who is this?	1 1 This is Timmy.	1	3
This is Karen. Karen is Timmy's sister. Who is this?	1 1 This is Karen.	1	3
It is early in the morning. It is seven o'clock in the morning. Is it early?	1 1 Yes, it is early.	1	3
Timmy and Karen are sneaking downstairs. They are going to the kitchen. Now Timmy and Karen are in the kitchen. They are in the kitchen together. They are talking. What are they doing?	3 2 They are talking.	1	6
Karen says: Timmy, has anyone seen you? Have they? Has anyone seen you? What does Karen say?	8 7 7 1 Has anyone seen you?	1	24

NARRATIVE	TARGET RESPONSE	SENTENCE POINT	DSS TOTAL
Timmy says: I don't think so. Karen says: Can Mommy still be sleeping? Can she? Can Mommy still be sleeping? What does Karen say?	8 Can Mommy still be 8 sleeping?	1	17
Timmy says: I think so. I think Mommy is still sleeping. Karen says: Did we wake her up? Did we? Did we wake her up? What does Karen say?	6 3 6 2 Did we wake her up?	1	18
Timmy says: No, Mommy is sleeping. She is not awake. Is Mommy awake?	1 7 No, Mommy is not awake.	1	9
Timmy says: Let's surprise Mommy. Let's make breakfast for Mommy. Let's surprise Mommy by making breakfast. What does Timmy say?	1 2 Let's surprise Mommy by 8 making breakfast.	1	12
Karen says: Yes, let's make breakfast. What should we make? What? What should we make for breakfast? What does Karen say?	2 6 3 6 What should we make for breakfast?	1	18
Timmy says: Let's make toast and orange juice. Karen says: Okay. Let's make toast and orange juice for breakfast.			

NARRATIVE	TARGET RESPONSE	SENTENCE POINT	DSS TOTAL
What will they make for breakfast?	3 4 3 They will make toast and orange juice for breakfast.	1	11
Timmy says: You make the toast, Karen. I will make the orange juice. What will Karen make?	4 Karen will make the toast.	1	5
What will Timmy make?	4 Timmy will make the orange juice.	1	5
Karen says: I will make the toast. Have you got the bread? Have you? Have you got the bread? What does Karen say?	8 1 7 Have you got the bread?	1	17
Timmy says: No, I haven't. The bread is in the breadbox. It is in the breadbox. Where is the bread?	1 The bread is in the breadbox.	1	2
Now Karen is getting the bread. She is getting the bread from the breadbox. What is she doing?	2 1 She is getting the bread from the breadbox.	1	4
Karen will toast the bread. Karen is putting the bread in the toaster. She is putting the bread in the toaster. What is she doing?	2 1 She is putting the bread in the toaster.	1	4
Timmy says: I will make the orange juice. I will make the Tang. Have you got the Tang? Have you? Have you got the Tang? What does Timmy say?	8 1 7 Have you got the Tang?	1	17

NARRATIVE	TARGET RESPONSE	SENTENCE POINT	DSS TOTAL
Karen says: No, it is in the cabinet. Timmy is opening the jar. He is putting some Tang into the pitcher. He is putting Tang into the pitcher. What is he doing?	2 1 He is putting Tang into the pitcher.	1	4
Now, he is pouring some water into the pitcher. He is mixing the Tang and the water together. He is mixing Tang and water together. What is he doing?	2 1 3 He is mixing Tang and water together.	1	7
Now Karen says: The toast is ready. The bread is toasted. Has the orange juice been made? Has it? Has the orange juice been made? What does Karen say?	8 Has the orange juice 7 been made?	1	16
The orange juice has been made. The toast and orange juice are ready. Everything is ready. The whole breakfast is ready. Is everything ready?	7 1 Yes, everything is ready.	1	9

LEVEL II: LESSON 29

CONCEPTS	ELICITED STRUCTURES		DSS VALUE
looking for someone, finding someone	**Primary emphasis**		
	personal pronoun –	*he, she, him*	2
VOCABULARY schoolyard, grocery store, storekeeper	main verb –	*must* + verb, *have* + verb + *-en*	7
FLANNEL-BOARD MATERIALS	interrogative –	reversal of auxiliary *have,* reversal with any two auxiliaries	8
paper figures: Mommy, Timmy, three boys, storekeeper, policeman, mailman paper cutouts: store front, school front, street, bed	negative –	*have* + *not,* uncontracted negative	7

MOMMY LOOKS FOR TIMMY

NARRATIVE	TARGET RESPONSE	SENTENCE POINT	DSS TOTAL
This is Mommy. This is Timmy's mommy. She is his mommy. Who is this?	1 1 This is Timmy's mommy.	1	3
Mommy wants to talk to Timmy. She wants to talk to him. What does she want to do?	2 2 2 She wants to talk to Timmy.	1	7
But Timmy is not here. He is not in the house. He is not in the back yard. He is not here. Is Timmy here?	1 7 No, Timmy is not here.	1	9
Mommy says: Where is Timmy? Where can he be? Where is he? What does Mommy say?	2 1 1 2 Where is he?	1	7
Mommy says: I must find Timmy. I want to talk to him. I must find him. What does Mommy say?	1 7 2 I must find him.	1	11

NARRATIVE	TARGET RESPONSE	SENTENCE POINT	DSS TOTAL
Mommy is going outside. She is going to look for Timmy. Mommy is looking for Timmy. What is Mommy doing?	1 Mommy is looking for Timmy.	1	2
Mommy is walking down the street. She is going to the schoolyard. She is going in the schoolyard. Mommy sees some boys. Mommy says: Has Timmy been here today? Has he? Has he been here today? What does Mommy say?	8 2 7 Has he been here today?	1	18
The boys say: No, we haven't seen Timmy. We haven't seen him today. What do they say?	3 7 7 2 We haven't seen him today.	1	20
Mommy goes to the grocery store. She is looking for Timmy. Mommy sees the storekeeper. Mommy says: Has Timmy been here today? Has he? Has Timmy been here today? What does Mommy say?	8 7 Has Timmy been here today?	1	16
The storekeeper says: No, he hasn't. I haven't seen him today. I haven't seen Timmy today. What does the storekeeper say?	1 7 7 I haven't seen Timmy today.	1	16
Mommy goes outside. She is looking for Timmy.			

NARRATIVE	TARGET RESPONSE	SENTENCE POINT	DSS TOTAL
She sees a policeman. Mommy says: Have you seen Timmy? Have you? Have you seen Timmy? What does Mommy say?	8 1 7 Have you seen Timmy?	1	17
The policeman says: No, I haven't seen him. I haven't seen him today. What does the policeman say?	1 7 7 2 I haven't seen him today.	1	18
Mommy starts to go back home. She is looking for Timmy. She sees a mailman. Mommy says: Have you seen Timmy? Have you? Have you seen him today? What does Mommy say?	8 1 7 Have you seen Timmy?	1	17
The mailman says: No, I haven't seen him. Not today. I haven't seen Timmy today. What does the mailman say?	1 7 7 I haven't seen Timmy today.	1	16
Mommy is getting worried. She can't find Timmy. She can't find him anywhere. Mommy says: Where can he be? Where? Where can he be? What does Mommy say?	2 6 2 4 Where can he be?	1	15
Mommy is worried. She is worried because she can't find Timmy. She is thinking: Where can he be? I have looked everywhere. Oh! Oh! Mommy thinks of something! Mommy says: Could Timmy be inside?			

NARRATIVE	TARGET RESPONSE	SENTENCE POINT	DSS TOTAL
Could he be sleeping? Could he? Could he be sleeping? What does Mommy say?	8 2 8 Could he be sleeping?	1	19
Mommy runs upstairs. She looks in Timmy's bedroom. There is Timmy. He is sleeping. Mommy found Timmy. He was sleeping all the time. What was he doing?	2 2 3 He was sleeping all the time.	1	8

LEVEL II: LESSON 30

CONCEPTS	ELICITED STRUCTURES		DSS VALUE
remember/forget, finding the way, asking for help	**Primary emphasis**		
	personal pronoun	– *he, she, him, his, her*	2
		– *we, us, our, they, them, their*	3
VOCABULARY	main verb	– *-s, -ed,* copular *am, are,* auxiliary *am, are*	2
remember, forget, which, policeman, sidewalk, drinking fountain		– *can, will* + verb, obligatory *do* + verb	4
FLANNEL-BOARD MATERIALS	secondary verb	– early-developing infinitive	2
paper figures: Bobby, Karen, Mommy, policeman	interrogative	– reversal of obligatory *do*	6
paper cutouts: slide, swings, teeter-totter, drinking fountain, intersecting sidewalks	wh-question	– *whose, which, which* + noun	8
	Secondary emphasis		
	main verb	– *should* + verb, obligatory *did* + verb	6
	secondary verb	– later-developing infinitive	5
	conjunction	– *because*	6

FINDING THE WAY HOME

NARRATIVE	TARGET RESPONSE	SENTENCE POINT	DSS TOTAL
This is Bobby. Who is this?	1 1 This is Bobby.	1	3
This is Karen. Who is this?	1 1 This is Karen.	1	3
Karen and Bobby live in a house. They live in a red house. This is their house. Where do they live?	3 1 They live in a red house.	1	5
Whose house is this?	1 1 3 This is their house.	1	6
Bobby's and Karen's house is near the park.			

NARRATIVE	TARGET RESPONSE	SENTENCE POINT	DSS TOTAL
Their house is near the park. Bobby and Karen like to go to the park. They like to play in the park. What do they like to do?	3 1 5 They like to go to the park.	1	10
Bobby and Karen go to the park every day. They go to the park with Mommy. Mommy takes them to the park. But Mommy is busy today. She is too busy to go to the park. Mommy says: I can't take you to the park today. I am too busy. I am too busy to take you to the park. What does Mommy say?	1 2 3 1 I am too busy to take you to the park.	1	8
Can Mommy take Bobby and Karen to the park?	4 4 No, Mommy can't take 3 Bobby and Karen to the park.	1	12
Bobby and Karen are sad. They want to go to the park today. They are sad because they want to go to the park today. Why are they sad?	3 2 6 3 They are sad because they 1 2 want to go to the park today.	1	18
Bobby says: Can we go to the park? Can we go by ourselves? Can we go to the park by ourselves? What does Bobby say?	6 3 4 Can we go to the park 5 by ourselves?	1	19
Mommy says: You can go to the park by yourselves.			

NARRATIVE	TARGET RESPONSE	SENTENCE POINT	DSS TOTAL
You can go if you are careful. You can go by yourselves if you are careful. What does Mommy say?	1 4 5 You can go by yourselves 5 1 2 if you are careful.	1	19
Bobby and Karen are walking to the park. They are walking. They are walking to the park. What are they doing?	3 2 They are walking to the park.	1	6
Bobby says: We can slide down the slide. We can swing on the swings. We can ride on the teeter-totter. Which one should we do first? Which one? Which one should we do first? What does Bobby say?	8 6 3 6 Which one should we do first?	1	24
Karen says: Let's ride on the teeter-totter. Bobby and Karen are riding on the teeter-totter. They are riding on the teeter-totter. What are they doing?	3 2 They are riding on the teeter-totter.	1	6
Now Bobby is thirsty. He wants a drink of water. He says: Which way is the drinking fountain? Which way? Which way is the drinking fountain? What does Bobby say?	8 11 Which way is the drinking fountain?	1	11
It is over there. Bobby and Karen are getting a drink. They are getting a drink. What are they doing?	3 2 They are getting a drink.	1	6

NARRATIVE	TARGET RESPONSE	SENTENCE POINT	DSS TOTAL
Karen says: I'm tired. Let's go home now. I want to go home. What does Karen say?	1 1 2 I want to go home.	1	5
Why does she want to go home?	2 2 2 She wants to go home 6 2 1 because she is tired.	1	16
Bobby says: I want to go home, too. I want to have lunch. Let's go home now. What does Bobby say?	1 2 Let's go home now.	1	4
Why does he want to go home?	2 2 2 He wants to go home 6 2 2 2 because he wants to have lunch.	1	19
Oh, dear! Look at all the sidewalks. There are lots of sidewalks in the park. Bobby says: Which sidewalk goes to our house? Which one? Which sidewalk goes to our house? What does Bobby say?	8 2 3 Which sidewalk goes to our house?	1	14
Bobby can't remember. He can't remember. He forgot the way home. He can't remember the way home. Did Bobby remember the way home?	7 6 No, Bobby didn't remember the way home.	1	14
Karen can't remember either. She forgot the way home. Did Karen remember the way home?	2 2 No, she forgot.	1	5
Karen says: Where is the sidewalk to our house?			

NARRATIVE	TARGET RESPONSE	SENTENCE POINT	DSS TOTAL
Which way do we go? Which way? Which way do we go? What does Karen say?	8 6 3 4 Which way do we go?	1	22
Bobby and Karen can't remember the way home. They forgot the way home. Karen says: What can we do? What? What can we do? What does Karen say?	2 6 3 4 What can we do?	1	16
What should they do? Who might help them? Can you guess?	(Elicit responses from the children.)		
Bobby says: I know what to do. I'm going to ask someone to help us. I'm going to ask our friend, the policeman. I'm going to ask the policeman to help us. What does Bobby say?	1 2 2 I'm going to ask the 5 3 policeman to help us.	1	14
What is he going to do?	2 1 2 He is going to ask the 5 3 policeman to help them.	1	14
Bobby says: Mr. Policeman, my name is Bobby. This is my sister, Karen. We live in the red house near the park. We forgot our way home. We can't remember the way home. What does Bobby say?	3 4 4 We can't remember the way home.	1	12
Bobby says: Which way should we go? Which way?			

NARRATIVE	TARGET RESPONSE	SENTENCE POINT	DSS TOTAL
Which way should we go? What does Bobby say?	8 6 3 6 Which way should we go?	1	24
Bobby says: Will you help us find our house? Will you? Will you show us the way to go? What does Bobby say?	6 1 4 3 Will you show us the 3 way to go?	1	18
The policeman says: I will help you get home. I will show you. I will show you the way. What does the policeman say?	1 4 1 I will show you the way.	1	7
What is the policeman going to do?	1 The policeman is going 2 3 to show them the way.	1	7
The policeman says: This is the way to your house. This sidewalk goes to your house. Now Bobby and Karen are running home. They are hurrying. They are running fast. What are they doing?	3 2 They are running fast.	1	6
Are they going slow?	3 2 No, they are going fast.	1	6
Karen says: I see a red house. Whose house is that? Whose? Whose house is that? What does Karen say?	8 1 1 1 Whose house is that?	1	12
Bobby says: That is our house. We are almost home!			

LEVEL II: LESSON 31

CONCEPTS

inside, outside, behind, in, under, counting, hiding

VOCABULARY

hide-and-seek, living room, closet, fooled

FLANNEL-BOARD MATERIALS

paper figures: Bobby, Karen, Mommy
paper cutouts: chair, couch, TV set, bed, closet door, table, bathtub

ELICITED STRUCTURES		DSS VALUE
Primary emphasis		
personal pronoun	– *he, she, him, her*	2
	– *we, they, their, them*	3
main verb	– *can, will* + verb, obligatory *do* + verb	4
secondary verb	– early-developing infinitive	2
negative	– *isn't*	5
interrogative	– reversal of modal, reversal of obligatory *do, does, did*	6
Secondary emphasis		
main verb	– *-s,* copular *am, are,* auxiliary *am, are*	2
	– obligatory *did* + verb	6
negative	– *can't*	4
conjunction	– *and*	3

HIDE-AND-SEEK

NARRATIVE	TARGET RESPONSE	SENTENCE POINT	DSS TOTAL
This is Karen. Who is this?	1 1 This is Karen.	1	3
This is Bobby. Who is this?	1 1 This is Bobby.	1	3
Bobby's is Karen's brother. He is Karen's brother. He is her brother. Who is he?	2 1 2 He is her brother.	1	6
This is Mommy. Who is this?	1 1 This is Mommy.	1	3
She is Bobby's and Karen's mommy. She is their mommy. Who is she?	2 1 3 She is their mommy.	1	7

NARRATIVE	TARGET RESPONSE	SENTENCE POINT	DSS TOTAL
Bobby says: Mommy, can I go outside? Can I? Can I go outside to play? What does Bobby say?	6 1 4 Can I go outside 3 to play?	1	15
What does Bobby want to do?	2 2 2 He wants to go outside 3 to play.	1	10
Mommy says: No, Bobby, you can't. No, you can't. Can Bobby go outside? Can he?	2 4 No, he can't.	1	7
Mommy says: You can't go outside. It is raining. You can't go outside because it is raining. What does Mommy say?	1 4 4 You can't go outside 6 1 1 because it is raining.	1	18
Bobby is sad. He is not happy. Is he happy?	2 1 7 No, he is not happy.	1	11
Bobby is sad because he can't play outside. He is sad because he can't play outside. Why is he sad?	2 1 6 2 He is sad because he 4 4 can't play outside.	1	20
Karen says: Can we play inside, Mommy? Can we play a game? Can we play a game inside? What does Karen say?	6 3 4 Can we play a game inside?	1	14
Mommy says: Yes, you can. Karen says: I know a game.			

NARRATIVE	TARGET RESPONSE	SENTENCE POINT	DSS TOTAL
I know a game we can play. I know a game we can play inside. What does Karen say?	1 1 3 I know a game we 4 can play inside.	1	10
What game can they play? Can you guess?	(Elicit responses from the children.)		
Karen says: We can play hide-and-seek. We can play that inside. We can play hide-and-seek inside. What does Karen say?	3 4 3 We can play hide-and-seek inside.	1	11
Karen says: Let's play hide-and-seek. Let's play. Let's play hide-and-seek. What does Karen say?	1 2 3 Let's play hide-and-seek.	1	7
What game are they going to play?	3 2 2 They are going to play 3 hide-and-seek.	1	11
Karen says: Do you know how to play hide-and-seek? Do you? Do you know how to play hide-and-seek? What does Karen say?	6 1 4 8 5 Do you know how to play 3 hide-and-seek?	1	28
Bobby says: Yes, I do. Karen says: Okay, Bobby, you hide. You hide first. You hide. What does Karen say?	1 1 You hide.	1	3
Karen says: I will count to ten while you hide. I will count to ten.			

NARRATIVE	TARGET RESPONSE	SENTENCE POINT	DSS TOTAL
I will count to ten while you hide. What does Karen say?	1 4 3 8 I will count to ten while 1 1 you hide.	1	19
Bobby is going to hide. He is going to hide. What is he going to do?	2 1 2 He is going to hide.	1	6
Karen shuts her eyes. She shuts her eyes and counts to ten. Let's count with Karen.	(Children count in unison.)		
Karen is opening her eyes. Now Karen is going to look for Bobby. She is going to look. She is going to look for Bobby. What is she going to do?	2 1 2 She is going to look for Bobby.	1	6
Karen says: Here I come, ready or not. What does Karen say?	1 1 5 Here I come, ready or not.	1	8
Karen is looking for Bobby. She is looking for Bobby. What is she doing?	2 1 She is looking for Bobby.	1	4
Karen is looking in the living room. She is looking for Bobby in the living room. Where is she looking?	2 1 She is looking in the living room.	1	4
Karen is looking behind the chair. She is looking behind the chair. Where is she looking?	2 1 She is looking behind the chair.	1	4
Bobby is not there. He isn't there. He isn't behind the chair. Is he behind the chair?	2 1 5 No, he isn't behind the chair.	1	9

NARRATIVE	TARGET RESPONSE	SENTENCE POINT	DSS TOTAL
Karen is looking behind the couch. She is looking behind the couch. Where is she looking?	2 1 She is looking behind the couch.	1	4
Bobby is not there. He isn't there. He isn't behind the couch. Is he behind the couch?	2 1 5 No, he isn't behind the couch.	1	9
Karen is looking behind the TV. She is looking behind the TV. Where is she looking?	2 1 She is looking behind the TV.	1	4
Bobby is not there. He isn't there. He isn't behind the TV. Is he behind the TV?	2 1 5 No, he isn't behind the TV.	1	9
Is Bobby anywhere in the living room?	1 5 No, Bobby isn't anywhere in the living room.	1	7
Karen says: Mommy, Bobby is not in the living room. I can't find Bobby. Mommy says: Did you look for Bobby in the bedroom? Did you? Did you look in the bedroom? What does Mommy say?	6 1 6 Did you look in the bedroom?	1	14
Karen says: No, I didn't. Karen is looking in the bedroom. She is looking in the bedroom. Where is she looking?	2 1 She is looking in the bedroom.	1	4
Karen is looking under the bed.			

NARRATIVE	TARGET RESPONSE	SENTENCE POINT	DSS TOTAL
She is looking under the bed. Where is she looking?	2 1 She is looking under the bed.	1	4
Bobby is not there. He isn't there. He isn't under the bed. Is he under the bed?	2 1 5 No, he isn't under the bed.	1	9
Karen is looking in the closet. She is looking in the closet. Where is she looking?	2 1 She is looking in the closet.	1	4
Bobby is not there. He isn't there. He isn't in the closet. Is he in the closet?	2 1 5 No, he isn't in the closet.	1	9
Is Bobby anywhere in the bedroom?	2 1 5 No, he isn't anywhere in the bedroom.	1	9
Karen says: Mommy, I can't find Bobby. He isn't in the bedroom. Mommy says: Did you look in the kitchen? Did you? Did you look in the kitchen? What does Mommy say?	6 1 6 Did you look in the kitchen?	1	14
Karen says: No, I didn't. Karen is looking in the kitchen. She is looking in the kitchen. Where is she looking?	2 1 She is looking in the kitchen.	1	4
Karen is looking under the table. She is looking under the table. Where is she looking?	2 1 She is looking under the table.	1	4

NARRATIVE	TARGET RESPONSE	SENTENCE POINT	DSS TOTAL
Bobby isn't there. He isn't there. He isn't under the table. Is he under the table?	2 1 5 No, he isn't under the table.	1	9
Is he anywhere in the kitchen?	2 1 5 No, he isn't anywhere in the kitchen.	1	9
Karen can't find Bobby. She can't find Bobby anywhere in the house. Karen says: Mommy, I can't find Bobby. I can't. I can't find him. What does Karen say?	1 4 4 2 I can't find him.	1	12
Karen says: He isn't in the living room. He isn't in the bedroom. He isn't in the kitchen. Mommy says: Did you look for Bobby in the bathroom? Did you? Did you look in the bathroom? What does Mommy say?	6 1 6 Did you look in the bathroom?	1	14
Mommy and Karen are looking in the bathroom. They are looking in the bathroom. Where are they looking?	3 2 They are looking in the bathroom.	1	6
Karen says: Oh, oh! Look, Mommy! Bobby is hiding in the bathtub. He is hiding in the bathtub. Where is Bobby hiding?	1 Bobby is hiding in the bathtub.	1	2

NARRATIVE	TARGET RESPONSE	SENTENCE POINT	DSS TOTAL
Bobby says: I fooled you. I was hiding in the bathtub. Karen says: Let's play again, Bobby. It's my turn to hide. Let's play again. What does Karen say?	1 2 Let's play again.	1	4

LEVEL II: LESSON 32

CONCEPTS	ELICITED STRUCTURES		DSS VALUE
going around the block, safety, danger of streets	**Primary emphasis**		
	main verb –	copular *am, are, were,* auxiliary *am, are*	2
VOCABULARY	–	*can, will* + verb, obligatory *do* + verb	4
cross, sidewalk, street	secondary verb –	early-developing infinitive	2
FLANNEL-BOARD MATERIALS	interrogative –	reversal of obligatory *do,* reversal of modal	6
paper figures: Mommy, Timmy, Bobby, Mrs. Jones, mailman	wh-question –	*when, how, how* + adjective	5
paper cutouts: bike, mailbox, rake, broom, house front	**Secondary emphasis**		
	personal pronoun –	*he, she*	2

TIMMY RIDES HIS NEW BIKE

NARRATIVE	TARGET RESPONSE	SENTENCE POINT	DSS TOTAL
This is Timmy. Timmy is a boy. Timmy is the boy in our story. Who is this?	1 1 This is Timmy.	1	3
Timmy has a new bike. The bike has shiny wheels. It is bright red. This is Mommy. This is Timmy's mommy. She is his mommy. Who is this?	1 1 This is Mommy.	1	3
Timmy says: I want to ride my bike. When can I ride my bike? When can I go? When can I ride my bike? What does Timmy say?	5 6 1 4 When can I ride 1 my bike?	1	18

NARRATIVE	TARGET RESPONSE	SENTENCE POINT	DSS TOTAL
Mommy says: You can ride your bike now. You can ride today. You can ride your bike now. What does Mommy say?	1 4 1 You can ride your bike now.	1	7
Mommy says: You can ride your bike today, Timmy. But don't cross the street! Don't go in the street. Don't cross the street! What does Mommy say?	4 4 Don't cross the street.	1	9
Mommy says: Stay on the sidewalk. Stay on the sidewalk with your bike. Why should Timmy stay on the sidewalk with his bike?	(Elicit answers from the children.)		
Timmy will be safe on the sidewalk. There are cars in the street. Timmy is happy. Timmy says: I am going to ride my bike. I am going to ride it. I am going outside. I am going to ride my bike. What does Timmy say?	1 2 2 1 I am going to ride my bike.	1	7
Timmy says: I am going to stay on the sidewalk. I am going to ride my bike on the sidewalk. I am going to stay on the sidewalk. What does Timmy say?	1 2 2 I am going to stay on the sidewalk.	1	6
Timmy says: I won't go in the street. I will stay on the sidewalk.			

NARRATIVE	TARGET RESPONSE	SENTENCE POINT	DSS TOTAL
I won't go in the street. What does Timmy say?	1 5 4 I won't go in the street.	1	11
Timmy gets on his shiny bike. He rides to the corner of his block. He turns the corner and sees a man! He sees a man at the mailbox. The man has on a blue suit. He has a blue hat. He is carrying a big bag with letters in it. Who do you think it is?	(Elicit answers from the children.)		
Timmy says: Hello, Mr. Mailman! How are you, today? How are you? What does Timmy say?	5 2 1 1 How are you?	1	10
The mailman says: I am fine. I am carrying letters. I am delivering mail. I am carrying letters. What does the mailman say?	1 2 I am carrying letters.	1	4
The mailman says: I have letters in my bag for everyone on the block. I have a package for your house, Timmy. I have one for your house. Timmy says: How big is the package? How big is it? How big is the package? What does Timmy say?	5 1 1 How big is the package?	1	8
The mailman says: The package is little. It is little. It is for your mommy. I will give it to your mommy.			

NARRATIVE	TARGET RESPONSE	SENTENCE POINT	DSS TOTAL
What is the mailman going to do?	1 The mailman is going 2 to give the package to Timmy's mommy.	1	4
The mailman says: Timmy, what are you doing? What are you doing today? What are you doing? What does the mailman say?	2 4 1 2 What are you doing?	1	10
Timmy says: I am riding my new bike. I am riding around the block. I am riding my bike around the block. What does Timmy say?	1 2 1 I am riding my bike around the block.	1	5
Timmy says: Good-bye now! The mailman says: Good-bye. Timmy rides to the next corner. He sees Mrs. Jones. Mrs. Jones is raking leaves. She is raking leaves. What is she doing?	2 1 She is raking leaves.	1	4
Timmy is waving to Mrs. Jones. He is waving. He is waving to Mrs. Jones. What is he doing?	2 1 He is waving to Mrs. Jones.	1	4
Timmy says to himself: Mrs. Jones is working. I am playing. Mrs. Jones is working, but I am playing. She is working, but I am playing. What does Timmy say to himself?	2 1 5 1 She is working, but I 2 am playing.	1	12

NARRATIVE	TARGET RESPONSE	SENTENCE POINT	DSS TOTAL
Timmy says to himself: I am riding my bike. I am having fun. Timmy rides to the next corner. He turns the corner, and he sees a friend. Timmy sees his friend Bobby. He sees Bobby. Timmy says: Hi, Bobby! See my new bike. Do you want to ride my bike? Do you want to ride my bike? Do you? Do you want to ride my bike? What does Timmy say?	6 1 4 2 Do you want to ride 1 my bike?	1	15
Bobby says: I don't know how to ride a bike. How do you do it? I don't know how. How do you do it? What does Bobby say?	5 6 1 4 1 How do you do it?	1	18
Timmy says: I will show you. You can ride on the back of my bike. Let's go to my house. Let's ride to my house. What does Timmy say?	1 2 1 Let's ride to my house.	1	5
Timmy says: I think my mommy has cookies for us. Bobby says: Good. I want some cookies. I am hungry. I want some cookies. Timmy says: Let's go. Bobby gets on the back of Timmy's new bike. They ride to the corner. They turn the corner. Timmy sees his house. He sees his mommy.			

NARRATIVE	TARGET RESPONSE	SENTENCE POINT	DSS TOTAL
His mommy is sweeping the sidewalk. She is sweeping the sidewalk. What is she doing?	2 1 She is sweeping the sidewalk.	1	4
Timmy and Bobby say: Can we have some cookies? Can we? Can we have some cookies? What do they say?	6 3 4 3 Can we have some cookies?	1	17
Mommy says: Yes, you can. You can have a cookie. You can have some cookies. What does Mommy say?	1 4 3 You can have some cookies.	1	9
Mommy says: Have you been a good boy, Timmy? Did you stay on the sidewalk? Timmy says: Yes, I stayed on the sidewalk. I didn't go in the street. I didn't ride in the street. What does Timmy say?	1 7 6 I didn't ride in the street.	1	15
Timmy says: I stayed on the sidewalk. I rode all the way around the block. I stopped at every corner. And now I am back again. Mommy says: Good for you. Come inside and we'll have cookies. Timmy says: When can I ride my bike again? When can I?			

NARRATIVE	TARGET RESPONSE	SENTENCE POINT	DSS TOTAL
When can I ride my bike again? What does Timmy say?	5 6 1 4 1 When can I ride my bike again?	1	18
Mommy says: You were a good boy. You can ride your bike tomorrow. You were good so you can ride your bike tomorrow. What does Mommy say?	1 2 5 1 You were good so you 4 1 can ride your bike tomorrow.	1	15

Section III

Use of Interactive Language Development Teaching with Twenty-Five Clinical Children

THIS SECTION PRESENTS the findings of a three-year study of Interactive Language Development Teaching at the Northwestern University Speech and Language Clinics. A primary goal of this effort was to demonstrate that the theoretical formulations of a developmental model of grammar described in *Developmental Sentence Analysis* (Lee, 1974) and related psycholinguistic research findings, including those from cross-sectional and longitudinal normative studies with DSS procedures (Koenigsknecht, 1974), can be applied effectively by a speech and language clinician treating children with oral-language problems. Central to the rationale underlying the Interactive Language Development Teaching approach is objective, continuing assessment of a child-client's use of morphological forms and syntactic structures. It is important to measure the growth in the number and maturity of such forms and structures the child is able to incorporate within an utterance. The goal in such clinical teaching is to present grammatical structures in sequences that build upon those structures the child has already mastered; but since the level of development must be compared with the normal developmental patterns for emerging combinations of language structures, ongoing assessment is necessarily prerequisite to and concomitant with treatment. In such an approach to analysis and treatment, the child's spontaneous language usage is viewed as the end product of language learning. The clinician must continually analyze similarities and differences between the child-client's use of grammar in such spontaneous formulations and the typical grammatical patterns of normal children at a similar developmental stage. Such pattern comparisons permit the clinician to treat deviant syntactic development in the context of a normal developmental sequence. The amount and nature of the differences in grammatical development can be operationally defined and systematically treated. A critical shortcoming of most speech and language treatment programs is the inadequacy of such objective measures of the child-client's progress throughout the period of clinical training. It must be shown that the clinical child uses the grammatical structures presented in clinical lessons in his spontaneous responses to stimulus materials not drilled on or used in the treatment program. In the ensuing discussion, comparison of pre-treatment DSS, which revealed the language level at which these children were functioning prior to enrollment in therapy, with post-treatment DSS, which showed their level of language functioning at the end of the therapy period, is used to assess objectively the effectiveness of Interactive Language Development Teaching.

In the area of child language disabilities, clinical researchers attempting to establish the effectiveness of clinical procedures face another limitation, even if they have developed useful measures of the behavior under treatment. They cannot ethically use control groups. It would be unconscionable to withhold clinical training for any period of time from any child who needs it and would be likely to gain from it. This precludes designs in which one group of children receives treatment while treatment is withheld from a comparable group in order to show that the treatment produced results. The value of the DSS procedures and normative data lies in the fact that the progress of clinical children can be compared with the rate of progress of normally developing children who are at the same stage of language development. It is possible to estimate a clinical child's over-all language growth in months and compare it to the number of months the child has been in a treatment program. Clinical children have been slowed or reduced in their language development relative to normally developing children. Therefore, if a clinical treatment approach could effect a rate of gain equal to that of normal children, or even surpass it, the clinician could reasonably assume the effectiveness of the approach.

PROCEDURES

Treatment Format

Interactive Language Development Teaching was used with twenty-five children over a three-year period at the Northwestern University Speech and Language Clinics. During the course of the study, there were six language groups consisting of four or five children, usually four. The typical pattern was for the groups to be seen for one-hour clinical sessions four times a week in three treatment blocks of eight weeks. There was generally a nontreatment vacation period of approximately four weeks after both the first and the second eight-week treatment blocks. Thus, the interval between the immediate pre-treatment and immediate post-treatment testing sessions was approximately thirty-two weeks, or eight months. The statistical calculation of the exact time between the pre- and post-treatment assessment revealed a mean treatment interval of 8.3 months for the twenty-five clinical children. The structure of the lessons, including the writing and presenting of the story-conversations, followed the Interactive Language Development Teaching procedures described in Section I. Language-development stories similar to those in Section II were presented. The developmental level of language structures included within a series of lessons depended on the capabilities of the children in the group and the rate of progress evidenced in the course of treatment.

Clinicians

Seventy-five graduate students in speech and language pathology participated in the treatment program, each for one eight-week block. Thus, for each eight-week period there were as many graduate-student clinicians involved in the program as there were children in the group, usually four. Thus, typically, each clinician on a rotating basis conducted every fourth group story-lesson. All clinicians had completed at least one course in child language development prior to involvement in this project. All lessons were under the direct supervision of a faculty clinical supervisor holding the master's degree in speech and language pathology.

The extensive pre- and post-treatment speech and language measures were taken by a speech and language pathologist, at a master's-degree level, who was not directly involved in the treatment program. A clinical psychologist, at the doctoral-degree level, experienced in assessing functioning in language-impaired children, also conducted pre- and post-treatment assessments.

Children in Training

Interactive Language Development Teaching was used with twenty-five monolingual children from middle-class homes in the North Shore area of Chicago. At the beginning of their treatment period the children were in the preschool age range of three years, two months, to five years, nine months. The mean age of the twenty-five subjects at the beginning of treatment was 52.3 months, with a standard deviation of 5.1 months; at the end of the treatment period their mean age was 60.6 months. All the children included in this study had normal hearing, evidenced no general neuromuscular problems, and were within the range of normal on selected intelligence measures. All of the subjects evidenced reduced expressive-language functioning. The mean delay in grammatical development for the twenty-five subjects on their pre-enrollment language sample, as estimated with DSS procedures, was 21 months.

Pre- and Post-Treatment Clinical Measures

The twenty-three pre- and post-treatment tests and subtests included in this analysis were: Developmental Sentence Scoring (Lee and Canter, 1971; Lee, 1974), Northwestern Syntax Screening Test–Receptive and Expressive Sections (Lee, 1969, 1971), Peabody Picture Vocabulary Test (Dunn, 1959), Stanford-Binet Intelligence Scale Form L-M (Terman and Merrill, 1960), Preschool Attainment Record (Doll, 1966), Spencer-McGrady Sentence Repetition (unpublished test of ability to repeat sentences of increasing length with generally increasing grammatical load; Spencer, 1958, and McGrady, 1964), Oral Commissions Subtest from Detroit Tests of Learning Aptitude (Baker and Leland, 1967), Illinois Test of Psycholinguistic Abilities–Total and Individual Subtests (Kirk, McCarthy, and Kirk, 1968), Draw-a-Man Test (Harris, 1963), Developmental Test of Visual-Motor Integration (Beery and Buktenica, 1967), Memory Span for Digits Forward, Northwestern University Articulation Proficiency Test (Canter and Collins, unpublished research manual). Separate consideration was also given to the group's performance within individual component categories of the DSS, the mean developmental scores or mean scores per entry within the DSS grammatical categories, and the number of entries per sentence within the DSS grammatical categories.

FINDINGS

Pre-Treatment Measures

Obtained means, standard deviations, and minimum and maximum values for the raw scores on the twenty-three pre-treatment clinical measures are presented in Table 1. A similar listing of the means, standard deviations, and minimum and maximum values for the age-equivalent scores listed in months for sixteen of these pre-treatment measures which could

Table 1. Means, Standard Deviations, Minimum and Maximum Values for Raw Scores on Pre-Treatment and Post-Treatment Measures and Difference Means with t-Values for Comparisons over 8-Month Interval (25 Subjects, Pre-Treatment Mean Age of 52.3 Months, Post-Treatment Mean Age of 60.6 Months)

Test or Subtest	Pre-Treatment			Post-Treatment			Comparison		
	Mean	Standard Deviation	Range	Mean	Standard Deviation	Range	Difference Mean	t-Value*	p less than
Developmental Sentence Score	3.84	1.53	1.30–7.66	6.04	1.89	3.22–9.66	+ 2.20	5.59	0.001
NSST–Expressive Section	7.0	9.7	0–24	12.6	9.5	3–33	+ 5.6	2.17	0.04
NSST–Receptive Section	21.9	5.8	8–30	25.8	4.1	16–31	+ 3.9	4.83	0.001
Peabody Picture Vocabulary Test	43.1	12.6	15–60	52.0	8.9	29–63	+ 8.8	6.99	0.001
Stanford-Binet Intelligence Test	99.9	14.0	76–121	105.7	17.8	75–142	+ 5.8	2.48	0.02
Preschool Attainment Record	76.0	12.0	47–96	87.8	13.6	59–108	+11.8	3.98	0.001
Spencer-McGrady Sentence Repetition	2.0	1.4	0–5	4.1	1.9	1–7	+ 2.1	6.54	0.001
Oral Commissions (DTLA)	11.8	4.7	2–18	15.0	2.4	6–18	+ 3.3	4.12	0.001
ITPA–Total Score	114.9	35.2	43–184	150.4	35.5	86–205	+35.5	7.82	0.001
Auditory Reception	13.0	6.0	0–24	18.7	7.1	7–32	+ 5.8	6.06	0.001
Auditory Association	13.2	5.9	1–26	16.6	5.2	7–25	+ 3.5	5.82	0.001
Auditory Sequential Memory	10.4	4.5	1–18	12.9	4.9	3–24	+ 2.5	3.01	0.01
Visual Reception	13.2	6.2	1–27	17.4	5.0	9–27	+ 4.2	3.52	0.01
Visual Association	12.6	5.3	1–20	16.5	5.2	3–24	+ 3.9	3.35	0.01
Visual Closure	9.8	4.5	0–19	12.0	4.7	5–22	+ 2.2	2.35	0.03
Visual Sequential Memory	9.2	4.2	0–18	10.9	4.3	4–20	+ 1.6	1.85	0.07
Manual Expression	15.8	6.4	4–29	18.0	6.0	6–29	+ 2.2	2.24	0.04
Verbal Expression	11.5	3.6	5–19	16.1	6.0	6–27	+ 4.6	4.51	0.001
Grammatic Closure	6.8	4.5	0–17	11.8	4.1	4–20	+ 5.0	5.09	0.001
Draw-a-Man (Goodenough-Harris)	4.7	3.2	0–11	6.2	3.0	0–10	+ 1.5	2.97	0.01
Developmental Test of Visual-Motor Integration	4.7	2.1	0–9	6.7	2.6	3–11	+ 2.0	5.07	0.001
Memory Span for Digits	2.7	1.1	0–4	3.2	0.8	2–5	+ 0.5	2.70	0.01
NU Articulation Proficiency Test	32.0	12.3	13–54	39.6	12.0	15–67	+ 7.6	3.61	0.001

*$df = 24$.

TABLE 2. MEANS, STANDARD DEVIATIONS, MINIMUM AND MAXIMUM VALUES FOR AGE-EQUIVALENT SCORES IN MONTHS ON PRE-TREATMENT AND POST-TREATMENT MEASURES AND DIFFERENCE MEANS WITH t-VALUES FOR COMPARISONS OVER 8-MONTH INTERVAL (25 SUBJECTS, PRE-TREATMENT AGE OF 52.3 MONTHS, POST-TREATMENT MEAN AGE OF 60.6 MONTHS)

	PRE-TREATMENT			POST-TREATMENT			COMPARISON		
TEST OR SUBTEST	Mean	Standard Deviation	Range	Mean	Standard Deviation	Range	Difference Mean	t-Value*	p less than
Developmental Sentence Score	31.3	7.9	21–60	42.1	12.1	28–69	+10.8	5.45	0.001
NSST–Expressive Section	26.0	5.2	24–47	32.8	13.4	24–70	+ 6.8	2.56	0.02
NSST–Receptive Section	39.3	11.5	24–60	47.3	10.6	26–64	+ 8.0	3.72	0.001
Peabody Picture Vocabulary Test	54.8	15.4	27–78	67.9	14.2	36–90	+13.1	7.18	0.001
Stanford-Binet Intelligence Test	52.7	7.8	36–70	63.0	10.1	44–86	+10.3	7.68	0.001
ITPA–Total Score	51.1	9.0	33–69	60.2	9.1	44–74	+ 9.1	7.62	0.001
Auditory Reception	48.0	11.1	25–70	59.5	15.4	37–90	+11.5	5.42	0.001
Auditory Association	55.8	12.6	30–87	62.3	11.1	43–84	+ 6.5	4.82	0.001
Auditory Sequential Memory	42.0	10.8	24–60	48.5	11.9	26–78	+ 6.5	3.76	0.001
Visual Reception	59.6	17.1	25–99	70.0	11.4	49–88	+10.4	3.25	0.01
Visual Association	53.7	12.2	30–72	63.5	13.3	34–86	+ 9.8	3.44	0.01
Visual Closure	49.6	11.7	25–73	55.0	12.2	35–81	+ 5.4	2.09	0.04
Visual Sequential Memory	50.0	12.3	25–78	55.2	13.6	34–87	+ 5.2	1.90	0.07
Manual Expression	58.7	18.1	30–99	65.0	17.7	34–99	+ 6.3	2.12	0.04
Verbal Expression	51.9	8.9	34–68	61.1	13.4	37–84	+ 9.2	3.96	0.001
Grammatic Closure	46.7	14.0	26–72	61.7	8.9	39–80	+15.0	5.32	0.001

*df = 24.

appropriately be converted to age-equivalent listings is contained in Table 2. The ensuing discussion utilizes both Tables 1 and 2. The reader should keep in mind that the age-equivalent scores shown in Table 2 are conversions for some of the raw scores listed in Table 1. For the twenty-five pre-treatment clinical cases, the DSS ranged from 1.30 to 7.66, with a mean DSS of 3.84 and standard deviation of 1.53. The mean estimated age-equivalent score in months on the DSS was 31.3, with a standard deviation of 7.9. Thus, as estimated by the over-all DSS, the average delay in grammatical development for these children was twenty-one months at the time of their enrollment in the treatment program.

Reductions in performance were evident on the two other expressive-language tasks which place some demand on the syntactic skills of the subjects, namely, the Expressive Section of the NSST — on which, at the time of their enrollment, the children's group mean score was more than two standard deviations below the mean score expected of three-year-old children — and the Spencer-McGrady Sentence Repetition measure — on which their mean score was substantially below that expected of four-year-old children.

The group performance was clearly below age-level expectations on the two measures of auditory sequential memory. The mean pre-treatment performance on the Memory Span for Digits Forward was less than the three-digit span normally obtained by three-year-old children. Performance on the Auditory Sequential Memory Subtest of the ITPA was reduced by nearly a full year relative to age-level expectations. The sequential-memory difficulties seemed specific to the auditory modality, since scores on the Visual Sequential Memory Subtest of the ITPA were at a level appropriate for the chronological age of the children.

These clinical children generally did poorly on the pre-treatment application of the Grammatic Closure Subtest of the ITPA. Items in this test tap primarily the usage of various morphological forms in a sentence-completion picture-explanation task.

Two other measures that displayed a general impairment in the speech and language skills of these clinical children were the Receptive Section of the NSST and the Northwestern University Articulation Proficiency Test. On the NSST–Receptive Section, a screening instrument which samples comprehension of selected syntactic structures, the mean score for the group was more than one year below the group's mean chronological age. On the general test of articulation proficiency these clinical cases obtained a mean score of 32.0 correct consonant single productions out of a possible 67 items.

It is also important to consider those measures on which these clinical cases scored at or above their age-level expectations as a group. As shown in Tables 1 and 2, the obtained means on the Stanford-Binet Intelligence Scale, the Illinois Test of Psycholinguistic Abilities–Total Score, and the Preschool Attainment Record were at a level appropriate for the chronological age of the children. Subjects' pre-treatment intelligence quotients as computed from the Stanford-Binet Intelligence Scale ranged from 76 to 121, with a mean of 99.9 and a standard deviation of 14.0. The children's composite performance within the range of normal on the ITPA and the PAR also indicated that their general level of functioning was commensurate with their chronological age. The severe expressive-language problems they exhibited represented specific problems in language learning and usage.

The pre-treatment results from two basic receptive-language measures were also normal. These were the Peabody Picture Vocabulary Test, a measure of receptive vocabulary for single words, and the Oral Commissions Subtest of the DTLA, a measure of comprehension of sequenced basic commissions. The requirements for comprehension of syntax on the Oral Commissions Subtest are minimal.

It is interesting to note that differences appeared between the group's performances on the two subtests from the ITPA which assess expressive skills. The mean scores for both the Manual Expression Subtest, 58.7 months, and the Verbal Expression Subtest, 51.9 months, were appropriate for the age of the clinical group, but there was a six-to-seven-month advantage on the gestural measure. On the other hand, the better performance on the Verbal Expression Subtest in contrast to all other expressive-language measures, including the DSS, the NSST–Expressive Section, the Sentence Repetition task, and the Grammatic Closure Subtest, reflects the fact that more advanced morphological forms and syntactic structures are not needed for scoring well on the Verbal Expression Subtest, in which the required task is basically to provide names for discrete, relevant, and factual concepts specific to stimulus items.

Further inspection of Tables 1 and 2 shows that these clinical children achieved normal results as a group for the auditory and visual reception and association subtests of the ITPA. Another general finding was that they scored within normal limits on the three visual-motor skill measures: the Developmental Test of Visual-Motor Integration, the Draw-a-Man Test, and the Visual Closure Subtest of the ITPA.

Pearson product-moment correlations were computed between the pre-treatment DSS scores and the other pre-treatment measures obtained by the twenty-five children seen for Interactive Language Development Teaching. As shown in Table 3, there were significant positive correlations between performance on the DSS and each of the four expressive-language measures, with NSST–Expressive Section $r_{xy} = 0.68$, with Spencer-McGrady Sentence Repetition $r_{xy} = 0.50$, with Verbal Expression $r_{xy} = 0.66$, and with Grammatic Closure $r_{xy} = 0.45$. The two measures of auditory sequential memory were each positively correlated with the overall DSS also, with Auditory Sequential Memory $r_{xy} = 0.51$ and with Memory Span for Digits Forward $r_{xy} = 0.40$. Significant positive correlations were indicated, in addition, between the pre-treatment DSS scores and the pre-treatment results of the PPVT $r_{xy} = 0.45$, the Oral Commissions Subtest $r_{xy} = 0.69$, the ITPA–Total $r_{xy} = 0.49$, the Auditory Association Subtest $r_{xy} = 0.36$, the Visual Association Subtest $r_{xy} = 0.39$, and the Draw-a-Man Test $r_{xy} = 0.43$. Correlation measures between the DSS and the following were not statistically significant: NSST–Receptive Section

TABLE 3. PEARSON PRODUCT-MOMENT CORRELATIONS BETWEEN THE PRE-TREATMENT DSS AND OTHER PRE-TREATMENT MEASURES FOR 25 SUBJECTS

Pre-Treatment Measures	r_{xy}*
NSST–Expressive Section	0.68†
NSST–Receptive Section	0.30
Peabody Picture Vocabulary Test	0.45†
Stanford-Binet Intelligence Scale	0.26
Preschool Attainment Record	0.34
Spencer-McGrady Sentence Repetition	0.50†
Oral Commissions (DTLA)	0.69†
ITPA–Total Score	0.49†
Auditory Reception	0.27
Auditory Association	0.36†
Auditory Sequential Memory	0.51†
Visual Reception	0.24
Visual Association	0.39†
Visual Closure	0.20
Visual Sequential Memory	0.01
Manual Expression	0.07
Verbal Expression	0.66†
Grammatic Closure	0.45†
Draw-a-Man (Goodenough-Harris)	0.43†
Developmental Test of Visual-Motor Integration	0.31
Memory Span for Digits	0.40†
NU Articulation Proficiency Test	0.31

*$df = 23$

†$p < .05$

r_{xy} = 0.30, Stanford-Binet Intelligence Scale r_{xy} = 0.26, Preschool Attainment Record r_{xy} = 0.34, Auditory Reception Subtest r_{xy} = 0.27, Visual Reception Subtest r_{xy} = 0.24, Visual Closure Subtest r_{xy} = 0.20, Visual Sequential Memory Subtest r_{xy} = 0.01, Manual Expression Subtest r_{xy} = 0.07, Developmental Test of Visual-Motor Integration r_{xy} = 0.31, and Northwestern University Articulation Proficiency Test r_{xy} = 0.31.

In summary, on the pre-treatment measures these clinical children were found to be functioning, over-all, within a normal range of intelligence but to have severe expressive-language problems. Deficits in language usage were most clearly shown on measures of expressive usage of grammar. Comprehension of spoken syntax was also reduced. The difficulties these preschool children would face in school or education settings if their oral-language skills were not improved would be massive.

Post-Treatment Measures

Obtained means, standard deviations, and minimum and maximum values for the raw scores on the twenty-three post-treatment clinical measures are presented in Table 1. As in the earlier discussion of the pre-treatment measures, a display of the means, standard deviations, and minimum and maximum values for the age-equivalent scores listed in months is provided for sixteen of these post-treatment measures in Table 2. Important information is contained in both Tables 1 and 2 on the differences in performance by the twenty-five children prior to and following their enrollment of approximately eight months in the Interactive Language Development Teaching program. Under the third general column, labeled "Comparison," the first subcolumn contains information on the mean of the differences between the pre- and post-treatment scores for the clinical children, raw scores being shown in Table 1 and age-equivalent scores in Table 2. The final two subcolumns contain a summary of the comparisons made with a correlated *t*-formula (Ferguson, 1971). In the following discussion, reference is made to both raw scores and age-equivalent scores. The 0.05 level of confidence was selected as the minimum in reporting significance for the results of the statistical treatment of the data.

Following enrollment of approximately eight months in Interactive Language Development Teaching, the mean age of the children was 60.6 months. As shown in Table 1, following the treatment period there were gains in the raw scores for every one of the twenty-three measures. With the single exception of the Visual Sequential Memory Subtest, on which pre- and post-treatment group performances were within the normal range, the *t*-comparisons revealed these gains to be statistically significant.

Although improved performance on the measures might be expected with increasing age of the subjects and possibly some regression toward the mean, the rate and nature of the positive changes for these clinical children provided useful information about the Interactive Language Development Teaching form of language intervention.

An important premise, central to the interpretation of the before-and-after comparisons, was that clinical children have been reduced or slowed in their language development relative to normally developing children. If presenting grammatical structure with the interactive approach effected a rate of gain equal to or surpassing the rate of progress of normally developing children who are at the same stage of language development, the effectiveness of the approach would be clearly demonstrated. Developmental Sentence Analysis of the spontaneous language usage of these children following the treatment period resulted in DSS scores ranging from 3.22 to 9.66, with a mean DSS of 6.04 and standard deviation of 1.89. The mean DSS increase for the twenty-five subjects was 2.20. At the end of the treatment period the mean estimated age-equivalent score in months on the DSS was 42.1 months, with a standard deviation of 12.1. The mean gain per child was 10.8 months on this objective measure of the use of morphological forms and syntactic structures in the spontaneous formulation of utterances. When this over-all language growth of 10.8 months is compared to the 8.3 months these clinical children were enrolled in treatment, the effectiveness of Interactive Language Development Teaching is supported. These results indicated that the grammatical structures presented clinically through emphasis in the story-conversations were later used by these children in spontaneous formulations in conversation with an adult.

Gains were evidenced also on the Grammatic Closure Subtest of the ITPA. The obtained mean increase of 15.0 months on the expressive measure of morphological forms and grammatical features placed the performance of these clinical children within the normal range following approximately eight months of treatment. Significant gains were also shown on the Spencer-McGrady Sentence Repetition measure, reflecting improved ability to repeat sentences of increasing length with generally increasing grammatical load. The two other measures which quite directly sample changes in syntactic skills were the Expressive and Receptive sections of the NSST. The mean increase in the Expressive section was 5.6 raw-score points, with an estimated age-equivalent gain of 6.8 months. Comprehension of syntactic structures, as measured with the screening instrument, was improved on the average by 8.0 months. In Interactive

Language Development Teaching both the receptive and expressive uses of syntax are emphasized. Although gains on the Receptive section were greater than on the Expressive section of the NSST, these language-delayed children were progressing during the treatment period at a rate approximating the normal progress seen at these stages of language development.

On the pre-enrollment measures, the group performance was clearly below age-level expectations on both measures of auditory sequential memory. Although, at the end of the treatment study, gains were evident on the Auditory Sequential Memory Subtest and the Memory Span for Digits Forward, these gains were minimal and were less than the gains normally expected during such an eight-month developmental period. Auditory sequential-memory difficulties continued for these youngsters. The important finding was that these clinical children, although they were operating under the continuing constraints of reduced and limiting auditory sequential-memory skills, improved their use of grammar at a rate faster than normally developing children at approximately the same stages of language development. The comprehension and spontaneous use of syntax improved during the course of enrollment in Interactive Language Development Teaching despite the existing auditory sequential-memory impairments.

The children's post-treatment performances on the Stanford-Binet Intelligence Scale, the Illinois Test of Psycholinguistic Abilities–Total Score, and the Preschool Attainment Record were in general within normal limits for their age level. The same pattern on these three more general measures of over-all level of functioning was obtained on the pre-treatment testing. Increases in age-equivalent scores on these tests exceeded the increase in the children's chronological ages. The mean gain in months on the Stanford-Binet Intelligence Scale was 10.3, while on the ITPA–Total Score it was 9.1. A mean gain of 11.8 raw-score points on the PAR was consistent with the growth shown on the other more general measures. The relationship between improved language skills and changes in performance on these measures, especially the Stanford-Binet Intelligence Scale and PAR, will be better understood when individual items on these scales are analyzed for language-task requirements and are subjected to statistical analyses.

Definite gains were shown in the course of treatment on the PPVT single-word receptive vocabulary measure, as well as on the Auditory Reception Subtest of the ITPA and the Oral Commissions Subtest of the DTLA. The age-equivalent increases on the PPVT — mean gain of 13.1

months — and on the Auditory Reception Subtest — mean gain of 11.5 months — surpassed the amount of change expected for this period. Over a series of Interactive Language Development Teaching story-lessons, considerable attention is given to concept development and to receptive and expressive vocabulary expansion.

The mean post-treatment score for the Manual Expression Subtest was 65.0 months, a net increase of 6.3 months, while for the Verbal Expression Subtest it was 61.1 months, a net increase of 9.2 months. Although pre-treatment scores for both subtests were appropriate for the age of the clinical group, there had earlier been a seven-month advantage on the gestural measure — an advantage that was narrowed at the end of the eight-month treatment period.

These clinical children had achieved normal results as a group for the Auditory Association, Visual Association, and Visual Reception subtests of the ITPA on the pre-enrollment testing. At post-treatment testing there were age-equivalent gains of 6.5 months, 9.8 months, and 10.4 months, respectively, on these measures. Performance on the three visual-motor skill measures — the Developmental Test of Visual-Motor Integration, the Draw-a-Man Test, and the Visual Closure Subtest of the ITPA — also progressed normally during this period. The articulatory skills of the children evidenced modest improvement during this same period, as shown by a mean increase of 7.6 correct consonant singles on the Northwestern Articulation Proficiency Test.

Individual categories of the DSS. Separate consideration was also given to the clinical cases' pre- and post-treatment performance on syntactic structures within the individual grammatical categories of the DSS. Table 4 contains the means and standard deviations of the group's pre- and post-treatment scoring within each DSS category. The measures are based on the sum of the weighted scores for a given DSS component category divided by the number of DSS sentences in the language sample. Across a language sample it is sensitive to both the number of entries per sentence, reflective of utterance length, and the weightings assigned to the entries, reflective of the maturity of syntactic usage. Thus it is an indication of not only the developmental level or maturity of syntactic usage within the category but also the typical frequency of usage of structures within the category. Table 4 also contains a summary of the univariate analyses of variance (Winer, 1971) for the effect of treatment on each category over the eight-month period.

A comparison of the pre- and post-treatment means by category revealed that group scores increased in the Indefinite Pronoun–Noun Modifier,

TABLE 4. MEANS AND STANDARD DEVIATIONS OF PRE- AND POST-TREATMENT SCORES PER DSS SENTENCE WITHIN DSS COMPONENT CATEGORIES AND SUMMARY OF THE UNIVARIATE ANALYSES OF VARIANCE FOR TREATMENT EFFECT OVER 8-MONTH INTERVAL (25 SUBJECTS)

CATEGORIES	PRE-TREATMENT		POST-TREATMENT		COMPARISON		
	Mean	Standard Deviation	Mean	Standard Deviation	F-RATIO	DEGREES OF FREEDOM	p LESS THAN
Indefinite Pronouns	0.89	0.42	1.07	0.31	3.00	1,48	0.09
Personal Pronouns	1.13	0.52	1.62	0.57	10.15	1,48	0.01
Main Verbs	0.77	0.45	1.45	0.65	18.23	1,48	0.001
Secondary Verbs	0.21	0.14	0.32	0.21	4.03	1,44	0.05
Negatives	0.24	0.18	0.38	0.30	2.71	1,42	0.11
Conjunctions	0.44	0.40	0.44	0.31	< 1.00	1,33	
Interrogative Reversals	0.24	0.23	0.19	0.21	< 1.00	1,21	
Wh-Questions	0.06	0.05	0.10	0.07	2.58	1,26	0.12
Sentence Point	0.31	0.19	0.55	0.20	19.23	1,48	0.001

Personal Pronoun, Main Verb, Secondary Verb, Negative, Wh-Question, and Sentence Point categories. Statistically significant increases were obtained on four individual DSS categories involving Personal Pronouns, Main Verbs, Secondary Verbs, and Sentence Points. Degrees of freedom for the comparisons varied, depending on the number of clinical language samples containing items from the grammatical category under study. Mean scores for Conjunctions remained constant on the pre- and post-samplings of spontaneous speech. There was a slight decrease in the mean scores for Interrogative Reversals. A similar pattern of decreasing scores on the question forms was seen in the normative studies with the DSS procedure (Koenigsknecht, 1974).

The mean score per DSS sentence within the grammatical categories shown in Table 4 involved both the developmental level and frequency of usage of the syntactic structures under study. To better understand the possible influences of Interactive Language Development Teaching on the grammatical usage of these children, two additional measures were computed. The first, which related directly to the length of a child's utterances, was based on the number of scorable entries within each category divided by the number of DSS sentences on the language sample (Table 5). The next measure, the mean developmental score, was derived by dividing the weighted sum for a category by the number of DSS entries in that category. This is a general measure of the maturity of syntax usage (Table 6).

The means and standard deviations of the pre- and post-treatment measures for the number of entries per DSS sentence and for the mean developmental scores are listed in Table 5 and 6, respectively. Summaries of the univariate analyses of variance for the effect of treatment on each category over the eight-month period are also included. As shown in Table 5, the mean number of entries per DSS sentence increased in the Indefinite Pronoun–Noun Modifier, Personal Pronoun, Main Verb, Secondary Verb, and Negative categories. Statistical significance for this measure was obtained on three of the grammatical categories, including Personal Pronouns, Main Verbs, and Secondary Verbs.

Mean developmental scores or mean scores per DSS entry increased in the Indefinite Pronoun–Noun Modifier, Personal Pronoun, Main Verb, Secondary Verb, Negative, Interrogative Reversal, and Wh-Question categories (Table 6). These gains in mean scores per entry were statistically significant for Main Verbs, Negatives, and Wh-Questions. Only the mean developmental score within the Conjunction category decreased over the eight-month treatment period. In the statistical analysis of the normative data for the DSS (Koenigsknecht, 1974), the Conjunction category

TABLE 5. MEANS AND STANDARD DEVIATIONS OF PRE- AND POST-TREATMENT NUMBER OF ENTRIES PER DSS SENTENCE WITHIN DSS GRAMMATICAL CATEGORIES AND SUMMARY OF THE UNIVARIATE ANALYSES OF VARIANCE FOR TREATMENT EFFECT OVER 8-MONTH INTERVAL (25 SUBJECTS)

	PRE-TREATMENT		POST-TREATMENT		COMPARISON		
CATEGORIES	Mean	Standard Deviation	Mean	Standard Deviation	F-RATIO	DEGREES OF FREEDOM	p LESS THAN
Indefinite Pronouns	0.48	0.20	0.54	0.16	1.58	1,48	0.21
Personal Pronouns	0.60	0.25	0.84	0.24	10.75	1,48	0.01
Main Verbs	0.47	0.20	0.77	0.27	19.38	1,48	0.001
Secondary Verbs	0.08	0.04	0.11	0.06	3.34	1,44	0.07
Negatives	0.06	0.04	0.07	0.05	< 1.00	1,41	
Conjunctions	0.12	0.13	0.12	0.08	< 1.00	1,33	
Interrogative Reversals	0.09	0.07	0.08	0.06	< 1.00	1,26	
Wh-Questions	0.05	0.04	0.05	0.04	< 1.00	1,21	

Table 6. Means and Standard Deviations of Pre- and Post-Treatment Mean Developmental Scores or Mean Score per Entry within DSS Grammatical Categories and Summary of the Univariate Analyses of Variance for Treatment Effect over 8-Month Interval (25 Subjects)

Categories	Pre-Treatment		Post-Treatment		Comparison		
	Mean	Standard Deviation	Mean	Standard Deviation	*F*-Ratio	Degrees of Freedom	*p* less than
Indefinite Pronouns	1.84	0.44	1.97	0.32	1.42	1,48	0.24
Personal Pronouns	1.85	0.32	1.91	0.27	< 1.00	1,48	
Main Verbs	1.59	0.42	1.87	0.38	6.24	1,48	0.02
Secondary Verbs	2.97	1.47	2.98	1.10	< 1.00	1,44	
Negatives	3.76	1.06	4.87	1.27	9.46	1,41	0.01
Conjunctions	4.32	1.75	3.85	1.16	< 1.00	1,33	
Interrogative Reversals	2.50	1.44	3.12	1.88	< 1.00	1,26	
Wh-Questions	1.08	.29	2.90	2.37	7.00	1,27	0.02

was the only grammatical category not to reveal significant changes in mean developmental scores with increasing age of the subjects.

SUMMARY

Interactive Language Development Teaching was used with twenty-five clinical children over a three-year period at the Northwestern University Speech and Language Clinics. The mean age of the children upon enrollment in treatment was four years and four months. All the children included in this study had normal hearing, evidenced no general neuromuscular problems, and were within the range of normal on selected intelligence measures; however, they had severe expressive-language problems. Deficits in language usage were most clearly shown on measures of expressive usage of grammar. The mean delay in grammatical development for the twenty-five subjects on their pre-enrollment language sample, as estimated with the DSS procedure, was twenty-one months. Comprehension of spoken syntax was also reduced.

Extensive pre- and post-treatment speech, language, and learning measures were taken by a speech and language pathologist and by a psychologist, neither of whom was directly involved in the treatment program. The mean treatment interval for the twenty-five children was eight months. In addition to the twenty-three major clinical measures taken, consideration was also given to the group's performance within individual component categories of the DSS. For all measures the means of the differences between the pre- and post-treatment scores were computed and analyzed for statistical significance. During the treatment period the children made gains on the raw scores for every one of the clinical measures. With the single exception of the Visual Sequential Memory Subtest of the ITPA, on which pre- and post-treatment group scores were within the normal range, the comparisons showed these gains to be statistically significant. Although improved performance on the measures might be expected with increasing age of the subjects, the rate and nature of the positive changes for these subjects provided useful information about the effectiveness of Interactive Language Development Teaching.

Clinical children have been slowed or reduced in their language development relative to normally developing children. If presenting grammatical structures with the Interactive Language Development Teaching approach effected a rate of gain equal to or surpassing the rate of progress of normally developing children who are at the same stage of language development, the effectiveness of the approach would be clearly demonstrated.

Developmental Sentence Analysis revealed that the mean gain per child on the estimated age-equivalent score for the DSS was 10.8 months on this objective measure of the use of morphological forms and syntactic structures in spontaneous language usage. When this over-all language growth of 10.8 months was compared to the 8.3 months these clinical children were enrolled in treatment, the effectiveness of Interactive Language Development Teaching was supported. The grammatical structures presented clinically, through emphasis in the story-conversation lessons, were later used by these children in spontaneous formulations in conversation with an adult. Significant gains were also shown on other measures of the children's comprehension and expressive use of grammar.

Several useful findings resulted from the pre- and post-treatment comparisons. For example, on the pre-enrollment measures the group performance was clearly below age-level expectations on measures of auditory sequential memory. Although, at the end of the treatment study, gains were evident on these measures, these gains were minimal and less than those normally expected during such an eight-month developmental period. The auditory sequential-memory difficulties continued for these youngsters. The important finding was that these clinical children, although they were operating under the continuing constraints of reduced and limiting auditory sequential-memory skills, improved their use of grammar at a rate faster than normally developing children at approximately the same stages of language development. The comprehension and spontaneous use of syntax improved during the course of enrollment in Interactive Language Development Teaching despite the existing auditory sequential-memory deficits.

The clinical cases' pre- and post-treatment performances on syntactic structures within the individual categories of the DSS were also studied. Mean developmental scores or mean scores per DSS entry increased in the Indefinite Pronoun–Noun Modifier, Personal Pronoun, Main Verb, Secondary Verb, Negative, Interrogative Reversal, and Wh-Question categories. The mean number of entries per DSS sentence increased in the Indefinite Pronoun–Noun Modifier, Personal Pronoun, Main Verb, Secondary Verb, and Negative categories.

In this investigation, Developmental Sentence Analysis and Interactive Language Development Teaching were used to help clinical children match and exceed the rate of progress of normally developing children who are at the same general stage of grammatical development. The results demonstrate the effectiveness of clinical intervention through the clinical presentation of grammatical structure to children with language problems.

References

BAKER, HARRY J., and BERNICE LELAND
1967 Detroit Tests of Learning Aptitude. Rev. ed. Indianapolis, Ind.: Bobbs-Merrill Company, Inc.

BEERY, KEITH E., and NORMAN A. BUKTENICA
1967 Developmental Test of Visual-Motor Integration. Chicago: Follett Publishing Company.

CANTER, GERALD J., and NORMAN H. COLLINS
1965 Northwestern University Articulation Proficiency Test: Consonant Singles. Unpublished research manual.

DOLL, EDGAR A.
1966 Preschool Attainment Record. Circle Pines, Minn.: American Guidance Service, Inc.

DUNN, LLOYD M.
1959 Peabody Picture Vocabulary Test. Circle Pines, Minn.: American Guidance Service, Inc.

FERGUSON, GEORGE
1971 Statistical Analysis in Psychology and Education. New York: McGraw-Hill Book Company.

HARRIS, DALE B.
1963 Goodenough-Harris Drawing Test Manual. New York: Harcourt, Brace & World, Inc.

KIRK, S., J. MCCARTHY, and W. KIRK
1968 The Illinois Test of Psycholinguistic Abilities. Rev. ed. Urbana, Ill.: University of Illinois Press.

KOENIGSKNECHT, ROY A.
1974 Statistical Information on Developmental Sentence Analysis. In Laura L. Lee: Developmental Sentence Analysis. Evanston, Ill.: Northwestern University Press.

LEE, LAURA L.
1969, 1971 The Northwestern Syntax Screening Test. Evanston, Ill.: Northwestern University Press.

LEE, LAURA L.
1974 Developmental Sentence Analysis. Evanston, Ill.: Northwestern University Press.

LEE, LAURA L., and SUSAN M. CANTER
1971 Developmental Sentence Scoring: A Clinical Procedure for Estimating Syntactic Development in Children's Spontaneous Speech. Journal of Speech and Hearing Disorders 36:315–40.

MCGRADY, HAROLD
1964 Verbal and Nonverbal Functions in School Children with Speech and Language Disorders. Doctoral dissertation, Northwestern University.

SPENCER, ELLEN M.
1958 An Investigation of the Maturation of Various Factors of Auditory Perception in Preschool Children. Doctoral dissertation, Northwestern University.

TERMAN, LEWIS M., and MAUD A. MERRILL
1960 Stanford-Binet Intelligence Scale. Boston: Houghton Mifflin Company.

WINER, B. J.
1971 Statistical Principles in Experimental Design. New York: McGraw-Hill Book Company.